# PROGRAMMING
## FOR
# BEGINNERS

# TABLE OF CONTENTS

# SWIFT

*Basic Fundamental Guide for Beginners*

# PHP

*Basic Fundamental Guide for Beginners*

# JAVA

*Basic Fundamental Guide for Beginners*

# JavaScript

## *Basic Fundamental Guide for Beginners*

# HTML

*Basic Fundamental Guide for Beginners*

xi

# CSS

*Basic Fundamental Guide for Beginners*

# SWIFT

---

*Basic Fundamental Guide for Beginners*

# Introduction

Congratulations on purchasing *SWIFT :Basic Fundamental Guide For Beginners* and thank you for doing so.

There are plenty of books on this subject on the market, thanks again for choosing this one! Every effort was made to ensure it is full of as much useful information as possible, please enjoy!

Swift is among the new languages which you can use to code for OS X apps as well as the IOS apps. The language for technology is to learn to code, and there is no better way to take your coding skills than learning to code using Swift language. You will learn how you can solve real-world problems at a go as well as work in a creative manner. Swift language will help you build apps which every apple user would want to use. With Swift language, you have the ability to create something which can change the world.

Still a new language, Swift provides a change for the macOS and apple developers. Experienced apple developers will have something new to learn while the new developers have a chance to learn Swift language. Swift language is one of the best languages for every iOS and macOS developer. Every new language has a lot of things to learn. And that is also true with the Swift language.

In this book, we shall help you experience the fun of coding with Swift language. Writing code can sometimes be tiresome, it can also be intriguing. There is something lovely and enjoyable while writing a line of code, not forgetting the greatest joy that one feels after creating an app which solves a problem in the world. It is said, the best way to become a professional developer is to practice to code. If that is the case, we can get started! In case you start to feel like this is not for you, don't give up. Keep reading and I am sure you may surprise yourself.

# Chapter 1

## Introduction To Swift Programming

S wift is the new language to use to develop in apps in Apple. The language is applied in OS X and IOS devices. Swift replaces Apple's IOS and OS X languages. The greatest thing with Swift is that it has been designed to work well with the Objective-C.

There are a few beginners to Swift programming who start to learn the language with some expertise in other languages such as C, Objective - C and the C++.

Regardless of your level of experience, Swift is the right language to get started. In this chapter, we shall help you kick the ball rolling.

Some of the important devices which you will need to have to run your Swift programs include:

- Mac Laptop or computer. If you have the latest Mac, you will be good to go because it has sufficient memory and processor speed.

- The XCode. This is the IDE for building iOS apps and the OS X apps. You can get it for free if you visit the App store for Mac.

These are some of the important things which you need to have. They are enough to help you begin coding in Swift. However, if you can still add some additional tools, it can be very beneficial on your side. Still, if you don't have the extra tools, no need to worry. They include:

- A device of the iOS if you are going to work on the iOS platform. While you can still go ahead and develop an apple app without having a testing device, you will be shocked by the results when

4

you begin to see some of the reviews written by people. Just developing an apple app by following what is written in blog posts is something difficult. I will suggest you look for a real apple device. With an Apple device, things become easier. Unless you plan to develop something which does not need a user interface. This could be a large component of a given app.

- Internet access. Don't worry if you don't have a strong internet access. You can still develop even though you will experience some limitations. There are a few operations including uploading your app into the app store which will need you to have an internet connection.

- Sufficient disk space. Sufficient disk space means your internal disk or even external disk connected to your Mac. You need to ensure you have a backup alternative for all your projects.

Apple has a discussion forum the same way Android developers have a forum. I will suggest that you join the Apple forums to be able to associate and communicate with fellow developers.

## Set up your mac

Here we help you learn how you can prepare your Mac ready to develop in Swift. We provide you with the basic steps.

## First, Sign Up As A Developer:

The basic tools of a developer are free; this means you can begin to learn Swift programming immediately. However, Apple needs you to sign up as a developer on their developer website before you get the chance to use many of their developer tools and features. Some of the features you need don't require registration. There are crucial features which will need you to register, especially, when it comes to testing your App.

Besides the registration, there is a point where you will have to sign the non-disclosure agreement. Here, you will receive an invitation to participate in a developer program which you might have to pay some fee. However, if you aren't stable financially or perhaps you have a limited budget, you can opt not to join the program. Something which you should note is that the guidelines for developing apps in Apple change with time. It is also different from one country to another. Always go back to the developer website to familiarize yourself with the latest information and rules.

## Have Your Credentials Ready:

To sign up with Apple, you have to provide your Apple ID. Remember that your Apple ID is not private. Only the password is confidential. You can have more than one Apple IDs. In certain cases, you will find developers who have an additional Apple ID for their own use.

## Choose Your Program:

Apple has several developer programs for you to register. The easiest program is the individual program which now costs about $99 per year, as well as a separate program for the OS X and IOS. If you decide to enroll for the two, you will have to pay about $198.

Still, you can enroll as a business entity. This will help you to come up with teams made up of individual developers. At the same time, you can share the code among your developers. Also, it has programs for educational institutions. But, make sure you have an Apple ID to use it for your development.

## Getting Ready Your Environment:

The environment you are going to use to develop your Swift program will be the XCode and the Mac. Ensure that you have installed the XCode. XCode is provided freely, and it is easy to install. If you have access to a computer lab at school, XCode could be a component already at the lab.

There are no complicated settings to use XCode with Swift language. All you need to do is to select Swift language instead of the objective C in the pop-up menu which comes up. You will need to further get the latest Swift documentation and SDK. However, this is part of the basic installation process.

**The Source Control:**

The source control comes in-built with the XCode alongside the Git and Subversion. As a result of its architecture, Git has been closely combined with XCode compared to Subversion. Using any of these tools helps you store your code in the repository. Make it a practice to store your code in the repository so that you can download your source code at any time.

A source control allows you to use your source code at any time and any place, as long as you have a mac computer and internet connection.

# Chapter 2

# Working With Collections In Swift

S wift language has three types of collection. They include the arrays, sets and the dictionaries. All these collection types help one store values. Arrays consist of a collection of ordered items. The sets comprise of unordered collections of special values while the dictionaries comprise of unordered collections of "key-value associations".

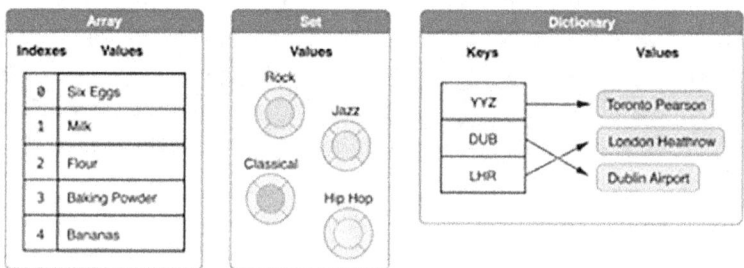

All the above three types of collections are clear concerning the kinds of values which they can store as well as the keys. What this means is that it is difficult for one to insert a wrong type of value into a given collection by mistake.

Furthermore, you can still be sure about the type of values which you want to extract from a given collection.

**Note:**

We implement dictionary, sets and arrays in Swift language as a generic collection.

## The "Mutability" Of The Collections:

Well, if you decide to create a dictionary, array or set and then allocate it a variable, we consider the created collection to be mutable. We say it is mutable because you have the ability to modify the collection once it is created. You can do this by either subtracting, adding or even perform some modification of the items inside. If you opt to allocate a set, dictionary or array to a constant, the collection becomes "**immutable**". Thus, we can't change the size and contents.

## Note:

It is a nice practice to have immutable collections in almost all situations especially when the collection is not supposed to be modified. By doing this way, it makes everything easy for one to read and understand the code. Furthermore, a compiler in Swift will help improve the level of performance of the collection.

## Arrays:

Arrays hold values of related items in an ordered list. The values can still appear in the array many times at various positions.

## Note:

The Swift's array type has been bridged to the Foundation's NSArray class.

## Array Type:

We write the Swift array in full like **Array<Element>,** in this case, the Element refers to the type of values found in the array. It is possible to write the array type in a different way which is fast and short [Element]. Even though both forms are similar, most developers prefer to use the second method because of how easy it is.

## Empty Array in Swift:

In Swift language, the initializer syntax allows one to create an empty array:

```
1   var someInts = [Int]()
2   print("someInts is of type [Int] with \(someInts.count) items.")
3   // Prints "someInts is of type [Int] with 0 items."
```

You should pay attention here and see that the **someInts** variable has been referred to **[Int] right from the type** of initializer.

At the same time, if we have the context already with the type of information such as typed constant or variable, it is possible to go ahead and build an empty array which has literal, this can be written with the []:

```
1   someInts.append(3)
2   // someInts now contains 1 value of type Int
3   someInts = []
4   // someInts is now an empty array, but is still of type [Int]
```

## Array Which Have A Default Value.

When dealing with arrays in Swift, it offers one the ability to create an array of a certain size which will hold the default values. You do this by setting the initializer with a default value of the correct type. This is called **repeating.** The number of times the value appears in the array is referred to as **count**:

```
1   var threeDoubles = Array(repeating: 0.0, count: 3)
2   // threeDoubles is of type [Double], and equals [0.0, 0.0, 0.0]
```

## How To Create An Array By Combining Two Arrays:

In Swift language, it is possible to have a new array by just integrating two existing arrays by using the addition symbol. The only thing to consider is that the arrays should be compatible.

```
1    var anotherThreeDoubles = Array(repeating: 2.5, count: 3)
2    // anotherThreeDoubles is of type [Double], and equals [2.5,
        2.5, 2.5]
3
4    var sixDoubles = threeDoubles + anotherThreeDoubles
5    // sixDoubles is inferred as [Double], and equals [0.0, 0.0,
        0.0, 2.5, 2.5, 2.5]
```

## Using The Array Literal To Create An Array:

Swift permits one to initialize an array by using the array literal, the array literal is the shortest form for one to write one or even more values of an array collection. The array literal consists of a collection of values. The values have been split using commas and enclosed with square brackets as shown below:

[ value 1 ,   value 2 ,   value 3 ]

This example will create an array to store the values:

```
1    var shoppingList: [String] = ["Eggs", "Milk"]
2    // shoppingList has been initialized with two initial items
```

In the above example, we have declared a variable called shoppingList to be an array of string values. Since this array contains values which have been detailed to be of string type, it can only contain string values. In this case, we have the array initialized with two string values.

You should note that the "shoppingList" array has been created using the *var* keyword instead of the constant keyword *let* because additional

11

items will be added to the array. In this example, we say the array literal has two String values. This resembles the "shoppingList variable declaration", and that is the reason why it is possible to assign the array literal as a means to make the array hold two initial values. As you can now see, with the "Swift's inference type "you should not worry so much with describing the array if you would like to initialize it using the array literal which contains the values similar type. The "shoppingList" list initialization could, therefore, be written in a short form as:

```
var shoppingList = ["Eggs", "Milk"]
```

Since we have all the values existing in the array literal of the same kind, Swift can refer to that [String] as the correct type for one apply for the "shoppingList" variable.

## Access And Modify An Array:

Arrays in Swift are accessed and modified with the help of properties and methods. Or you can still use the subscript syntax. If you want to know how many items the array holds, the read only count is an important way to know:

```
1  print("The shopping list contains \(shoppingList.count) items.")
2  // Prints "The shopping list contains 2 items."
```

The Boolean isEmpty property allows one to perform a check to determine if the count property is equal to 0.

```
1  if shoppingList.isEmpty {
2      print("The shopping list is empty.")
3  } else {
4      print("The shopping list is not empty.")
5  }
6  // Prints "The shopping list is not empty."
```

You can add or create a new item at the end of the array by just calling the arrays append (_:) method:

```
1   shoppingList.append("Flour")
2   // shoppingList now contains 3 items, and someone is making
    pancakes
```

Then again, you can append an array to one of the most compatible items using the addition assignment symbol (+=):

```
1   shoppingList += ["Baking Powder"]
2   // shoppingList now contains 4 items
3   shoppingList += ["Chocolate Spread", "Cheese", "Butter"]
4   // shoppingList now contains 7 items
```

We extract a value from an array with the help of the subscript syntax, what we do is specify the index of the value which we want to extract inside the square brackets.

```
1   var firstItem = shoppingList[0]
2   // firstItem is equal to "Eggs"
```

Please note that in any array, the first item begins with the index 0 and not 1. Swift arrays are zero-indexed.

Again, the subscript construct allows you to modify the value of a specific index.

```
1   shoppingList[0] = "Six eggs"
2   // the first item in the list is now equal to "Six eggs" rather
    than "Eggs"
```

Whenever you choose to apply the subscript construct, the index which you will as??? has to be valid. For instance, if you decide to write shoppingList [shoppingList.count] = "Salt", it will result in a "runtime error".

You can further try to take advantage of the subscript syntax which will help you change the values immediately. The subscript syntax does not care whether the replacement set of values contains diverse length compared to the one being replaced. In the example below, we replace the "Chocolate Spread", "Cheese", and "Butter" with "Bananas" and "Apples".

```
1   shoppingList[4...6] = ["Bananas", "Apples"]
2   // shoppingList now contains 6 items
```

If your goal is to successfully insert an item into the array at a precise index, use the insert (_:at:) method:

```
1   shoppingList.insert("Maple Syrup", at: 0)
2   // shoppingList now contains 7 items
3   // "Maple Syrup" is now the first item in the list
```

The above call to the method insert will insert a new item having the value "Maple Syrup" at the start of the shopping list, shown by the 0 index.

Alternatively, you can do away with an item from the array using the method remove (at:). This method will do away with an item at a given index and still return it back.

```
1   let mapleSyrup = shoppingList.remove(at: 0)
2   // the item that was at index 0 has just been removed
3   // shoppingList now contains 6 items, and no Maple Syrup
4   // the mapleSyrup constant is now equal to the removed "Maple
    Syrup" string
```

Note:

If you attempt to change a value whose index does not fall inside the array's existing limits, you will activate a runtime error. You should first confirm whether an index is correct before you can proceed to compare the array's property *count*. The highest and correct index is the -1. This is because of the previous reason we mentioned array indexing. It starts from zero, but when the count is 0, it means we have no correct indexes.

If we have some gaps in the array, they get closed down when the item is removed. This means the value at the index 0 will be equal to "Six eggs".

The method removeLast () should allow you to eliminate the last item instead of the remove (at:) to avoid the chances of querying the array's count property.

```
1   let apples = shoppingList.removeLast()
2   // the last item in the array has just been removed
3   // shoppingList now contains 5 items, and no apples
4   // the apples constant is now equal to the removed "Apples"
    string
```

**Iterate Over An Array:**

The for-in loop is important when you want to iterate over a whole set of values using the for-in loop:

15

```
1    for item in shoppingList {
2        print(item)
3    }
4    // Six eggs
5    // Milk
6    // Flour
7    // Baking Powder
8    // Bananas
```

If you want the whole integer index for every item together with its value, you make use of the enumerated () method which will iterate the array. Every object array and the enumerated () method will create a tuple. The integers begin at zero and move up one for every item. If you opt to enumerate an entire array, the integer will match the item indices. However, you can choose to reduce the tuple and translate it into temporary constants as well as variables in the process of iteration.

```
1    for item in shoppingList {
2        print(item)
3    }
4    // Six eggs
5    // Milk
6    // Flour
7    // Baking Powder
8    // Bananas
```

## Sets:

When we started to look at this Chapter, we discussed something about the set. If you can remember well, we said that it can store a collection of similar items without the presence of an organization. If order is not a big deal, then a set is one of the best to use. Sometimes, you can choose to use a set if the type of order for the items is not very important.

## Hash Values - Set Types:

Set types should have the ability to be "hashable" so that it can allow items storage. The set type needs to offer a way for one to compute the hash value for itself. A hash value simply refers to that value which remains the same no matter the objects. This could be if c==d, then c. hashValue == d. hashValue.

In Swift, String, Bool and Double are some of the set types which are "hashable by default". The enumeration case values with no related values are hashable by default.

Another important point to remember is that we can convert the custom types to be dictionary types by aligning the custom types to the Swift protocols. The types which align to the hashable protocol need to have a gettable int feature referred to as hashValue. The value which is returned by the type's hashValue is not needed to be similar across many different implementations of the same program.

Since the Hashable property is Equitable, the types which conform to it should have the equals operator (==) implementation. The Equitable property requires the conforming nature of == to take the equivalence relation. This means, the implementation of the == has to fulfill the conditions below for all the values of the a, b and c.

- a==a
- a==b
- a==b&& b == c meaning a == c

## The Set Type Syntax:

Swift set type has the following construct "Set<Element>", in this situation Element is the type which the set allows to store. Unlike arrays, the sets will not permit an equivalent shorthand.

17

## Creating And Initializing Empty Set

The syntax below will help you if you want to create and initialize empty set:

```
1   var letters = Set<Character>()
2   print("letters is of type Set<Character> with \(letters.count)
        items.")
3   // Prints "letters is of type Set<Character> with 0 items."
```

Meanwhile, let's assume that the context contains information. Then, it becomes easy to create an empty with the empty array literal.

```
1   letters.insert("a")
2   // letters now contains 1 value of type Character
3   letters = []
4   // letters is now an empty set, but is still of type
        Set<Character>
```

## Creating A Set Using Array Literal:

It is possible to initialize a set by the help of an array literal. This is in fact one of the easiest ways to adopt if you want to quickly write more than one value from the set collection. You can look at the example below which creates a set favoriteGenres:

```
1   var favoriteGenres: Set<String> = ["Rock", "Classical", "Hip
        hop"]
2   // favoriteGenres has been initialized with three initial items
```

In this example, the favoriteGenres variable shall be declared as the "set of String Values". This is written as Set<String>. It is written this way because the set has a specific value type of String. It can only store String values. In this illustration, the "favoriteGenres se???? has been

18

initialized with the three String values which have been written inside the array literal.

Again, note that the "favoriteGenres" set has been declared as a variable but not a constant. The reason is the items are removed and added.

# Chapter 3

# Control Statements And Decisions In Loops

When we have a code implemented line after line, we call that sequential flow. With the sequential interruption, the code can be interrupted in several ways:

- You can use the flow controls. This refers to the code structures which will interfere with the general flow of the code. The term flow control describes the conditional statements and other different types of loops. Often, they divert the flow by making the app jump out of the current function. This forces the next line of code to perform a given action rather than the line of code located in the source file.

- By use of closures and functions. This refers to the part of the code which is executed as a response to specific conditions. Some of these conditions can include events or even certain references inside code which trigger asynchronous or synchronous processes. This will also interfere with the net-line structure to begin the procedure of responding to the event.

All the above concepts have different types of implementation based on the language used. This chapter will discuss some of the basic control statements in Swift to give you a head start.

## Loops:

Every programming language has at least loops. Therefore, if Swift is not the first language you are learning, perhaps you have encountered loops at one point or the other while learning another computer programming language. Similar to other languages, Swift supports loops. However, you will see some slight difference when using loops in Swift. This is unique because it is not found in other languages.

We have two types of loops:

- The for loop which consists of a counter

- The while loop which depends on a specific condition

Again, we have another type of loop called polling loop. You may have used this one at one point in your life. The function of the poll loop is to confirm whether a certain action such as the button of the user's communication link is active or down. To implement a polling loop in Swift, the While loop helps you achieve that operation. However, kindly note that polling loops aren't that cheap. If you would like to monitor their conditions, they must be related to computer' resources.

## The For Loop In Swift:

For loops exist in nearly every programming language. It forms the core of programming languages. One reason for this is that the for loop command will allow you to implement certain parts of your code in a repeated manner depending on control.

In Swift, we have two types of for loops:

- The for-in loops

- The for-condition-increment

We shall look at the above types of for loop in the next sections.

Don't think the above for loops are new. No! In fact, they existed since the start of computer languages. However, you will realize that the for-in type of loop is mostly associated with the object-oriented programming. Still, if this is not your first time learning programming, for-in loops should not be new to you. We shall learn more about the for-in loops compared to other loops because they aren't that common. In addition, Swift developers find themselves using it regularly compared to other loops.

## We Start With The For-In Loops:

Even though they might appear new, they aren't. The for-in loops are not new to Swift programming. They are applied in many other object oriented languages such as C++. They are important when you want to work with a collection of objects. Instead of objects indexed in arrays.

Array objects tend to have a definite sequence. In other words, we can't have array elements holding the same index. If choose to create a for loop which will process every array element, then you should take advantage of the for loop. It is one of the best approaches to follow.

However, it happens sometimes when you have a collection of items that the objects aren't indexed and in no particular order. We can look at it like the objects or elements are in a random order. In this kind of situation, the objects are said to belong to a specific collection. Furthermore, the objects get identified individually using different methods rather than the index. There are also certain situations where the individual objects aren't identified because of how difficult it is.

Flicking through an array in a random order is very annoying, but in big situations, the order of presentation is not necessary. Your goal is to handle every appointment, every friend or bank account. As long as you are going to access every element and remove none, you are good to go.

The idea behind the syntax of for-in loop depends on two protocols:

- Generator

- Sequence

The Generator has a next function which is the main core. Now, anyone who has a class or creates a class which contains the sequence protocol will have the ability to access the next function which can now be adopted by the iterator. Regardless of the way the next function shall be ordered, it is upon the decision of the class or structure. This means it could either be random or ordered. Looking from a higher level of Swift perspective, the next is not defined. In real life, next is associated with contexts such as "next candidate in line", "next session" and so forth. When writing your Swift code, it is encouraged to imagine that we have no pre-arranged order unless you are sure that we have one.

The basic syntax to use for-in loops:

```
for <item> in <collection> {
   <statements>
}
```

You should not misinterpret the italicized terms as part of them, they are just basic descriptions which point to missing syntax elements. They consist of:

- <item> This one will point to a specific object in the collection. It holds a different element for every loop evaluation.

- <collection> This can contain any class or structure which assumes the nature of the sequence protocol. Don't even care to search it in the Swift documentation.

- <statements> These point to the code statements in Swift.

The steps below create a code which you can test with for-in type of loop:

1. Create a collection which belongs to the for-in loop. You can do that by declaring statements such as:

```
var elements = [1, 3, 5, 17, -1]
```

23

In the above example, our declared collection is a variable. However, it could be of any other type, not necessarily a variable.

2. Now, create the for-in loop. Look at this example:

```
for myElement in elements {
   // do something with myElement
}
```

You remember that this is a loop declaration. No need to have a different declaration for the myElement. If you do so, you shall have declared a separate variable. This loop will then work on the collection you had referenced in the first step. In this case, the myElement will contain every value of the loop. So, you can still use it inside the loop. The following are some of the for-in loops variations:

- To carry out a trial on a given item. Usually, you do a test on an item but you can also make use of it as an operation. There are times when you can carry out both. For instance, when the code below is placed inside the loop, it determines if the value of the iterated element can be a negative number. It will print out that particular value:

```
if myElement < 0 {
   println ( " \(myElement.description) is a negative
      number")
}
```

- Breaking out from a loop. Let's say that you are scanning a collection by looking for the lowest or even highest numeric value, you'll need to search all the values in the collection. This means that this kind of variation won't be of much help. Meanwhile, if you want to determine a specific value or even a value which will satisfy a given condition, this is the best to use. When carrying out this search, you'll want to stop once you find what you have been looking for. To end the loop from that point, you need to add the break statement. This statement will exit you

24

from the loop and continue execution on the next line. Here is an example:

```
if myElement < 0 {
    println (  " \(myElement.description) is a negative
      number")
    break;
}
```

- **Finding Every Item In Each Iteration:** As you might remember, the item in every for-in loop has the element from the collection. This element can be a value, as it has been indicated in the code below, but still, it can be an object. In the example of an ordered collection, like an array, you might want to know the index of an element number. Since this kind of information does not belong to the for-in loop, you will have to calculate it. To carry out the calculation, you will have to create a counter. This counter will build a special value for every element inside the loop. Here are the steps to follow if you want to create one:

1. Declare counter variable outside the loop. Ensure that the variable is declared using var, but not with let. You can do it this way: *var index = 2*

2. While within the loop, perform a counter increment: index ++

Now, here is how the body of your loop will be:

```
var index = 0
if myElement < 0 {
    println (  " \(myElement.description) at \(index) is
          a negative number")
    }
index++
```

- **Ignore the item:** In some cases, you don't really need to modify the item returned from every iteration. In the above case, you can choose to replace it with an underscore character as shown below:

25

For _in elements {

But, just in case you would like to reference the item later, you should apply the technique described previously.

- **Dictionary iteration:**

It is possible to do a dictionary iteration the same way you can iterate any other collection. The only variation happens when the item located in the syntax is a tuple consisting of a key and value for the dictionary element. Here is how a for-in loop for a dictionary will appear:

```
for (myKey, myValue) in myDictionary {
  //do something with myKey and myValue
}
```

Here is a code which uses the for-in loop to control a collection of items:

```
// Playground - noun: a place where people can play

var elements = [1, 3, 5, 17, -1]

var index = 0;

for myElement in elements {

  // do something with myElement
  if myElement < 0 {
    println ( " \(myElement.description) at
      \(index.description) is a negative number")
  }

  index++
}
```

## Now, Let's Turn Our Attention To The For-Condition-Increment Loops

As you know the for-condition–increment is the basis of for statements if you have learned another different programming language. When it comes to Swift for-condition loops, there is no difference. It is more or less the same as other languages with only one distinction. You don't have to place the loop control in the parentheses. You can have it, but it is not supposed to be. The general construct for the for-condition–increment is:

```
for <initialization>; <condition>; <increment>{
   <statements>
}

for <initialization>; <condition>; <increment>{
   <statements>
}
```

Similar to the for-in loop, we have some components which should not be confused with the syntax of the for-condition. For instance, the < and > aren't part of the syntax. Others include:

- <Initialization>: This simply initializes the counter. You should declare the index counter before you use it.

- <condition>: It will specify the condition based on the way the counter continues to increment. This type of condition is evaluated for each cycle in the loop, then the counter is incremented until the point when the condition fails.

- <increment>: This describes the expression one should use to increase the counter. The most common increment is the myCounter ++, which will increase the counter by 1, still, you can choose any type of increment you want.

- <statements>: These often point to the Swift code statements.

An example of how the for-condition loop is applied in code is shown below:

```
for (myElementCounter=0; myElementCounter <5;
   myElementCounter ++) {
```

You can choose to include the parenthesis but you don't have to. A more practical example is shown below:

```
// Playground - noun: a place where people can play

var elements = [1, 3, 5, 17, -1]

var myElementCounter = 0;

for myElementCounter =0; myElementCounter <5;
  myElementCounter ++ {

  // do something with myElement
  if elements[myElementCounter] > 15 {
    println (  " \(elements[myElementCounter].description)
      at \( myElementCounter.description) is greater than
      15")
  }
}
```

## Swift While Loops:

Similar to other languages, Swift has While loops. The basic syntax for the Swift while loops only needs a condition. Here is how it looks:

```
while myValue < 10 {
  // do something
}
```

If we review the above loop, myValue becomes the condition. Don't forget that you need to alter the value of myValue. If it does not change and the loop continues to run, the loop may be infinite. You should also underline that the condition in a while loop can at times be an expression. This means that a while loop can resemble the for-conditioning-increment loop in certain cases.

```
var myValue = 5
while myValue++ < 10 {
  // do something
}
```

Here, you should notice that there are three components of the for-condition-increment. It is the declaration of the myValue as well as the

28

initial value. In Swift, it should have the initialization, condition and increment. The while loops exist in two forms:

- Do while loop. You must have come across this while learning another programming language. With the following form, often the action gets executed at least once before the condition. It takes the form of a do < action > while <condition>

- While<condition> do < action>. In this type of while loop, we have our condition evaluated first. Now, when the condition is found to be true, the action will be performed.

All the above types of while conditions are the same in the way they are applied in other languages. The only exception could be that the condition defined in other languages has to within the parentheses.

## Conditions In Swift

In the Swift language, the if statements are used and applied in a similar fashion as other languages but there are some changes when it comes to the switch statements.

## The If Statements

Sometimes, you should realize that it is easy to talk about if statements because how they are used in other languages is the same in Swift. The syntax includes:

```
if <condition> {
    <statements>
}
```

In the same fashion, an if –else statement will have two branches:

```
if <condition> {
  <statements for true>
} else {
  <statements for false>
}
```

The greatest distinction is in the way the Swift language applies the if statement. You don't need to place the condition within the parentheses.

Still, you can have it, but no need to place it. One other difference is that the condition in swift can assume a Boolean expression or variable of any kind which takes the BooleanType convention. It is not easy to identify the above differences by just looking at the syntax examples.

## Switch Statements:

The basic syntax of the switch statement includes:

```
switch <control expression> {
  case <pattern 1>:
    <statements>
  case <pattern 2> where <condition>:
    <statements>
  case <pattern 3> where <condition,
      <pattern 4> where condition>:
    <statements>
  default:
    <statements>
}
```

As I said before, Switch statements in Swift tend to have certain variations from Switch statements in other computer programming languages. The list of differences highlights some of the issues developers have experienced over the years while working with the C-type switch statements. These issues are solved with the help of the features in Swift:

- Falling through: Every developer has encountered this situation. In most languages, you must include the break statement, not unless control jumps to the following case statement. However,

30

the Swift switch statement solves this by passing the control to the first statement that comes after the switch statement.

- Exhaustiveness: In the Swift switch statement, the statement has to go round all potential value for the control expression. But still, you can achieve this goal by using a default case.

- Guard clause: Swift allows you to have a guard statement which starts with the where. What this means is that you can have more than one case statement which matches a single control expression value. The guard clause resembles the AND statement. It enhances the basic case statement using extra aspects.

## Transferring Control:

Swift still has some transfer statements. The continue and break statement are not different from the other languages such as PHP, C, and Java.

- Continue: You are free to apply the continue statement in whichever type of loop statements described in this Chapter. It puts an end to a specific iteration and moves to the next.

- Break: It will end a loop iteration. Control switches back to the initial statement after the switch statement.

- Fallthrough: With this statement, it emulates the property of the case statements within the switch statement. If it has been located within a switch statement, then control is passed to next case.

# Chapter 4

# Swift Functions

**B**efore we can begin to look at Functions in Swift, I want you to remember those days you were a high school kid. But this time, I want you to try and recall the topic of algebra. I believe you weren't sleeping during that lesson, but paying attention. Well, if you can recall well, your mathematics teacher introduced and explained the topic of function. In mathematics, you came to learn that a function is a mathematical formula which accepts some inputs, performs certain operations and produces a given output.

The most important components of a function include:

- The name

- The input

- The expression

- The result

Most functions are written in the mathematical form. However, they can still be described in the human natural language.

**Writing Functions in Swift Language:**

Swift's syntax for functions is a bit different from the mathematical functions. The overall syntax includes:

```
func funcName(paramName : type, ...) -> returnType
```

You should look at the example below to help you understand the syntax
of functions in Swift:

From the above example, there is something new which you need to
learn on line 7. The "func" keyword helps Swift developers to declare a
swift function. The declaration takes the name of the function,
independent name of the variable or a parameter name surrounded by
parentheses.

After the parameter, we have two characters which imply that this
specific type of function should return a value of Double type. Next,
there is the opening curly brace which identifies the start of a function.
On line 8, we have declared a Double type of variable called result. This
will store the value which will??? the result of the function. You should
realize that it is similar to the function's return type previously declared
on line 7.

We have the initial mathematical function written on line 10 together
with the *result* of the expression. On line 12, we have the result taken
back to the caller with the return keyword. Any moment you would want
to exit a function and go back to the return calling party, the keyword
*return* becomes useful.

Now, we want to call the function we have created. In your text editor, type the below lines of code and watch out the results in the Results sidebar:

```
var outdoorTemperatureInFahrenheit = 88.2
var outdoorTemperatureInCelsius = fahrenheitToCelsius(outdoorTemperature
-> InFahrenheit)
```

From the above screenshot, we have declared a new variable called *outdoorTemperatureInFahrenheit* and assigned it a value. Remember that Swift refers the type in the above example to be of Double. The value is later transferred to line 16 where there is a function. Here, a new variable called *outdoorTemperatureInCelsius* is then declared. On the output sidebar, we see a value with repeating decimal to be the result of the function. If you review the result, you will notice that 32.2222 degrees Celsius is equal to the 88.2 degrees Fahrenheit. Now, you can sit back and relax as you enjoy using your temperature conversion tool.

Well, if you have followed closely what we have done on this particular example. You should give yourself a trial by writing the inverse of the method with the help of this formula.

$$f(x) = \frac{x * 9}{5} + 32$$

Move on and try to code it up by yourself. Once you have finished coding up, you should compare it with the code below:

```
func celsiusToFahrenheit(celsiusValue : Double) -> Double {
    var result : Double

    result = (((celsiusValue * 9) / 5) + 32)

    return result
}

outdoorTemperatureInFahrenheit = celsiusToFahrenheit(outdoorTemperature
    InCelsius)
```

The method on line 18-24 converts the Celsius to Fahrenheit and returns a value. You can see that if we pass the previous Celsius value we get the Fahrenheit value.

Here, you have successfully built two Swift functions which perform something important. You should try and play around with other values.

## Not Just Numbers Alone:

Swift function goes beyond the mathematical concept we have seen above. In a wider perspective, the functions are flexible and strong enough to accommodate more than one parameter. In addition, it can accept types rather than numeric types.

Let's consider writing a Swift function which will accept more than one parameter and return a value rather than a double.

```swift
func buildASentence(subject : String, verb : String, noun : String) -> String
    return subject + " " + verb + " " + noun + "!"
}

buildASentence("Swift", "is", "cool")
buildASentence("I", "love", "languages")
```

Once you are through with typing, you need to review your work. You should notice that we have declared a new function buildASentence, which holds three parameters. All the parameters belong to the string types. The function will also return a String type too. Line 29 holds the line which returns the result.

To be clear, we have the function called both on line 32 and 33. This outputs the results in the output sidebar. You should be free to use your own values for the parameters.

## Paremeters AD NAUSEAM

Can you visualize creating a life changing banking application for the Apple, and you would want to develop a means to add some random number of certain account balances. You just want to create a Swift function which will perform the addition. The challenge you are facing is that you aren't sure the number of accounts which you want to be added up at a specific time. The trick to use is the Swift's variable parameter passing syntax.

```
// Parameters Ad Nauseam
func addMyAccountBalances(balances : Double...) -> Double {
   var result : Double = 0

   for balance in balances {
      result += balance
   }
}
```

```
8      var result : Double
9
10     result = (((fahrenheitValue - 32) * 5) / 9)          31.2222222222222
11
12     return result                                        31.2222222222222
13  }
14
15  var outdoorTemperatureInFahrenheit = 88.2               88.2
16  var outdoorTemperatureInCelsius = fahrenheitToCelsius    31.2322222222222
       (outdoorTemperatureInFahrenheit)
17
18  func celsiusToFahrenheit(celsiusValue : Double) -> Double {
19     var result : Double
20
21     result = (((celsiusValue * 9) / 5) + 32)             88.2
22
23     return result                                        88.2
24  }
25
26  outdoorTemperatureInFahrenheit = celsiusToFahrenheit     88.2
       (outdoorTemperatureInCelsius)
27
28  func buildASentence(subject : String, verb : String, noun : String) -
       > String {
29     return subject + " " + verb + " " + noun + ":"       (2 times)
30  }
31
32  buildASentence("Swift", "is", "cool")                   "Swift is cool"
33  buildASentence("I", "love", "languages")                "I love languages!"
34
35  // Parameters Ad Nauseam
36  func addMyAccountBalances(balances : Double..., names : String) ->
       Double {
37     var result : Double = 0          ⊙ ...  must be on the last parameter  (3 times)
38
39     for balance in balances {
40        result += balance                                 (9 times)
41     }
42
43     return result                                        (3 times)
44  }
45
```

```
    return result
}

addMyAccountBalances(77.87)
addMyAccountBalances(10.52, 11.30, 100.60)
addMyAccountBalances(345.12, 1000.80, 233.10, 104.80, 99.90)
```

The function's Parameter is better called variadic parameter because it has the ability to represent an unknown number of parameters.

If you look at line 36, we have our balances parameter declared to be of type double. It is followed by (…) and a return of type double. The existence of the ellipsis makes Swift to know that there should be another parameter of type double when the function gets called. The function call runs from line 4-48. For every call, the function had a different value.

## First Class Functions:

This is one of the unique and outstanding things with Swift functions. They are simply first-class objects. Hope that looks interesting? First-class objects provide one with the capability to deal with a function just like any other ordinary value. The choice is yours, either opt to assign a function to a variable or even a constant to become a parameter to the next function. Let's use the illustration of what happens in a bank. We have cash withdrawal and cash deposit. Right?

Let's say that every Monday, you deposit a specific amount and then when the week nears to end you withdraw a different amount. The code below gives you the example of how this scenario is implemented:

```
var account1 = ( "State Bank Personal", 1011.10 )
var account2 = ( "State Bank Business", 24309.63 )

func deposit(amount : Double, account : (name : String, balance : Double)) ->
   (String, Double) {
   var newBalance : Double = account.balance + amount
   return (account.name, newBalance)
}
```

```
func withdraw(amount : Double, account : (name : String, balance : Double)) ->
-> (String, Double) {
   var newBalance : Double = account.balance - amount
   return (account.name, newBalance)
}

let mondayTransaction = deposit
let fridayTransaction = withdraw

let mondayBalance = mondayTransaction(300.0, account1)
let fridayBalance = fridayTransaction(1200, account2)
```

In this example, we have created two accounts both on line 77 and 88. Every account is a tuple comprising of an account balance and account name. Line 80 we declare a function called deposit which takes two types of parameters:

- The tuple called account

- The amount called Double

40

The tuple consists of two members:

- Name-type string

- Balance –type double-shows the funds in the account

The tuple type has still been declared as the return type.

We go to line "81", we have declared a variable to show new balance. The variable holds the total of the account tuple plus the amount passed by the variable. The result of the tuple is created on line 82 and then returned.

When you turn to line 90 and 91, there are two new constants declared and allocated to functions respectively by name: withdraw and deposit. Given that we deposit the money on Monday, this transaction is passed to the deposit function. The same happens for the withdrawals, we make withdrawals on Friday, therefore, the Friday transaction is passed the Withdraw function.

The lines "93 and 94" will output the results of both transactions. The results sidebar has the results.

### "Throw me a function"

The same way we have a function which can return String, int or Double. "A function can also return another function". You can check the lines of code below:

```
func chooseTransaction(transaction: String) -> (Double, (String, Double)) ->
  (String, Double) {
  if transaction == "Deposit" {
    return deposit
  }

  return withdraw
}
```

The function chooseTransaction accepts a String as the parameter, which it then applies it to determine the banking transaction type. The same function will return a function, the function accepts a tuple of String, Double, and String. Now, let's examine this code in close proximity. First, the line opens with the function definition and one single parameter. Next, we have characters which have to hold the return type value.

Then, the return type which is, in reality, has two: the tuple of Double, double and String together with the return function of the characters.

Finally, we have the "return type", which consist of a tuple of String and Double.

In the figure above, we have two functions on line 80 and 85. The two functions are bank transactions which we saw previously. They contain the function definition which takes two parameters and later has a return tuple which is comprised of the double and string.

On line 97, we have a comparison taking place of the transaction parameter string against "Deposit" string and in case we have a match found, the deposit function is given back on line 98. Now, we have two functions which have the ability to output two functions. How do you apply it"? You could be asking yourself that question or perhaps you are wondering whether you apply the function in another variable then call it? Well, here is the solution:

```
// option 1: capture the function in a constant and call it
let myTransaction = chooseTransaction("Deposit")
myTransaction(225.33, account2)


// option 2: call the function result directly
chooseTransaction("Withdraw")(63.17, account1)
```

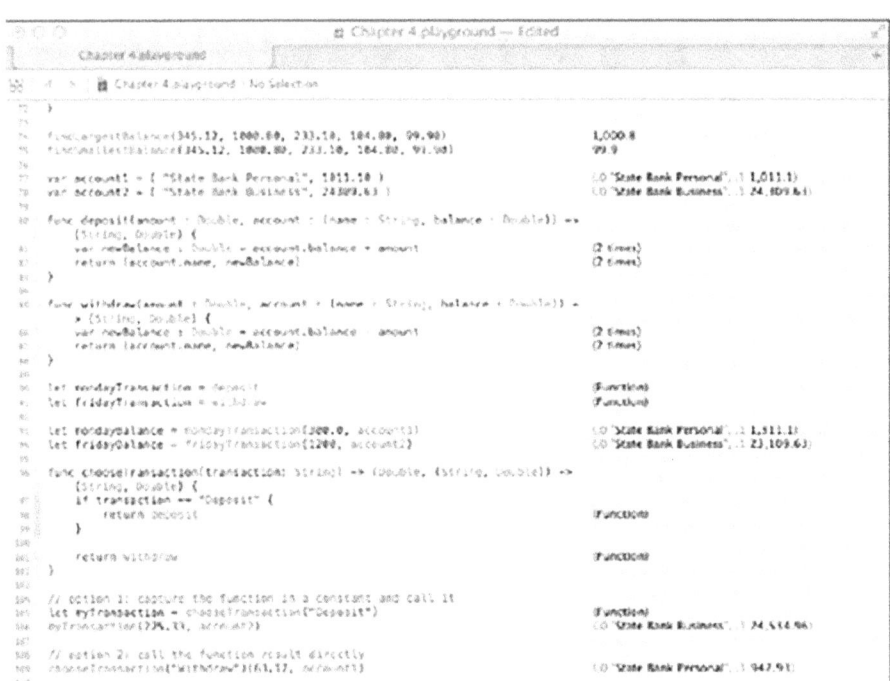

Get time and review the screenshot above especially on line 105. You should manage to identify the returned function. The function has later been called at line 106.

There is an alternate style on line 109. Here, we have the "chooseTransaction function" called to accept access to the withdraw function. Rather than letting a constant hold the result, the returned function gets instantly pressed into a service using parameters.

**Function In A Function:**

So far, you understand the concept of "functions returned by functions" which is later given to constants. Now, let's look at declaring a function within another function. This is known as nested functions. If you have heard of nested loops, then the same concept will apply with some little variations.

First, why are nested functions important? Good question. Whenever you would like to hide, isolate a particular functionality which does not require to get exposed to the outer layers. You can look at the screenshot below:

```
// nested function example
func bankVault(passcode : String) -> String {
    func openBankVault(Void) -> String {
        return "Vault opened"
    }
```

```swift
func closeBankVault(Void) -> String {
   return "Vault closed"
}
if passcode == "secret" {
   return openBankVault()
}
else {
   return closeBankVault()
}
}

println(bankVault("wrongsecret"))
println(bankVault("secret"))
```

When you review line 112, we have a new function, bankVault defined. It takes a single parameter of String type and later return a String.

On line 113 and 116, there are two types of function:

- OpenBankVault

45

- CloseBankVault

The above two functions don't take a parameter or return a String.

When we go to line 119, we have the "passcode parameter" compared with the string "secret". Suppose a match is found, bank vault gets opened by the call of the OpenBankVault function. If not, the bank vault will remain closed.

If look at line 113 and 116, we have a new Swift keyword: Void. This is the same in other languages. It generally means "emptiness". We use the Void keyword as a placeholder when we declare empty parameter lists.

Between the lines 127 and 128, the code will output the results of the method both the correct and incorrect passcode. You should just pay attention that "OpenBankVault and CloseBankVault function" are encircled by a function, and they remain unknown when we jump outside the function.

In general, the greatest advantage with nesting functions is the protection of functions. You should always apply nested functions anytime you want to have functions which work together. You can look at the picture below to develop a much better understanding of the concepts.

## Default Parameters:

So far you have learned a ton of important topics about Swift functions. You have seen how to apply it in the code. As you may have discovered, Swift functions give you a great ability to develop real-world solutions to daily problems. Still, we have another intriguing feature which Swift functions provide us with. This is called the default parameter values. It will give you the freedom to create functions which hold a parameter that has a "prefilled" value.

Take, for example, a developer who would want to build a function which can create checks. This function will have two parameters: the amount and the person to whom the check has to reach. Obviously, in a real-world scenario, these are the crucial aspects of the information

47

which you would want to know. However, in the meantime, you should imagine a function which can take the default payee and later the amount just in case there is not information relayed. Below you will see an example of the above description:

```
func writeCheck(payee : String = "Unknown", amount : String = "10.00") ->
-> String {
    return "Check payable to " + payee + " for $" + amount
}

writeCheck()
writeCheck(payee : "Donna Soileau")
writeCheck(payee : "John Miller", amount : "45.00")
```

You notice the way we have defined the function:

```
func writeCheck(payee : String = "Unknown", amount : String = "10.00") ->
-> String
```

Now, only one thing remains and that is the passing of the parameters actual values. In the above example, we are assigning the payee with "Unknown" as the default while amount has been set to "10.00". This is the approach to use in Swift programming when you want to have a function assume the default parameters. Simply assign the parameter with the value name.

Well, how does one call such a function? There are basically three ways of doing it as shown in the same code:

- You pass no parameters when you call the function
- You pass a single parameter
- You pass both parameters

So, in the first scenario where we don't have any parameters passed, we use the default values defined to show the returned string. In the cases which have remained, we have the values which have been passed applied in the default values.

Don't forget that whenever you want to call a function declared to accept the default parameters, it is vital to pass both the name of the parameter and colon. With default parameters, you experience the flexibility of making use of a known value rather than passing it explicitly. But, they aren't applicable for every function.

## What is contained in the name?

You know how easy it is to declare functions in Swift language? But, how about if I told you that parameters in Swift language can accept not only a text once defined by the func keyword? This is to mean that for every Swift parameter, there is an optional "external parameter" which occurs before the name of the parameter. The external names simply improve the clarity and function description.

```
func writeCheck(payer : String, payee : String, amount : Double) -> String {
    return "Check payable from \(payer) to \(payee) for $\(amount)"
}

writeCheck("Dave Johnson", "Coz Fontenot", 1000.0)
```

```
// option 1: capture the function in a constant and call it
let myTransaction = chooseTransaction("Deposit")          (Function)
myTransaction(225.23, account2)                           (.0 "State Bank Business", .1 24,534.06)

// option 2: call the function result directly
chooseTransaction("Withdraw")(63.17, account1)            (.0 "State Bank Personal", .1 947.93)

// nested function example
func bankVault(passcode : String) -> String {
    func openBankVault(Void) -> String {
        return "Vault opened"                             "Vault opened"
    }
    func closeBankVault(Void) -> String {
        return "Vault closed"                             "Vault closed"
    }
    if passcode == "secret" {
        return openBankVault()                            "Vault opened"
    }
    else {
        return closeBankVault()                           "Vault closed"
    }
}

println(bankVault("wrongsecret"))                         "Vault closed"
println(bankVault("secret"))                             "Vault opened"

func writeCheck(payee : String = "Unknown", amount : String = "10.00")
    -> String {
    return "Check payable to " + payee + " for " + amount (3 times)
}

writeCheck()                                             "Check payable to Unknown for $10.00"
writeCheck(payee : "Donna Soileau")                     "Check payable to Donna Soileau for $10.00"
writeCheck(payee : "John Miller", amount : "45.00")     "Check payable to John Miller for $45.00"

func writeCheck(payer : String, payee : String, amount : Double) ->
    String {
    return "Check payable from \(payer) to \(payee) for $\(amount)"  "Check payable from Dave Johnson to Coz Fonten...
}

writeCheck("Dave Johnson", "Coz Fontenot", 1000.0)       "Check payable from Dave Johnson to Coz Fonten...
```

The above function is not similar to the previous functions between lines 130 -132. Here are the differences:

- We have an extra parameter called payer to determine the source of the check

- There are no default parameters

If you review line 142, you will discover that the function "writeCheck" has three parameters. Just by looking at the name of the function, you can easily predict the function. If you are going to do a guess, a correct guess is that the parameter double is the amount. However, if you don't take time to look or familiarize yourself with the function declaration, you will not realize what the two parameter Strings are?

Using an external parameter, it will help offer a solution to this problem by providing an extra name to every parameter which needs to be passed whenever the function is called. This will make it appear clear to everyone who will read the code.

```
func writeBetterCheck(from payer : String, to payee : String, total amount :
  Double) -> String {
    return "Check payable from \(payer) to \(payee) for $\(amount)"
}

writeBetterCheck(from : "Fred Charlie", to: "Ryan Hanks", total : 1350.0)
```

# Chapter 5

# Structures and Classes in Swift

Classes in Swift resemble classes in other languages. But, one exception with classes in Swift is that they aren't the only ones which can produce the behaviors of classes. And this is the unique difference between Swift and many other languages.

Both the structure and enumeration of the Swift can have several methods the same way classes are. What this now implies is that whenever you want to perform a restructuring of your Swift app, you will require to re-evaluate some of your earlier decisions concerning what really makes up for class objects. There are situations when the structure and enumeration are needed.

We shall guide you on the basics of working with structures, classes, and enumerations in the Swift language. Since they are closely similar in Swift, we shall look at them as one.

### Classes, Structures, and Enumerations:

Having classes, enumerations and structures in Swift together show the similarities which they share. However, there is one specific difference which you need to pay attention to:

- Structures and enumeration are types of values.

This means that an instance of enumerations and structures are emulated whenever they are passed into a given function or allocated to a constant. As a result, there is a possibility of having many copies of the structure and enumeration, and for each copy, it contains its own unique values.

Meanwhile, classes are "reference types". So, when a class is allocated to a variable, we have a reference to the instance transferred. Since we have one instance which has been transferred to the variables, a modification of the values of the respectful instance takes place across all the specified copies.

You can look at the table below which has some of the features present in enumerations, classes and structures.

| Features in Classes, Structures, and Enumerations | | | |
|---|---|---|---|
| Feature | Classes | Structures | Enumerations |
| Instances | X | X | X |
| Properties | X | X | computed properties only |
| Methods | X | X | X |
| Subscripts | X | X | X |
| Initializers | X | X | X |
| Extensions | X | X | X |
| Protocols | X | X | X |
| Inheritance | X | | |
| Type casting | X | | |
| Deinitializers | X | | |
| ARC | X | | |

- Instances-An instance refers to an object which is the real representation of the class. There are specific object oriented languages where the class can still act as the instance.

- Properties-It upon your choice to either create properties which can be computed or stored when they are needed.

- Subscripts- It is possible to create subscripts which will allow you to gain access to specific features of an instance type depending on the subscript logic. Some of the examples consist of the multiple indexing types which belong to the multi-dimensional object. In some cases, they are retrieved just like they are a one-dimensional array. You can also use many dimensions.

- Initializers-This will help one prepare properties for a new instance.

- Protocols-it is possible to create methods inside a protocol which should be implemented using an object which mirrors the protocol.

- Extensions-The extensions will give you the ability to add properties and methods without the presence of the code which you want to add them.

- Inheritance-A class can inherit from another class with the help of a subclass. A class can contain any different amounts of subclasses.

- Deinitializers-This will help you to conduct a clean-up, especially of a class instance, want to be deallocated.

- The type Casting-It is possible to treat one class or sub class as a condition.

- ARC- This will permit one to have many instances of a class.

## Class Declaration:

This section will review some of the inner tasks of the structures, enumeration and class in Swift. The picture below indicates that majority of the code in Swift exists in the master view controller. This is the view which allows one to start and delete events. The "master view controller" will exchange communication with the detail view controller in the right side.

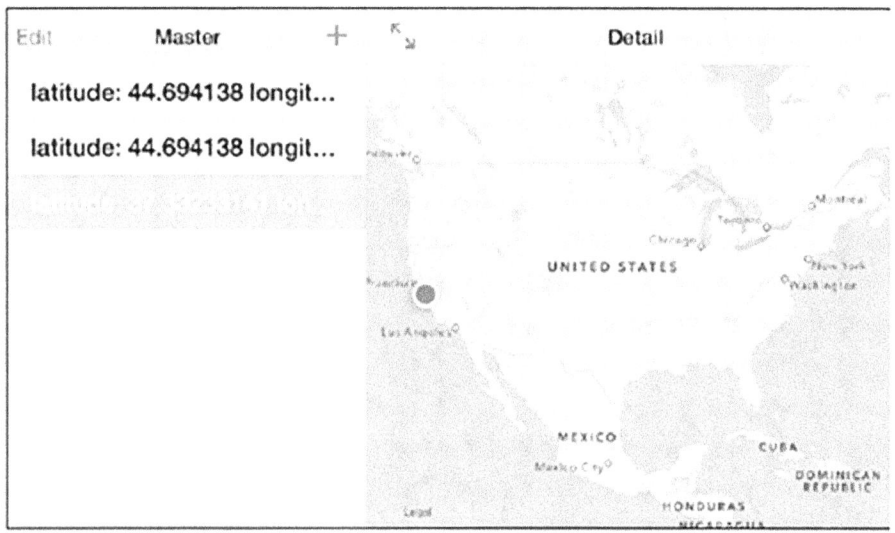

Detailed view controller often is executed using a simple class called DetailViewController. Because of the way this class is simple, we encourage you to take time and look at it so that you can develop the right notion of how classes operate.

In the figure below, we have the DetailViewController. From there, you should be able to realize that we have nothing complicated in the code, you should be fine with reading and understanding the whole class.

```
import UIKit
import MapKit

class DetailViewController: UIViewController {

    //@IBOutlet weak var detailDescriptionLabel: UILabel!
    @IBOutlet var mapView: MKMapView!


    var detailItem: AnyObject? {
        didSet {
            // Update the view.
            self.configureView()
        }
    }

    func configureView() {
        // Update the user interface for the detail item.
        /*if let detail: AnyObject = self.detailItem {
            if let label = self.detailDescriptionLabel {
                label.text =
            detail.valueForKey("timeStamp")!.description
            }
        }*/
    }

    override func viewDidLoad() {
        super.viewDidLoad()
```

Continuation:

```
        // Do any additional setup after loading
            the view, typically from a nib.
        self.configureView()
    }

    override func didReceiveMemoryWarning() {
        super.didReceiveMemoryWarning()
        // Dispose of any resources that can be
            recreated.
    }
}
```

The next section examines the code above in much detail so that you get familiar with the concept of Swift classes. What you need to realize is that many Swift classes go beyond what you have seen above, however, they all take this form.

A file of Swift will contain a class, an enumeration file, and a structure in any particular order.

## Import Declarations:

In Swift class, we have the section for declaring imports, which will import frameworks. Any time you are going to build an XCode class file for the Swift, you will have to place the import declaration.

Let's say you are not working in Swift but Objective –C. You will insert this statement in your file.

```
#import <Foundation/Foundation.h>
```

You should be careful to realize that the Objective C is a bit different. In Swift, we have the import declaration while for the Objective C is simply a compiler directive. Again in Swift, you will perform the import by using its actual name. When you turn to the OS X, we do the import by using both the name and the interface file. In reality, you should not have any worries concerning the import because they are already set up for you. Even if you don't see it there, you already have a template which you can adopt.

## Declaring A Class:

You have so far seen how we declare a class in Swift, it occupies a big space of the class declaration. You should be able to identify the first and last line of your class declaration. If you aren't sure, look at the example below:

```
class DetailViewController: UIViewController {
}
```

## Subclass Declaration:

You have seen that when we want to declare a class we need to begin with the class keyword which is followed by the class name, a colon and superclass name. If we go back to the code above, we can identify DetailViewController as the name of the class. This is a subclass of the UIViewController. Don't forget that there can only exist one superclass unless there is none.

## Base Class Declaration:

So far you have learned how to declare classes in swift, how to declare subclass and a superclass. But, what about the base class? Well, if you want to declare a base class. What you simply do is to remove the colon and the name of the superclass. Remember that a base class is a type of class without the superclass. Let's assume that DetailViewController was a base class, then, this is how we could have proceeded with the base class declaration:

```
class DetailViewController
```

## Using A Protocol:

If you have a class which will use more than one protocol, then they should be outlined after the superclass if it is present. If not, it should simply follow the colon.

## How To Declare A Subclass And Use A Protocol?

This is how it is done:

```
class DetailViewController: UIViewController, MyProtocol
```

## Base Class And Protocol:

```
class DetailViewController: MyProtocol
```

As you can see, you require the colon if you have both the protocol and superclass. If you have a base class which does not have a protocol, it does not need a colon.

When you have finished with class declaration, you need to place the body of your class inside the brackets.

## Declaration Of The Structure:

Where we have reached so far, declaring a structure is not a hard thing. They are just similar to the way we have done the classes. The only exception to pay attention to when declaring your structure is that they should not have a superclass. The only things which you need to describe are the protocols which are adopted by the structure.

## Declaring enum:

The same with a class, an enumeration declaration must begin with the enum keyword. Then you should follow with the name of the enum, then put a colon and if you have protocols you should include them. As you can see, this takes a similar approach to the way we did for the classes. However, there is only one possible scenario for a superclass. This is because enum does not inherit from another one. Below you can see an example of an enum declaration:

Enum MyHouse {

Just like structures and classes, the enum should also begin with capital letter.

Now, let's look at the body of an enum. The enum body should comprise of cases which are separated by commas. Every case should have a unique name. It could also describe more about the type of values it holds.

```
enum MyAnimals {
    case dog, cat, horse, cow
}
```

## Components and Subcomponents:

One of the popular applications of Swift enumeration involves the switch statement. Both of these two elements are very powerful in the Swift programming language, and they work in unison. You can take a look at a switch statement which makes use of enumeration:

```
enum MyAnimal {
   case dog, cat, horse, cow
}

var myPet = MyAnimal.cat

switch myPet {
case .cow:
   println ("moo")
case .cat :
   println ("meow")
case .dog:
   println ("woof")
case .horse:
   println ("neigh")
default:
   println ("silence")
}
```

You should play around with the above code to find out some of the results you get when you decide to alter the var statement. You will realize that we have a default statement since, with Swift, the switch statement is exhaustive. As an experiment, try to delete it and you will notice that you don't get any error because you have covered all possibilities.

You should attempt to add a donkey to become part of the cases. This will trigger an error message since the cases are not exhaustive. You should try to adddonkey or even a place a default case.

Again, you should try and add some raw integer values to the enumeration to make it appear more traditional. You can have a look at a different way to write the enumeration.

```
enum MyAnimal2:Int {
  case dog = 1, cat, horse = 3, cow
}
```

However, if you would like to declare an int type of enumeration, you need to try and access the raw values with the help of rawValue function using this form:

```
var myPet2 = MyAnimal2.cat.rawValue
```

## The Body:

When we examine the structure, class or enumeration, you often see methods inside the body, other times it is the properties and in some cases the variables. Besides the properties, functions and instance variables, classes have both actions and outlets. In other words, they are properties associated to storyboard elements. The process of creating the relation to the storyboard elements is the point at which it links your code to the user interface objects.

## The UI Actions And The Outlets For Classes Alone:

If they do exist, they carry this general construct:

```
@IBOutlet var mapView: MKMapView!
```

# Chapter 6

# Making Better Swift Apps

The Swift language was introduced in the September of 2014. Swift has language properties which improve the safety of the developer's code as well as make them code faster and in a manner which is reliable as compared to using the Objective-C. In this section, we share with you some tips on how to make better apps using the Swift language. These tips will help you build clean as well as help developers who are much conversant with the Objective-C to understand even the Swift language better. Here you will get tips for different levels, regardless of whether you are just starting out in the Swift language.

**Tips:**

**Enhance The Readability Of The Constants:**

One of the best ways you can make use of structs in the Swift language is to build a file which has all the constants. This is very important because the language will allow you to create nested structures such as:

```
import Foundation

struct Constants {

    struct FoursquareApi {
        static let BaseUrl = "https://api.foursquare.com/v2/"
    }

    struct TwitterApi {
        static let BaseUrl = "https://api.twitter.com/1.1/"
    }

    struct Configuration {
        static let UseWorkaround = true
    }

}
```

This type of nesting provides a namespace for the constants. For example, you can use the Constants FoursquareApi.BaseUrl to gain entry to the Foursquare's BaseUrl constant. This helps improve the readability and offers an extra layer to perform encapsulation.

## Keep away from "NSObject and @objc" to enhance the performance

By providing support to the Objective-C runtime makes the method calls to use automatic dispatch rather than the static dispatch. The overall effect is that the methods which help the "Objective-C runtime" will develop a four times performance boost.

## Make Use Of The Swizzling Method In Swift

This is a technique which replaces one method execution with another. Swift will enhance the code so that it can make a direct memory reference of searching up for the method location at the runtime as in the Objective-C. This means, Swizzling can't work in Swift classes, not unless:

- ExtendNSObject. You should not attempt this unless you are doing it for the swizzling method. It is very important to note that the swizzling method will operate on preexisting classes which contain the NSobject as part of their base class, however, we are much better using dynamic to select methods.

- Disable this optimization using the "dynamic keyword". This is the right choice and the option which is sensible especially when the codebase is fully in Swift.

- Make use of the @obj annotation on the swizzled method. This is right mostly when the method which you want to swizzle has been accessed by the objective-c.

**Tips For New Beginners In Swift**

**You Should Make It A Practice To Clean Up Your Asynchronous Code:**

Swift has one of the best syntaxes for one to write ending functions. Perhaps, if you have learned Objective-C, you will agree with me that we have completion blocks in the Objective –C. However, they were introduced later on, and their syntax was not really nice. As you can see below:

```
[self loginViaHttpWithRequest:request completionBlockWithSuccess:^(LoginOperation
  [self showMainScreen];
} failure:^(LoginOperation *operation, NSError *error) {
  [self showFailedLogin];
}];
```

Fortunately, Swift will make everything simple with the beautiful syntax.

```
loginViaHttp(request) { response in
  if response.success {
    showMainScreen()
  } else {
    showFailedLogin()
  }
}
```

## Regulate The Access To The Code:

As a new beginner, it is important to adopt the culture of using the right control modifiers so that you can encapsulate your code. If you have the correct code encapsulation, it will play a big role in understanding the various pieces of the code which we write and engage with. All this will be possible without the need to recall out thought process.

Swift language has with it popular access control means such as the internal, private and public. However, the protected access is not present in the access control modifier of the Swift language. The reason for the absence lies in the fact that a subclass has the ability to expose a method which is protected using the new public method. Furthermore, the protected method will not provide extra optimization chances for the Swift compiler especially when we have a random new override emerging. The last reason is that protected modifier will contribute to a poor code encapsulation since it stops the subclass helpers from getting access to information available to the subclass.

## Play Around With The Playgrounds:

A playground is one of the best places for new Swift developers. Here, you can try and build playgrounds which can help you do some testing and validation, share some concepts and validate the ideas with another. This can be achieved without heading to build a new project. If you would like to start a playground, you need to select it on the XCode launch.

Once you are on the playground, you should begin to code and see the results shown on the right.

You should take advantage of playgrounds and develop prototypes in Swift language.

## Make Use Of The Optional In The Right Manner:

We say a property is optional if it has a valid or nil value. It is possible to unwrap an optional by adhering to the optional name using an exclamation point. This should be similar to the optionalProperty! This is something which you don't want to encounter.

However, we have certain cases where the application of the implicitly unwrapped optional is allowed. IBOutletsis an example. The outlets are optional since IBOoutLets are declared at a specific point after the initialization, and all the non-optional features need to possess the initialization based on the rules of Swift.

## The NSNumber should be left behind:

The Objective-C uses primitives for both the numbers as well as the Foundation Objective –C. Some of the Swift types to use in place of the NSNUmber include:

- Float

- Double

- Swift

- Int

- Bool

We can still apply the NSNumber in the conversions between several types in the Objective-C, but Swift provides the idiomatic style of converting values.

## Tips On How You Should Not Develop Apps In IOS:

### 1. Don't Put Every File In The Root Folder

You should make use of folders to show groups in the XCode. This is just like in real life where you don't have all your utensils in one collection. Just try to be organized as this is the best way which you will end up building wonderful projects. You should be aware that in the XCode 9 folders are developed to take care of your groups.

## 2. Avoid having warning in your project

You should make it a practice to fix any type of warning which shows up in your project. It is a bad practice to have warnings remain in your project. Although warnings exist, that should not be the reason for you to leave them in your project. If you want to be a bit radical, you should play around with the build flag which will help you kill warnings.

## 3. Your source code should not be very long

It is always annoying when you open a source file, and get greeted with a long source code which will make you scroll and scroll before you reach the end. You should adopt the SwiftLint which can trigger a warning so that you can remain aware whenever your code starts to become big.

## 4. Don't write a lot of code which you might never use

Don't make this mistakes of returning something inside the if else block. Instead, apply this style when you want to return something:

```
if something {
    return true
}
return false
```

The next thing you should notice about this tip is that you need to develop the right knowledge about how Swift functions operate. Don't just copy and paste, try to do some little modification. You should take time to think about the problem you want to solve and avoid copying the same code in many places. Just get time and create new functions and use them in the right manner.

## 5. Reinventing the when might cost you

If you find the right and best practice, then use it. However, at all times it is good to do some research online about the problem before you can start to code. Don't forget that there are a lot of people who experience the coding problem. Most of the time, you will find someone who had a similar issue like the one you would like to solve. A visit to the StackOverflow can save your time and day. Make use of the advantage of a community. Don't be shy to ask questions on the internet.

## 6. Connecting third party libs manually is wrong

You make a habit to use dependency managers such as Swift Package Manager. Do not add dependencies manually. It looks ugly.

## 7. Minimize on the number of dependencies

If you find a native solution go with that. But, do not use too many dependencies. One way to avoid excessive use of dependencies is by only using dependencies for tasks which are complex.

## 8. Don't write async code if you don't have operations, promises and third party libs

In Swift programming, you will write async code. So, before you end up messing up things, you need to make use of promises because they are an extensive abstraction over the async tasks. They simplify your life so that you have an easy life.

## 9. Don't use the Singletons

They are the cause of all evils. You should put a stop to Singletons if you are a fun of using them. If you are not sure how you can stop using them, do some deep research on the internet.

# Conclusion

This book has been written to both macOS and IOS developers. Regardless of whether it is your first time to learn how to code or you are an experienced developer, there is something to learn here. If you are just getting started in Swift development, this book should be able to help you master the fundamentals in Swift programming.

The start of every journey in programming is to learn the language. For the IOS developers, this book starts the journey for you with the fundamentals of Swift programming language. This book generally prepares you to begin tackling complex stuff in the Swift language.

You should have realized that Swift language is not like the objective – C. Instead, it is much better and safe. Swift helps you get the best smart modern syntax. You have a language which is expressive and easy to understand. If you are done reading this book, the next step for you is to challenge yourself with even a complex Swift book. This will now help you grasp deep skills and concepts.

Practice to code every day, this book alone can't make you become an expert Swift developer. Perhaps you will need to put more effort into reading and writing code. Try several practical questions on building apps until when you feel confident of yourself. Remember, nothing comes on a silver platter. You have to dedicate your time and effort. We have done our part of helping you develop a basic understanding of Swift programming. Now, it is your chance to build and expand on that knowledge.

# PHP

---

*Basic Fundamental Guide for Beginners*

# Introduction to PHP

Is this your first time to code in PHP? Are you stuck in the MySQL database? Perhaps you don't know how to create sessions or cookies in PHP? This book will take you through a complete step-by-step process of learning PHP. Whether you have just started or you want to continue from where you left, get this masterpiece containing the fundamental concepts of PHP.

Besides that, we will explain everything in a friendly and interactive manner to make sure that you understand every concept. We will also provide you with screenshots of source code to type in your favorite text editor.

If your goal is to become a great PHP developer, then this book is for you. If you want to quickly master the basic fundamentals of PHP programming, then this book will help you do so. If you are tired of debugging your code and you want to learn how you can fix it up fast, then we have the solution for you.

PHP is an amazing language with easy-to-understand concepts. If you can learn PHP today, then you will manage to create anything from a simple contact form to a complete web application. You will even learn how to create a mailing list or a content management system.

That said, this book will teach you how to do that. We will also teach you how to build PHP applications to solve real-world problems. Since PHP is a web-based language, a little knowledge of HTML and CSS will help you. Still, if you're green on HTML and CSS. Don't worry, HTML and CSS are just easy as 1, 2, and 3.

# Chapter 1

## Starting Up and Running With PHP

### Introduction to PHP

Welcome to PHP. A popular programming language used by many people across the world.

PHP is an amazing language which you can use to build interactive and dynamic websites. When you are done writing your PHP program, you must have a Web server to run your code. PHP programs serve web pages to visitors based on their request. Put simply, it is a server side language. PHP has one prominent feature where you can embed your written code within the pages of HTML. This makes it very easy for anyone who wants to make dynamic content.

In the previous paragraph, you can simply say I described PHP as 'interactive and dynamic.'

As a beginner to PHP programming, you may be wondering about what exactly those two phrases mean. To save you time, when you hear a programmer describe a web page as being dynamic, they are simply trying to say that the contents of the page change automatically whenever the page is viewed. You can compare this with a static HTML file which never changes no matter how many people visit the page. Meanwhile, an interactive web page is one which accepts and responds to the input it receives from the visitors. A good example of an interactive website is a web forum. In a web forum, different users can post a message which is then displayed on the forum for everyone to see.

If you have been wondering what PHP stands for, then you are in the right place. PHP is an abbreviation for Hypertext Preprocessor. By just

74

knowing the full meaning of PHP, you can begin to tell some of the capabilities of the language. In simple terms, it processes information and unveils it as hypertext. Many developers prefer recursive acronyms and PHP is very appealing to developers.

In PHP, for you to see the results after you have written your code, you must run your program on a PHP server. Below are the steps to follow if you want to run your PHP program on a Web server:

1. First, a visitor will make a request for a web page by either typing the URL of the webpage or clicking on a link. The visitor can send data to the web server as well with the help of a form attached to the web page.

2. The server finds out which type of request it is, once it knows that the language is PHP. It begins processing the request.

3. Once the processing is completed, the visitor sees a page.

The most exciting thing takes place when the PHP program runs. Since PHP is a very flexible language, a single PHP script can perform a multitude of interesting tasks. Some of the tasks it can perform are:

- Process details in a form

- Read and write files on a web server

- It can process data kept in a web server which has a database

- Build dynamic graphics

Lastly, when any of the above tasks are done, a PHP script can show a customized HTML web page to the visitor.

## Why should I use PHP?

Most people new to PHP always ask this question. If you happen to be among them, here is something interesting for you, many internet service providers and web hosting firms have systems that are compatible with PHP. Today, a big population of developers use PHP, and they are very many because a majority of the websites are built on PHP programming.

Another powerful feature that you will get, if you choose to use the PHP language, is that it's cross-platform compatible. What this one simply means is that you can run your PHP programs on more than one platform. It doesn't matter if the platform you're using is Mac OS X, Windows, FreeBSD, and Solaris. Plus, the PHP engine is compatible with some of the popular web servers like Internet Information Server, Zeus, Apache, and lighttpd. This implies that if you want to develop your PHP program in, let's say, a Windows setup and later deploy it on Mac OS X, it is possible. In addition, the process of migrating your entire PHP program is easy. No stress involved.

Now, before we begin to discuss the basics of PHP language. I want to briefly show you the steps in setting up your PHP environment. Then, you can learn how to write a simple PHP code.

# First PHP Code

## What you should have

For you to actually run your first PHP script, you have to install and run a PHP Web server. You can pick any of the choices below:

- **Run localhost on your computer**

In this option, you will be running PHP on your computer. In other words, you will install a local PHP Web server on your machine. The easiest way you can achieve this is by looking online for a complete package. XAMPP is one of the best choices you should go for. This comes with the Apache Web server, MySQL database engine, PHP, and many other applications. No stress when it comes to the installation. Just a click of a button and you'll be done.

- **Run your coded scripts on a web host**

Now, if you have an active web hosting account which is designed to allow PHP, you can run your PHP scripts there. What you will do is use the FTP to upload your scripts. If you upload everything, then you can run the server to see the results. The disadvantage with a web server is that it is not fast compared to a local host.

## Your First Script

Below is a script of PHP that you will learn how to create.

```
<Code />

<!DOCTYPE html PUBLIC "-//W3C//DTD XHTML 1.0 Strict//EN"
  "http://www.w3.org/TR/xhtml1/DTD/xhtml1-strict.dtd">
<html xmlns="http://www.w3.org/1999/xhtml" xml:lang="en" lang="en">
  <head>
    <title>My first PHP script</title>
  </head>
  <body>
    <p><?php echo "Hello, world!"; ?></p>
  </body>
</html>
```

In the above script, the majority is made up of XHTML.

So, the <? Php and ?> tags pass a message to the Web server that everything in the tags is a PHP code. The line of code enclosed within the PHP tags is simple. It makes use of a built-in function called 'echo,' which prints a simple text ("Hello, world!") on the website. The PHP language has a lot of functions which we are going to learn in the following chapters. These functions are important to help a developer or programmer build applications.

You should pay attention to the semicolon (;) immediately after the line of PHP. The semicolon shows the end of the PHP line of code. Every time you finish writing your line of PHP, you should put a semicolon. However, if you are writing a single line of code like in the example above, then it is optional. You can choose to put it in or ignore it. But, not when you have more than one line of PHP script.

## Creating the PHP script

Now, for you to create a similar script like the one above, first, you must get a text editor. Nowadays, many computers have their own text editors such as:

78

- Windows notepad and the text editor for the MAC

However, if you feel like the above options are not the best for you, then you can choose to download Sublime text. Once you have your text editor ready, you should type the code below in the editor. Save it in any name but make sure you store in the pathway of your web server:

```
<html>
 <head>
  <title>PHP Test</title>
 </head>
 <body>
 <?php echo '<p>Hello World</p>'; ?>
 </body>
</html>
```

However, if you have a web hosting account, use FTP to upload your code before you run it.

## Test the script

We will now assume that you have done everything outlined above. The only thing remaining is to run your script. If you want to run your script, enter the following URLs into your web address:

- http://localhost/hello.php

For those who are working on an internet hosting account. Your code will resemble:

- http://www.youurl.com/hello.php

If everything runs well, then this is the output which you should get:

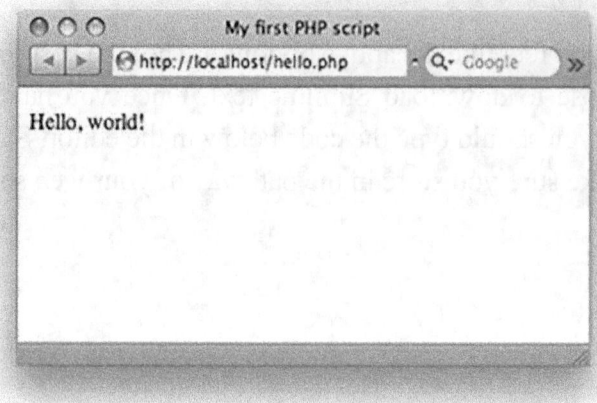

## Problems?

If you encountered problems along the way while running your PHP script, you may need to go back and assess your Web server. It could be that your Web server isn't set up correctly. If for example, if the PHP code was shown on the browser instead of something similar to the above image, then that means your web server was configured well.

## Next?

If the above web page displayed, congratulations! You can now write, save, and run your PHP program. You will improve the skills mentioned above in the next chapters. But for now, we are going to teach you the core basics of the PHP programming language.

# Chapter 2

# A Walk Through the PHP Language

At this point, you have now learned what PHP is and what some of its uses are. I believe you that you were able to run your first PHP program. Now, in this chapter, we are going to help you learn more about the core basics of PHP. This chapter will focus on:

- Variables

- PHP operators

- Constants

- Data types and many others

## Variables in PHP

One of the most important things in any programming language is variables. A variable can be described as a container which can carry certain values. With variables, some values can change in the process of execution. And it's this ability to manage dynamic values which makes the variables so powerful in programming.

For instance, let's look at this line of PHP code:

```
echo 4 + 4;
```

As you might predict, this script will print 8 when it's executed. This is beautiful, but let's say, you want to show the value of 3+ 4. The only way out is to write the code like the one shown below:

*echo 3 + 4;*

Now, this is when variables become useful. If you decide to use variables rather than numbers in your code, then your script becomes more flexible and useful. Here is an example to show you how variables can be used:

*Echo $a + $b;*

The line of code above is general. But, it gives you much flexibility because you can assign any numbers to variables *$a* and *$b*. In its current state, if you were to execute this code, it will show you the sum of the values of *$a* and *$b*.

*$a=4;*

*$b=3;*

*Echo $a + $b;*

## Naming variables

A variable is made of two parts. Those two parts consist of the variable name together with the value the variable carries. A good practice when it comes to naming your variables is to use names which are familiar to the task or operation performed. Similar to other programming languages, there are rules one must follow when giving names to variables:

- Variable names should have the dollar sign at the start

- After the dollar sign, a letter or underscore is permitted

Another important point which you need to remember is PHP variable names are case-sensitive. This means if you write *$Variable* and later write *$variable*, they are all different. I will suggest you pick one method which you will use to write all your variables and stick to that method. If you can do this, then you will avoid confusion. Again, while the length of a variable is not fixed, it is good to note that having a variable name with more than 30 characters looks abnormal. If you want to see what variables look like in PHP, then here is an example:

- *$_342*

- *$my_variable*

- *$y*

- *$number*

## Declaring a variable

Declaring a PHP variable is what many developers call 'creating a variable.' To declare a variable is not something hard to do because it's very easy. For example:

*$my_second_variable;*

If PHP recognizes a variable's name in the code, it immediately declares the variable.

Any time you declare a variable in PHP, it's recommended that you assign the variable a value. This procedure of allocating a value to your variable is called 'initializing.' Doing this has many advantages. For example, if someone else passes through your code, they would be able to tell what type of value the variable holds. If you fail to initialize a variable, then the default value assigned is null. Have a look at how you can declare and initialize a PHP variable by trying this example:

*$money=200;*

## Types of PHP data

All data types kept in PHP variables come in either one of the eight basic types. In the PHP language, there are four scalar data types. Data is said to be scalar if it contains just a single value. Below is a list of these data types:

- **Integer**

- **Float**

It is a floating point number like 9.34

- **String**

Consists of a series of characters such as 'How much?'

- **Boolean**

This can either be false or true

Besides the scalar types, PHP also has what we call 'compound data' types. A data type is said to be compound if it can have more than one value. Listed below are the compound data types found in PHP:

- **Array**

Represents an ordered map that has numbers or names linked to values

- **Object**

One that may have methods and properties

Lastly, PHP also has special data types. They are special since they neither contain compound or scalar data. However, they have a unique meaning:

- **Resource**

- **Null**

It might have null as the value. This means the variable does not hold any value

## PHP loose typing

Something else that you need to understand about PHP is it is a loosely-typed language. In other words, it is a language which does not care about the type of data kept in a variable. What this means is that it automatically changes the variable's data type. For example, you can initialize a variable as a double integer, but add a string value to it. This is not something you can do with other programming languages like Java, which is strongly-typed.

This feature of PHP is both negative and positive. It gives you the flexibility important in different situations, but on the other hand, you will not be notified if you happen to pass a wrong data type. You will not be notified of an error, but you may notice that the output of your code is not what you expected. The good news is that PHP has a way to test this.

## Expressions and Operators

Now, I believe you that you are already knowledgeable about the PHP variables, right? If somebody asks you to declare and initialize an integer variable, you are capable of doing it, right? But, programming could look dull if this is only what you could achieve with variables. This is when operators bring in a new flavor. Operators allow you to play around with the data stored in the variables so that you can come up with a new value. Take, for example, the code below. It uses the operator (-) to subtract the values of $a and $b to produce a new value:

- *echo $a-$b;*

In short, if you are still wondering what an operator is, it is a symbol with the ability to change one or more values, often resulting in a new value. On the other hand, an expression is anything which will translate into a value. This can consist of different combinations of functions, operators, variables, and values. In the previous example, *$a-$b* is an expression. Some other examples of expressions are:

- *$x - $y*
- *True*
- *$x + $y + $t*

Operands are the values and variables used together with an operator.

## Types of operators

There are 10 types of operators in PHP. They are:

- **Arithmetic operators**

These include addition, subtraction, multiplication, division, and modulus

- **Assignment operators (=)**

You have already seen its application

- **Bitwise operators**

- **Comparison operators**

This lets you make comparisons between one operand and the other one in different ways.

Here's a list of the comparison operators in PHP:

| Operator | Example | Result |
|---|---|---|
| == (equal) | $x == $y | true if $x equals $y; false otherwise |
| != or <> (not equal) | $x != $y | true if $x does not equal $y; false otherwise |
| === (identical) | $x === $y | true if $x equals $y and they are of the same type; false otherwise |
| !== (not identical) | $x !== $y | true if $x does not equal $y or they are not of the same type; false otherwise |
| < (less than) | $x < $y | true if $x is less than $y; false otherwise |
| > (greater than) | $x > $y | true if $x is greater than $y; false otherwise |
| <= (less than or equal to) | $x <= $y | true if $x is less than or equal to $y; false otherwise |
| >= (greater than or equal to) | $x >= $y | true if $x is greater than or equal to $y; false otherwise |

- **Incrementing and decrementing operators**

Usually used to subtract or add the value one over and over again

- **Logical operators**

These work on the Boolean values. A Boolean value can either be true or false

- **String operators**

PHP has only one string operator which is the concatenation operator or the (dot). What this string operator does is to join two strings to make them longer.

## Operator precedence

When dealing with a simple expression such as 4 + 9, it is very easy. Add 4 and 9 to get 13. But, let's examine a case where we have more than one operator, do you think we shall work it out the same way we did above? No! This is when operator precedence comes in to help. All operators in PHP have been ordered based on precedence. This means that an operator with higher precedence is always executed first before one which has a lower precedence. Below is a list of operators arranged according to precedence.

| Precedence of Some PHP Operators (Highest First) |
| --- |
| ++ -- (increment/decrement) |
| (int) (float) (string) (array) (object) (bool) (casting) |
| ! (not) |
| * / % (arithmetic) |
| + - . (arithmetic) |
| < <= > >= <> (comparison) |
| == != === !== (comparison) |
| && (and) |
| \|\| (or) |
| = += -= *= /= .= %= (assignment) |
| and |
| xor |
| or |

## Constants

PHP also allows you to define constants to hold values. One thing about the values of constants is that it remains the same. In addition, constants are defined once in a PHP script.

Don't confuse constants with variables in PHP. Constants are different from variables in the way they are defined, and they don't begin with the dollar sign. However, I will recommend that you make it a habit to define all your constants in uppercase letters. In addition, don't use reserved PHP keywords to define constants. If you do so, you may confuse PHP.

## Decisions and Loops

Up to this point, you have learned some of the basics of PHP. You know the number of data types in PHP, and you know the types of expressions in PHP as well as variables, right? All of the codes you have seen are categorized as a linear type of code. But, things become even interesting when you begin to use decisions and loops.

Simply put, a decision will allow you to either execute a given section of code or not depending on the results of a given test. Loops will permit the code to run repeatedly until that point when the code accomplishes a specific condition.

By integrating decisions and loops into your code, you will gain much control over your code, and you can make them dynamic. With the help of decisions and loops, you have a chance to display different kinds of content to your visitors depending on what buttons they click or where they live, among other conditions.

## Making decisions

Similar to other popular programming languages, PHP gives you the power to write a code which can make a decision, depending on the current result of an expression. With 'decisions,' you have the ability to develop complex codes.

## Decisions with 'If statements'

This is the easiest decision statement that one can understand. The basic nature of the 'if statement' is as follows:

*If (expression) {*

*// put here your code*

*}*

*// additional code goes here*

In this example, the code in the braces is executed only if the expression in the parenthesis is true.

Now, let's say the code is false, then that means the code in the braces will not be executed. However, it is important to highlight that any script after the closing brace will always be executed no matter the results of the test. So in the previous example, if the expression is true, then both the 'put here your code' and the 'additional code goes here' will run. But, if the expression is found to be false, then the 'put here your code' will not be executed, but the extra 'additional code goes here' will still be executed.

**Another 'else statement'**

You have seen that the 'if statement' will let you execute a code if an expression is true. But, if the expression is read as false, then the piece of code is skipped. Now, with an else statement, it gives you the ability to improve the decision-making process. Let's look at an example:

*If ($z >=20) {*

*echo "Z is greater than twenty";*

*} else {*

*echo "Z is less than 20";*

*}*

If $z is greater than or equal to twenty, then 'Z is greater than twenty' is displayed. However, if $Z is less than twenty, then 'Z is less than 20' is shown to the user. It is still possible to create a combination of a 'last else' statement with another 'if' statement, so you have plenty of alternative choices. PHP still offers you with a special 'else, if' in which you can combine an 'else' and 'if' statement. So you can have it like this:

*If (expression1) {*

*echo "Write your statement here";*

*} else if (expression2) {*

*echo "Write your second statement here";*

*} else {*

*echo "write your last statement here";*

*}*

## Switch statement

There are times when you will face a scenario where you want to test an expression against many different values, each having its own assigned task if the value matches. Have a look at this example that applies to the 'if,' 'else, if' and 'else' statements:

*If ($x === "open") {*

*// Open the file*

*} else if ($x == "save") {*

*// Save the file*

*} else if ($x == "logout") {*

*// logout the user*

*} else {*

*Print "Kindly select an option";*

*}*

The above example repeatedly compares the same variable with different values. Well, this is very tiresome. What if you want to have a different expression?

If you were to implement it with the PHP switch statement, things just get easier and fun. The switch statement makes things look simple and elaborate. You will use the expression 'once.' You can look at the example so that you can understand what I am saying:

```
Switch ($X) {

case "open":

//Open your file

break;

case "save":

// save your file

break;

case "logout":

//logout the user

break;

default:

print "kindly select an option";

}
```

You can see that despite the second example requiring additional lines of code, it is a clear approach that is easy to follow and maintain.

## Using the ternary operator

We already looked at operators in the previous sections, has and there is another operator known as the ternary operator. The ternary operator has the question mark as its symbol. Furthermore, the ternary operator evaluates three expressions:

*(expression 1)? expression2: expression3;*

The ternary operator is somehow similar to the 'if, else' construct. You can think of the ternary operator as a compact version of the 'if, else' style. The previous code can be interpreted like this: 'If the *expression1* is true, then the entire expression is equal to *expression1on2*, but if the *expression1* is evaluated as false, then the overall expression is equal to *expression1on3.*"

## Using loops to do repeated tasks

I hope you have learned how you can make decisions with a separate snippet of code based on a written condition. Now, I want to introduce to you something more powerful. I know you have heard of the word loop. As the name suggests, there is an act of repetition in a loop. So, a loop repeats a given task until a condition is attained. Similar to decisions, the condition in a 'loop' has to be in the form of an expression. For those of you who don't understand this, let me explain it to you. If the expression is going to be false, then the loop will stop. But, as long as it is true, the loop continues to run.

## While loops

This is the easiest type of loop that anyone can understand. A 'while' loop looks similar to the 'if' statement. Here is a 'while' construct:

```
While (expression) {

//Code

}
// More code
```

Looks simple, doesn't it? If the expression found in the parenthesis is evaluated and found to be true, the block of code in the braces is executed. Again, if the expression is evaluated and found to be true, then the block of code is executed again, and the pattern goes on. However, let's say the expression is false, what happens? The loop exits the condition, but the remaining code outside the parenthesis will be executed. Let us use a practical application of a 'while' loop:

```php
<? php
$books= 10;
while ($books > 0) {
echo "Selling a book... ";
$books - -;
echo "done. There are $books books left. < br / >";
}
echo "We are out of books!";
? >
```

## The 'do while' loop

In the 'while loop,' we evaluate the expression at the start. However, when it comes to the 'do while' we do the opposite. We first run part of the code before we test the expression. Look at this example:

```php
<? php
$w = 1;
$l= 1;
do {
$w++;
$l++;
$area = $w * $l;
} while ($area < 1000);
```

> echo "The smallest square over 1000 sq. ft in area is $w ft. x $l
> ft.";
>
> ? >

In this example, the code inside the loop will run before the condition is tested. What this means is that the variable *$area* will at least have a value before we arrive at the testing phase. Now, if the area will continue to have a value of less than 1000, then the loop will continue to run.

## The 'for' loop

So far you have learned about the while, and the 'do while' loop. But, there is one other type of loop that's more compact and neat, the 'for' loop. I would suggest that you use the 'for' loop when you have a specific number in your head which you want the loop to repeat. With the 'for' loop, you can create a counter variable which will record the number of loops. The syntax for a 'loop' is:

> *for (expression1; exression2; expression3) {*
>
> *// run the code*
>
> *}*
>
> *// Additional code goes here*

Looking at the above syntax, we realize that unlike the 'do while' loops which only have one expression in their parenthesis, the 'for loop' has three expressions. The expressions are described below in order:

- **Initialize**r

This runs only once. The 'for' statement initializes a counter first.

- **Loop test**

This has the same function as the single expression in the 'do while' loop. So, if the expression test is true, then the loop continues, but if it is false, then the loop exits.

- **Counting**

This is used to change the value of the counter

The code snippet below is a demonstration of the 'for loop.' Kindly study it:

```
for ($1=1; $1<= 10; $1++) {

echo "I have reached: $1 <br />";

}

echo "finished";
```

This example shows how efficient a 'for loop' can be.

## Loops and the break statement

When you are working with the 'do while' and many others, the loop will run until the point it is found to be false.

But, it is possible to exit a loop while it's in the middle by applying the 'break' statement. This operates the same way it does inside a switch construct.

Why should you break from this loop? Well, in some instances it is still right to exit out of the loop. For example, the infinite 'for' loop will continue to run and run until it exhausts the resources on the server.

Another reason why you might want to exit a loop is when you have completed doing whatever kind of process you wanted to achieve.

## Creating nested loops

Have you ever heard of a loop within a loop? Below is an example of how a 'nested' loop will look:

```
for ($t = 0; $t < 10; $t++) {
for ($u = 0; $u < 10; $u++) {
echo $t. $u. "< br / >";
  }
}
```

## Strings

When it comes to programming, a string is a series of characters. For example, 'many,' 'how are you,' and 'morning' are all valid strings. In essence, the web is entirely made up of a string of data. HTML and XHTML comprise of strings. This part will take you through some of the crucial things you need to be aware of regarding strings in PHP.

## Creating and accessing strings

To create a string variable is very simple, all it takes is to initialize your variable with a literal string value. For instance:

```
$yourstring= 'hello';
```

If you check the example above, the literal string is enclosed in single quotes. But, you can still use the double quotation marks. Something which you need to note is that both single and double quotation marks operate differently. A string enclosed with single quotation marks lets PHP use it exactly as it has been typed.

Here, the double quotation marks have several additional features:

- You can use special characters
- You can parse and replace

## Create a string using this method

Earlier, I had taught you how you can create a string, but there are different other ways as shown in the examples below:

*$yourstring= $mystring;*

*$yourstring = "how". "are". "you?";*

*$yourstring = ($x > 200)? "Bigger number": "Smaller number";*

## Length of a string

The function *strlen ()* will help you determine the length of a string. The function accepts the string value as the argument and outputs the length of the string. For example:

*$yourstring= "goalpost";*

*echo strlen ($yourstring). "<br/>"; // outputs 8*

## Gaining access to string characters

Do you want to learn how you can access individual characters in a string?

PHP offers you with an easy approach. Study this example to learn:

*$character = $string[index];*

## Arrays

At this point, you already know what a variable is in PHP. We said that a variable is a container which can hold a single value. However, there are specific types of variables which can store more than one value. An example of that variable is the array, and the other one is the object.

Arrays are an incredible feature in programming languages because it gives one the ability to work with huge sizes of data. As an excellent form of data storage, the two major properties of arrays are:

- An array has no fixed size, which means it can store millions of values

- It is very simple to manipulate multiple array values all at once

To begin with, let's first define an array.

Arrays are simply a unique form of a variable with added functionality. For example, arrays will help you store as many values in just one variable. Let's say, for example, you have a lot of soccer balls which you would like to store. If you want to store all your balls in a single variable, this is how your piece of code will look like:

*$ball1 = "Map";*

*$ball2 = " Success";*

*$ball3 = "Mountains";*

*Assume, now that you have a list of books.*

*$book1 = "Map";*

*$book2 = " Success";*

*$book3 = "Mountains";*

Well, suppose you wanted to loop through your list of books and pick one? Or let's assume that you don't have 3 books but 400? The best tactic to use here is the array. An array allows you to store all your books in one single variable name. Plus, you can access the array by using the array name.

In an array, each element stored has its own index to ensure that the process of accessing it becomes simple. PHP has three types of arrays, and we are going to discuss each type one by one.

## Numeric array

This is an array that has a numeric index. A numeric array assigns each array element a numeric index.

To create a numeric array, you can use two methods:

- In this first example, the index is automatically assigned:

*$books = array ("Tom and Mary", "The happy ending", "The Storm");*

- In this second example, the index is assigned manually:

*$books [0] = "Tom and Mary";*

*$books [1] = "The happy ending";*

*$books [2] = "The Storm";*

## Associative arrays

In this array, we will link the key with the value stored. But, when you want to store the type of data related to individual values, a numeric array is never the best to use. Instead, an associative array is the best option to go with.

This example uses an array to assign the age of various people:

*$ages = array ("David" =>22, "Peter" => 40, "Steve" =>37);*

You can then use the ID keys in a script like:

*<? php*

*$ages['David'] = "22"; $ages['Peter'] = "40"; $ages['Steve'] = "34"; echo "Peter is ". $ages['Peter']. " years old. ";?>*

This code will display Peter is 40 years old.

## Multidimensional arrays

When it comes to the multidimensional array, each element is an array. So, it is like we have an array of arrays. In the example below, we have created a multidimensional array with ID keys:

*$class=array*

*(*

*"Geoffrey" =>array*

*(*

*"Meghan",*

*"Eden",*

*"Hazard"*

*),*

*"Jameson" =>array*

*(*

*"Mike"*

*),*

*"White" =>array*

*(*

*"Cleveland",*

*"Edwin",*

*"Junior"*

*)*

*);*

*This array would look this if written together with the output:*

*Array*

*(*

*[Geoffrey]=>Array*

*(*

*[0]=>Meghan*

*[1]=>Eden*

*[2]=>Hazard*

*)*

*[Jameson]=>Array*

*(*

*[0]=>Mike*

*)*

*[White]=>Array*

*(*

*[0]=>Cleveland*

*[1]=>Edwin*

*[2]=>Junior*

*)*

*)*

If we want to display a single value from one of the arrays above, then we do that by using the following code:

> *echo "does". $class['Geoffrey'][2]. "belong to the Geoffrey class?";*

This code will display the following: "does Eden belong to the Geoffrey class?"

## Functions

A function is a block of code which performs a specific task. A function is defined by following a certain syntax, and then you can call the function from a different section of your code. The syntax that you should follow whenever you are creating a PHP function is:

*function nameOfFunction ()*

*{*

*//Script to be executed*

*}*

When creating PHP functions, one is always advised to give the function a name which corresponds to the task the function is going to do. The name of the function can even begin with an underscore or a letter, but it should start with a number. Here is an example of a function which will ask for my name:

*<? php*

*Function Askname ()*

*{*

*echo "What is your name?"*

*}*

*echo "Please, ";*

*Askname ();*

*?>*

The script will display the following: *"Please, what is your name?"*

## Function parameters in PHP

If we want to increase the functionality of the function, then we need to add more parameters. You can look at a parameter as a variable. Parameters appear inside the function parenthesis. Look at the example below which uses parameters, the function is going to print several first names, but it will still retain the last names:

```php
<? php function showName($fname) {

echo $fname. " Rael. <br />";

}

echo "My name is ";

showName ("Kai Jam");

echo "My brother's name is ";

showName("Hoda");

echo "My cousin's name is ";

showName("Stuart") ;>
```

See the output below:

My name is Kai Jam Rael.
My brother's name is Hoda Rael.
My cousin's name is Stuart Rael.

In this example, the function *showName ()* has one parameter. It is still possible for a function to have more than one parameter.

## Return values in PHP

If you want a function in PHP to return a value. We simply apply the 'return' statement. Consider this example:

```php
<? php function sum($x,$y) {

$total=$x+$y;

return $total;

}
echo "3 + 6 = ". sum (3,6);

?>
```

*The output of this code will be 3 + 6 = 7*

# Chapter 3

# PHP Form Handling

S o far, you are now familiar with the basics of PHP and the way the PHP program works. You have also learned some of the core basics of the PHP language. I am sure you can declare a variable, write a PHP function, and many other important things which a person knowledgeable with PHP is supposed to know. From this point on, you will learn how to build practical PHP applications. One of the most popular capabilities of PHP is the ability to receive input entered by a visitor through an application. The previous scripts which we have done don't actually allow a user to enter values. However, if you can add that feature where a user can enter some values and read the input, then your PHP program becomes more interactive.

A common practice is letting the visitor of a web application enter some data is by using the HTML form. I know you have filled in a lot of HTML forms. Popular HTML forms include the contact form and order forms where you can order products from an online shop.

### User input and PHP forms

The *$_POST* and *$_GET* are the two main methods used in PHP to get information from forms. The most important thing which you need to note down is that, whenever you are handling HTML forms together with PHP, all HTML form elements will also be present in your PHP code snippets.

This example has an HTML form and a submit button:

```
<html>
<body>
<form action=" home. Php" method=" post">
Your Name: <input type="text" name="firstname"/>
Your age: <input type="text" name="age"/>
<input type="Submit"/>
<form>
</body>
</html>
```

If the user submits the above form after entering the data, the form goes to the *home.php* file. The output of this form could be something like: "Welcome Mike! You are 30 years old."

Let's turn our attention to the PHP form validation. Whenever a user has entered data and clicked 'send,' it is important for the data to be validated by the client code. You can still perform browser validation. In fact, the browser validation is faster and reduces the server load.

However, if you are going to store your data in a database, it is recommended that you perform server validation. The best method to go with server validation is to post the form to the same page. Don't go to a different page. By doing this, you will help the user see the error message while they're in the same form.

*$_GET* is a built-in function which will help you collect values from a form using the method 'get.'

# The Function $_GET

We use the built-in *$_GET* function to gather values from a form using the method GET. When you use the GET method, any information that is sent will be visible to everyone. The information will be displayed in the address bar of the browser. In addition, there are limits to the amount of information you can send.

## So, when is it applicable to use the method get?

First, if you are fine with all of your variable names and values appearing in the URL, then you can use the method 'get.' But, you should never send your most sensitive data using this method. Again, large quantities of information are unfit for this method.

## The $_POST Function

The *$_POST* function is another function which can be used in the PHP forms to collect values from a form after it has been sent from the method 'post.' The greatest thing with this method is that it provides security for your data. Nobody can see the information which you are sending. In addition, there is no restriction on the amount of data which you can send. However, an 8MB max size is the default size for the post, but still, you can change this on the *post_max_size* in your *php.in* file.

```
<form action="welcome.php" method="post">
Name: <input type="text" name="fname" />
Age: <input type="text" name="age" />
<input type="submit" />
</form>
```

When the data is submitted in the example above. This is how the URL will look:

"http://www.example.com/welcome.php"

## The $_REQUEST Function

This function holds the details of the *$_POST, $_GET* as well as the *$_COOKIE.*

The *$_REQUEST* is a powerful function since it combines both the post and get. Before we can close this topic on form handling, it is also important to talk about the URL redirection. While it might not be related to the forms in a direct manner, URL redirection is something which you may have interacted with more than once. This is something you usually encounter when you fill out online forms.

Another helpful thing you can get by using the redirect feature is that you eliminate the possibility of users resubmitting the form when they reload the browser page. Instead, they refresh the page that they have been redirected to.

If you want to redirect your users to a given page, it will be very simple. No stress involved. All you need to do is write: *Location: HTTP header*, plus the URL you want to redirect.

The example below explains everything.

> *header ("Location: thankyou.html");*

# Chapter 4

## Introduction Databases and SQL

### Making a decision about the way you store your data

As a developer, you need to note that when you start building applications which require you to store data, you must know which method your application will use to store the data. To help you make this decision. Here are some things that you should think of:

- The people who will access the data

- How much will the size be after, let's say, 10 years?

- What is the limit of my data?

- Will my application access the data frequently?

- The frequency of updates you may need to perform.

Once you have considered the above points, then you need to make a decision on which approach you are going to use.

A database management engine is the most popular model used when you want to store, modify, and retrieve data.

### Database architectures

Before we can get started with the database topic, there are two options for database architecture which you can pick: a client-server and the embedded model.

An embedded database exists within the application which needs it. This means it runs on the same machine as the application host. In addition, it stores the data in the same host application machine.

Client-server models on, the other hand, these are flexible and powerful databases. Mostly, they are applied in networks. Database models come in two types:

- **Simple database model**

A simple type of database similar to an associative data array. Every data item is referenced using a single key. In this model, it is difficult to create a relationship between the data stored in the database.

- **Relational databases**

This gives one enormous ability and flexibility. It is among the most popular options. You will find that the relational database is common in the web sector. If you have ever heard someone mention RDBMS, then this is what they were referring to. Some examples of RDBMS in PHP include *PostgreSQL & MySQL*.

For this chapter, we will be focusing on the MySQL. The MySQL database model gives one of the following advantages:

- It is very popular across the web

- It is cheap and available in a majority of the web hosting accounts

- Very simple to use

- It is powerful, fast and can handle large complex data

- It is very easy to install, no complex steps to follow

- It can be installed for free

## Relational databases in depth

As the name suggests, a relational database will offer the ability for data to be associated and categorized using certain attributes. For example, a record of students can be grouped by age, height, or date. In a relational database, data is organized in a table of rows and columns.

This is an example of a database table:

| playerNumber | name | phoneNumber | datePlayed | nickname |
|---|---|---|---|---|
| 42 | David | 555-1234 | 03/03/04 | Dodge |
| 6 | Nic | 555-3456 | 03/03/04 | Obi-d |
| 2 | David | 555-6543 | 03/03/04 | Witblitz |
| 14 | Mark | 555-1213 | 03/03/04 | Greeny |
| 2 | David | 555-6543 | 02/25/04 | Witblitz |
| 25 | Pads | 555-9101 | 02/25/04 | Pads |
| 6 | Nic | 555-3456 | 02/25/04 | Obi-d |
| 7 | Nic | 555-5678 | 02/25/04 | Nicrot |

In the table above, you should be able to identify the rows and columns. You will see that the rows hold information about every player while the columns are identified with a heading. This is called the column name or field name.

## Normalization

In this table, you will notice that any time there is a match, all the details of a player have to be written down. It does not matter whether the details already exist or not. The end result is time wasting and repetition. Repetition of the same information such as the players' phone number is referred to as redundancy. Redundancy is unacceptable in a database. It wastes a lot of space and time.

Preventing redundancy is called 'normalization.' For instance, if we are to normalize the above table, we need to create another table for *playernumber*, *name*, *phonenumber*, and *nickname.* The table will look like this:

| playerNumber | name | phoneNumber | nickname |
|---|---|---|---|
| 42 | David | 555–1234 | Dodge |
| 6 | Nic | 555–3456 | Obi-d |
| 14 | Mark | 555–1213 | Greeny |
| 2 | David | 555–6543 | Witblitz |
| 25 | Pads | 555–9101 | Pads |
| 7 | Nic | 555–5678 | Nicrot |

You will now notice that on this table, each player only has one record. The player number is the unique field which identifies every player. Now that we have removed part of the players' information, we will create another table with the remaining details:

| playerNumber | datePlayed |
|---|---|
| 42 | 03/03/04 |
| 6 | 03/03/04 |
| 2 | 03/03/04 |
| 14 | 03/03/04 |
| 2 | 02/25/04 |
| 25 | 02/25/04 |
| 6 | 02/25/04 |
| 7 | 02/25/04 |

In this table, we have the *playerNumber* retained because it is the unique field which identifies each player. Now, if we can link up this second table and the previous one using the unique field, we can successfully associate a player and the date they played a match. In this example, we now say that the two tables are linked together using the *playerNumber* field. The *playerNumber* field in this last table is called the 'foreign key' because it points to the primary key in the previous table.

If you look at the above case, the only repeating information is the *playerNumber*. Therefore, we have saved a lot of space and time compared to the original table where we had to write all of the information. This type of relation is called 'one, too many' relations. This is because a single record of a player can be related to many other records if the player plays more than one game. The whole process that we have done is called normalization.

## SQL

SQL is an acronym that stands for structured query language. SQL gives you the ability to carry out any operation related to the database such as creating a database and many other tasks. Even though this chapter focuses on MySQL, we will also mention SQL since it is another version of MySQL. But, because the basics of SQL are similar to MySQL, then you can apply them to MySQL.

## MySQL Data types

Any time you create a MySQL data type, you must specify the type and size of every field. The data types in MySQL include numeric, string, and date.

# The numeric types of data

| Numeric Data Type | Description | Allowed Range of Values |
|---|---|---|
| TINYINT | Very small integer | –128 to 127, or 0 to 255 if UNSIGNED |
| SMALLINT | Small integer | –32768 to 32767, or 0 to 65535 if UNSIGNED |
| MEDIUMINT | Medium-sized integer | –8388608 to 8388607, or 0 to 16777215 if UNSIGNED |
| INT | Normal-sized integer | –2147483648 to 2147483647, or 0 to 4294967295 if UNSIGNED |
| BIGINT | Large integer | –9223372036854775808 to 9223372036854775807, or 0 to 18446744073709551615 if UNSIGNED |
| FLOAT | Single-precision floating-point number | Smallest non-zero value: $\pm 1.176 \times 10^{-38}$; largest value: $\pm 3.403 \times 10^{38}$ |
| DOUBLE | Double-precision floating-point number | Smallest non-zero value: $\pm 2.225 \times 10^{-308}$; largest value: $\pm 1.798 \times 10^{308}$ |
| DECIMAL(precision, scale) | Fixed-point number | Same as DOUBLE, but fixed-point rather than floating-point. precision specifies the total number of allowed digits, whereas scale specifies how many digits sit to the right of the decimal point. |
| BIT | 0 or 1 | 0 or 1 |

# Date and time data types

| Date/Time Data Type | Description | Allowed Range of Values |
|---|---|---|
| DATE | Date | 1 Jan 1000 to 31 Dec 9999 |
| DATETIME | Date and time | Midnight, 1 Jan 1000 to 23:59:59, 31 Dec 9999 |
| TIMESTAMP | Timestamp | 00:00:01, 1 Jan 1970 to 03:14:07, 9 Jan 2038, UTC (Universal Coordinated Time) |
| TIME | Time | –838:59:59 to 838:59:59 |
| YEAR | Year | 1901 to 2155 |

# String data types

| String Data Type | Description | Allowed Lengths |
|---|---|---|
| CHAR(n) | Fixed-length string of n characters | 0–255 characters |
| VARCHAR(n) | Variable-length string of up to n characters | 0–65535 characters |
| BINARY(n) | Fixed-length binary string of n bytes | 0–255 bytes |
| VARBINARY(n) | Variable-length binary string of up to n bytes | 0–65535 bytes |
| TINYTEXT | Small text field | 0–255 characters |
| TEXT | Normal-sized text field | 0–65535 characters |
| MEDIUMTEXT | Medium-sized text field | 0–16777215 characters |
| LONGTEXT | Large text field | 0–4294967295 characters |
| TINYBLOB | Small BLOB (Binary Large Object) | 0–255 bytes |
| BLOB | Normal-sized BLOB | 0–65535 bytes |
| MEDIUMBLOB | Medium-sized BLOB | 0–16777215 bytes (16MB) |
| LONGBLOB | Large BLOB | 0–4294967295 bytes (4GB) |
| ENUM | Enumeration | The field can contain one value from a predefined list of up to 65,535 values |
| SET | A set of values | The field can contain zero or more values from a predefined list of up to 64 values |

116

## SQL Statements

To succeed in working with databases and tables, you must learn and know how to apply SQL statements. Popular SQL statements include:

- SELECT

- UPDATE

- REPLACE

- INSERT

- DELETE

Other statements include:

- CREATE

- DROP

- ALTER

## Connecting to MySQL using PHP

Well, now you are familiar with the MySQL database terms. We can now take you through a brief study of connecting your database with MYSQL. There are two ways which you can use PHP to connect to the MYSQL database:

- MySQLi (MYSQL improved)

- PDO (PHP Data Objects)

As you can see, the existence of the two methods points that each method has an advantage and a disadvantage. Which one is the best could just lead to an endless debate which we might never finish. In this book, we are going to use the MySQLi method.

The MySQL improved extension has the MySQLi class. To connect your database using PHP, follow the steps below:

1. You will require your MySQL server address. However, if the database exists on the same server, it will possibly be the local host.

2. Create a PHP file name, and you can name it as *connect.php*.

3. Type the PHP code below in your *connect.php* file. Make sure that you replace the username, password, and *dname* with your own details:

```php
<?php

$mysqli= new mysqli ("localhost", "username", "password", "dname");

?>
```

4. Once the code has connected to the MYSQL, you can move on by selecting your database. You can also run SQL queries and do other operations that you want.

## Retrieving data using 'select'

One of the most interesting things with the databases is the speed at which you can retrieve data in whatever order you want. Consider it as a database which stores books. If you want to display the contents of the database organized by the last and first name, SQL can help you achieve this quickly by using the ORDER BY statement:

"SELECT username, firstname, lastname FROM books ORDER BY firstname;"

## Summarizing data

MySQL gives you the ability to summarize data instead of just presenting the actual data stored in the database. Use the following functions to summarize your data:

- *Sum()*

- *Avg()*

- *Max()*

- *Count ()*

# Chapter 5

## Manipulate MySQL Data With PHP

### Inserting records

The SQL statement INSERT INTO helps one place records into a database table:

*INSERT INTO name of table VALUES (v1, v2....);*

If you only want to insert specific values, letting the remaining fields become nulls, you can use:

*INSERT INTO name of table (field1, field2, ...) VALUES (v1, v2, ...);*

To insert data into a table using PHP, first, we need to use the INSERT INTO statement and write the SQL query with the required values. The basic SQL INSERT INTO looks this way:

*INSERT [INTO] name of the table (names of column) VALUES (values)*

The square brackets around INTO are optional. It serves as a way to improve readability. The column names can be placed in any order. But, the values in the parenthesis must appear exactly as in the columns.

The picture below has a code snippet of how the INSERT INTO is used:

120

```php
<?php
/* Attempt MySQL server connection. Assuming you are running MySQL
server with default setting (user 'root' with no password) */
$link = mysqli_connect("localhost", "root", "", "demo");

// Check connection
if($link === false){
    die("ERROR: Could not connect. " . mysqli_connect_error());
}

// Attempt insert query execution
$sql = "INSERT INTO persons (first_name, last_name, email) VALUES ('Peter',
'Parker', 'peterparker@mail.com')";
if(mysqli_query($link, $sql)){
    echo "Records inserted successfully.";
} else{
    echo "ERROR: Could not able to execute $sql. " . mysqli_error($link);
}

// Close connection
mysqli_close($link);
?>
```

We have to connect to the database first. Once the connection is done, the INSERT statement is executed. In this code, we are injecting data into a table of persons. The values we are inserting are the *fname, lname,* and email.

Once the records have been successfully inserted, a message will be displayed on the screen to inform us that the process has been successful. In case the process of inserting the records fails, an error message will be shown on the screen. Something else which you need to pay attention to is the way we have used the 'if, else' statement which we learned at the start of this book.

## Insertion in multiple rows

SQL is a useful language which can allow you to perform the insertion of many rows into a database table by writing a single line of query.

In this example, we have added more rows to the table:

```
01.  <?php
02.  /* Attempt MySQL server connection. Assuming you are running MySQL
03.  server with default setting (user 'root' with no password) */
04.  $link = mysqli_connect("localhost", "root", "", "demo");
05.
06.  // Check connection
07.  if($link === false){
08.      die("ERROR: Could not connect. " . mysqli_connect_error());
09.  }
10.
11.  // Attempt insert query execution
12.  $sql = "INSERT INTO persons (first_name, last_name, email) VALUES
13.              ('John', 'Rambo', 'johnrambo@mail.com'),
14.              ('Clark', 'Kent', 'clarkkent@mail.com'),
15.              ('John', 'Carter', 'johncarter@mail.com'),
16.              ('Harry', 'Potter', 'harrypotter@mail.com')";
17.  if(mysqli_query($link, $sql)){
18.      echo "Records added successfully.";
19.  } else{
20.      echo "ERROR: Could not able to execute $sql. " . mysqli_error($link);
21.  }
22.
23.  // Close connection
24.  mysqli_close($link);
25.  ?>
```

Looking at the above example, you can see that every row is distinguished by a comma and surrounded with parenthesis.

## Records update

The update statement is another useful statement which will let you make changes to the data stored in the table. We use the update statement together with the WHERE clause.

The basic form of an UPDATE statement looks like this:

> *"UPDATE table_name SET c1= value, c2 = value2, ...WHERE column_name=yourvalue"*

Something you should always remember is that whenever you update a table, make sure you can tell the primary key. A practical approach to this is writing a query to the database and indicating all the records. After this, you can show these results together with a link to the update page.

But, for now, let's create a SQL query that has the UPDATE statement and the WHERE construct. After we have done this, we will move on to execute the query by passing the query to a *mysqli_query ()* function which completes the update function.

In our update statement, we want to update the table person's email address if the person in the 'person table' has an id of 1:

```php
<?php
/* Attempt MySQL server connection. Assuming you are running MySQL
server with default setting (user 'root' with no password) */
$link = mysqli_connect("localhost", "root", "", "demo");

// Check connection
if($link === false){
    die("ERROR: Could not connect. " . mysqli_connect_error());
}

// Attempt update query execution
$sql = "UPDATE persons SET email='peterparker_new@mail.com' WHERE id=1";
if(mysqli_query($link, $sql)){
    echo "Records were updated successfully.";
} else {
    echo "ERROR: Could not able to execute $sql. " . mysqli_error($link);
}

// Close connection
mysqli_close($link);
?>
```

As you can see, we establish a connection first with the database. Once the connection is successful, our UPDATE statement is the next to be executed.

## Deleting a record

In the same way, you can update and insert records into a table. You can also delete the same values in the table with the help of the SQL statement. And don't forget that the DELETE statement is also used together with the WHERE construct to delete all records which fulfill a given condition. The DELETE construct is as follows:

*DELETE FROM tble_name WHERE condition*

However, something which you need to be careful with when using the DELETE command is that it is final. The moment a record is deleted, it will never be recovered. The record is gone forever. Don't confuse this with your computer where you have a recycle bin to go and restore your records. No! The action is permanent. The worst thing with this DELETE syntax is that the WHERE construct is optional. This means if you fail to put it in your code, every record is going to be deleted, and you will never recover it unless you have a backup. So, whenever you have to write the delete command, instead of the process being instant, you should display the records which you want to be deleted to the user to confirm everything first before you perform the deletion process.

Now, we can get into the practical side. In the picture below, the PHP code will delete the records of all those persons whose first name on the table is equivalent to John:

```php
01.  <?php
02.  /* Attempt MySQL server connection. Assuming you are running MySQL
03.  server with default setting (user 'root' with no password) */
04.  $link = mysqli_connect("localhost", "root", "", "demo");
05.
06.  // Check connection
07.  if($link === false){
08.      die("ERROR: Could not connect. " . mysqli_connect_error());
09.  }
10.
11.  // Attempt delete query execution
12.  $sql = "DELETE FROM persons WHERE first_name='John'";
13.  if(mysqli_query($link, $sql)){
14.      echo "Records were deleted successfully.";
15.  } else{
16.      echo "ERROR: Could not able to execute $sql. " . mysqli_error($link);
17.  }
18.
19.  // Close connection
20.  mysqli_close($link);
21.  ?>
```

## Building a member registration application

In this section, I'll walk you through the steps of building a user registration application. The registration system will give users the ability to create an account by providing details such as their username, password, email and they can also sign out if needed. Also, you will

124

learn how you can use PHP to restrict users from certain pages. In short, this practical application will make use of all the concepts we have learned in each of the chapters in this book.

## First, let's set up our database

Now, I want you to create a database and assign it your favorite name. I will call my database 'registration.' As I said at the start, always try to give your variables, databases, and so forth, names which relate to the operation or function you want to do. Our registration database will have a table called 'users.' Our 'users table' has the following fields:

- Email

- Username

- Password

- User id

Below is the picture of my table:

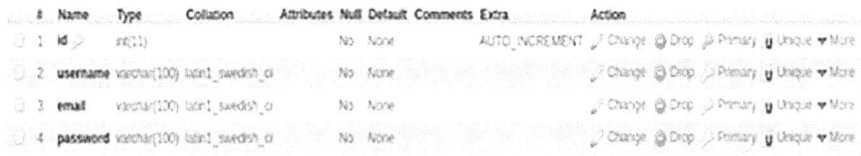

If you are not happy using the PHPMYADMIN wizard, you can go with the MySQL prompt. Just type the commands below:

```
CREATE TABLE `users` (
  `id` int(11) NOT NULL AUTO_INCREMENT PRIMARY KEY,
  `username` varchar(100) NOT NULL,
  `email` varchar(100) NOT NULL,
  `password` varchar(100) NOT NULL
) ENGINE=InnoDB DEFAULT CHARSET=latin1;
```

If you have successfully done that, then well done! You have successfully created a database. The next thing I would like you to do is to create a folder inside the root directory of your server. I want to assume that you are using WAMPP or XAMPP as your localhost. Locate the folder called *htcdocs* and create the folder inside it. Once you are done creating the registration folder, I want you to create the following files inside the registration folder:

- errors.php

- index.php

- login.php

- server.php

- style.css

If you have done that, open your files in your best editor. I am using Sublime Text 3.

## User registration

```php
<?php include('server.php') ?>
<!DOCTYPE html>
<html>
<head>
  <title>Registration system PHP and MySQL</title>
  <link rel="stylesheet" type="text/css" href="style.css">
</head>
<body>
  <div class="header">
    <h2>Register</h2>
  </div>

  <form method="post" action="register.php">
    <?php include('errors.php'); ?>
    <div class="input-group">
      <label>Username</label>
      <input type="text" name="username" value="<?php echo $username; ?>">
    </div>
    <div class="input-group">
      <label>Email</label>
      <input type="email" name="email" value="<?php echo $email; ?>">
    </div>
    <div class="input-group">
      <label>Password</label>
      <input type="password" name="password_1">
    </div>
    <div class="input-group">
      <label>Confirm password</label>
      <input type="password" name="password_2">
    </div>
    <div class="input-group">
      <button type="submit" class="btn" name="reg_user">Register</button>
    </div>
    <p>
        Already a member? <a href="login.php">Sign in</a>
    </p>
  </form>
</body>
</html>
```

Go to the *register.php* file in your text editor. You can either copy and paste the code below or type it.

This picture shows an HTML form. But, some of the things which you need to note is the method 'action' which has been assigned to the *register.php*. What this one means is that when the user selects the register button, all the data contained in the form will go back to the same page. If you can still remember, when I was talking about the PHP form handling I did recommend that you apply this technique. At the top of this same page, I have included the *server.php* because some of this data is going to be received by the server.

You should also be able to recognize that we have included the *errors.php* file as a way to show errors from the form. Something else which you should see is that we are using the 'post' and not the 'get' method because we don't want anyone to see our information. Remember that we will be submitting data which has a password. Plus, the 'post' method works for data of just about any size.

Also, in the header section, we have put *CSS* links. There is a style sheet called *style.css*. I believe you already understand the role of *CSS*. So, open your *style.css* file and type the code below:

```css
* {
  margin: 0px;
  padding: 0px;
}
body {
  font-size: 120%;
  background: #F8F8FF;
}

.header {
  width: 30%;
  margin: 50px auto 0px;
  color: white;
  background: #5F9EA0;
  text-align: center;
  border: 1px solid #B0C4DE;
  border-bottom: none;
  border-radius: 10px 10px 0px 0px;
  padding: 20px;
}
```

```css
form, .content {
  width: 30%;
  margin: 0px auto;
  padding: 20px;
  border: 1px solid #B0C4DE;
  background: white;
  border-radius: 0px 0px 10px 10px;
}
.input-group {
  margin: 10px 0px 10px 0px;
}
.input-group label {
  display: block;
  text-align: left;
  margin: 3px;
}
.input-group input {
  height: 30px;
  width: 93%;
  padding: 5px 10px;
  font-size: 16px;
  border-radius: 5px;
  border: 1px solid gray;
}
```

```css
.btn {
    padding: 10px;
    font-size: 15px;
    color: white;
    background: #5F9EA0;
    border: none;
    border-radius: 5px;
}
.error {
    width: 92%;
    margin: 0px auto;
    padding: 10px;
    border: 1px solid #a94442;
    color: #a94442;
    background: #f2dede;
    border-radius: 5px;
    text-align: left;
}
.success {
    color: #3c763d;
    background: #dff0d8;
    border: 1px solid #3c763d;
    margin-bottom: 20px;
}
```

By using the *CSS*, the form will look very beautiful. Now, it is time to write the script which is going to collect the information submitted from the HTML form and store it in the database. This is going to be completed in the *server.php*. So, go and open the *server.php* then type in the following code:

```php
<?php
session_start();

// initializing variables
$username = "";
$email    = "";
$errors = array();

// connect to the database
$db = mysqli_connect('localhost', 'root', '', 'registration');

// REGISTER USER
if (isset($_POST['reg_user'])) {
  // receive all input values from the form
  $username = mysqli_real_escape_string($db, $_POST['username']);
  $email = mysqli_real_escape_string($db, $_POST['email']);
  $password_1 = mysqli_real_escape_string($db, $_POST['password_1']);
  $password_2 = mysqli_real_escape_string($db, $_POST['password_2']);

  // form validation: ensure that the form is correctly filled ...
  // by adding (array_push()) corresponding error unto $errors array
  if (empty($username)) { array_push($errors, "Username is required"); }
  if (empty($email)) { array_push($errors, "Email is required"); }
  if (empty($password_1)) { array_push($errors, "Password is required"); }
  if ($password_1 != $password_2) {
  array_push($errors, "The two passwords do not match");
  }

  // first check the database to make sure
  // a user does not already exist with the same username and/or email
  $user_check_query = "SELECT * FROM users WHERE username='$username' OR email='$email' LIMIT 1";
  $result = mysqli_query($db, $user_check_query);
  $user = mysqli_fetch_assoc($result);

  if ($user) { // if user exists
    if ($user['username'] === $username) {
      array_push($errors, "Username already exists");
    }

    if ($user['email'] === $email) {
      array_push($errors, "email already exists");
    }
  }

  // Finally, register user if there are no errors in the form
  if (count($errors) == 0) {
    $password = md5($password_1);//encrypt the password before saving in the database

    $query = "INSERT INTO users (username, email, password)
          VALUES('$username', '$email', '$password')";
    mysqli_query($db, $query);
    $_SESSION['username'] = $username;
    $_SESSION['success'] = "You are now logged in";
    header('location: index.php');
  }
}
// ...
```

In this code, we are using sessions help track the users. A session is started by creating the *session_start()* at the top of the file. The comments in the code try to explain everything that is happening. However, there are a few things which I would like to talk about.

The 'if statement' helps determine whether or not the *reg_user* button located on the registration form has been clicked. Don't forget that if you go to our form, specifically on the submit button, the name attribute assigned to it is the *reg_user* which is the one being referenced to in the 'if statement.'

All data submitted from the form has to be analyzed to confirm that whatever the user entered was correct. Passwords have to be checked to ensure that they match. If the user keyed in every detail, then this means that there are no mistakes when the form is submitted. The details of the user will be successfully entered into the 'users' table. This way, the user registration would be successfully completed. Another important point to pay attention to is that the password entered into the 'users' table will be hashed. This means it will be secured so that no one can tamper with it. An advantage which comes with hashing your password is, if a hacker gains entry into your database, they will not manage to read your password.

In our current code, you can't see the error messages because we haven't written the *error.php* code. Well, if you want to display errors, type the following code into the *error.php* file:

```php
<?php  if (count($errors) > 0) : ?>
  <div class="error">
    <?php foreach ($errors as $error) : ?>
      <p><?php echo $error ?></p>
    <?php endforeach ?>
  </div>
<?php  endif ?>
```

In our registration page, we have created it in such a way that whenever a user successfully registers, the application will take them straight to the page called *index.php*.

Now, let's examine the user login. If there is something that's quite easy to build, it's the login page. Just open your text editor and type the code below:

```php
<?php include('server.php') ?>
<!DOCTYPE html>
<html>
<head>
    <title>Registration system PHP and MySQL</title>
    <link rel="stylesheet" type="text/css" href="style.css">
</head>
<body>
    <div class="header">
        <h2>Login</h2>
    </div>

    <form method="post" action="login.php">
        <?php include('errors.php'); ?>
        <div class="input-group">
            <label>Username</label>
            <input type="text" name="username" >
        </div>
        <div class="input-group">
            <label>Password</label>
            <input type="password" name="password">
        </div>
        <div class="input-group">
            <button type="submit" class="btn" name="login_user">Login</button>
        </div>
        <p>
            Not yet a member? <a href="register.php">Sign up</a>
        </p>
    </form>
</body>
</html>
```

Most of the things in this code resemble what was on the *register.php* page.

Now, when it comes to writing the code that will sign in the user, we have to do that in the *server.php*. So, open your *server.php* code and type this code at the end of the file:

```
// LOGIN USER
if (isset($_POST['login_user'])) {
  $username = mysqli_real_escape_string($db, $_POST['username']);
  $password = mysqli_real_escape_string($db, $_POST['password']);

  if (empty($username)) {
    array_push($errors, "Username is required");
  }
  if (empty($password)) {
    array_push($errors, "Password is required");
  }

  if (count($errors) == 0) {
    $password = md5($password);
    $query = "SELECT * FROM users WHERE username='$username' AND password='$password'";
    $results = mysqli_query($db, $query);
    if (mysqli_num_rows($results) == 1) {
      $_SESSION['username'] = $username;
      $_SESSION['success'] = "You are now logged in";
      header('location: index.php');
    }else {
      array_push($errors, "Wrong username/password combination");
    }
  }
}
?>
```

Again, what this code does is that it checks whether or not the user has entered data in all the fields correctly and verify that all the credentials which were provided matched with the ones stored in the database. If they match the code, then it will log them in. Once the user is signed in already, they will be directed to the page where they will be told that they were logged in successfully.

Now, it is time to find out what is going on in the *index.php* file. Open the file and type in the following code:

134

```php
        <?php endif ?>

        <!-- logged in user information -->
        <?php  if (isset($_SESSION['username'])) : ?>
            <p>Welcome <strong><?php echo $_SESSION['username']; ?></strong></p>
            <p> <a href="index.php?logout='1'" style="color: red;">logout</a> </p>
        <?php endif ?>
    </div>

    </body>
    </html>


<?php
  session_start();

  if (!isset($_SESSION['username'])) {
    $_SESSION['msg'] = "You must log in first";
    header('location: login.php');
  }
  if (isset($_GET['logout'])) {
    session_destroy();
    unset($_SESSION['username']);
    header("location: login.php");
  }
?>
<!DOCTYPE html>
<html>
<head>
  <title>Home</title>
  <link rel="stylesheet" type="text/css" href="style.css">
</head>
<body>

<div class="header">
  <h2>Home Page</h2>
</div>
<div class="content">
    <!-- notification message -->
    <?php if (isset($_SESSION['success'])) : ?>
        <div class="error success" >
            <h3>
            <?php
                echo $_SESSION['success'];
                unset($_SESSION['success']);
            ?>
            </h3>
        </div>
```

In this code, we use the 'if clause statement' to check if the user signed in already. If they're not logged in yet, they will be taken to the login interface. This means that this page is only visible to users who are already logged in. Now, if you want to make certain pages accessible only to the users who have logged in, all it takes is to have this snippet of code appear at the top of the file.

In the second 'if' statement, we want to check if the user has already clicked the 'sign out' button. If it is evaluated as 'true,' the user is then logged out and taken back to the main page to log in. If you have done everything up to this point, then try to run your whole application. Attempt to register yourself as the new user. You can now personalize this site so that it suits your needs.

# Chapter 6

# PHP Sessions, Cookies, and Authentication

As you continue to build your web projects, there are complicated applications which will require you to monitor your visitors and users. You may not have built a login system, but you might need some certain details of your users. Some of these details could be the sessions of your users.

Different technologies have been created to help you accomplish this. Some of these technologies include browser cookies and HTTP authentication. These technologies will allow you to monitor your visitors through the use of a seamless process.

## PHP Cookies

A cookie is a data object which a web server will store on your hard drive using the web browser. It can have any kind of alphanumeric information as long as it does not exceed 4KB, and it can be recovered from your computer and taken back to the server. Some of the popular uses of cookies include tracking session of users, storing the shipping cart, storing data from different visits, holding login details, and other functions.

Cookies are a private thing, this means, that not everyone can read them besides the website owner. This means that if a cookie is released by 'example.com,' it can only be recovered using the same domain. This is done as a way to secure the data and prevent external websites from having access to information which they are not allowed to have.

As a result of the internet's modern architecture, many websites can now release their own cookies. Cookies received from different domains are called third-party cookies. Third-party cookies are usually created by advertising firms as a way for them to collect information about a user as they visit different websites.

Since each website can have its own cookies, many browsers have an option to let users switch their cookies off both for the third-party and the server's domain. Luckily, when you turn off your cookies, you also turn off the third-party cookie for websites.

The exchange of a cookie takes place at the transfer of headers. This happens way before we send the HTML of a web page. The moment the HTML has been sent, it becomes difficult to send a cookie.

Well, learning how to send a cookie is not hard, the most important thing to know is that the HTML exchange should not take place before you have it sent. To define your cookie, you need to write the *setcookie* function. This function comes with the following basic syntax:

*Setcookie (name, value, exptre, path, domain, secure, httponly);*

If I want to create a cookie with a given name, and only want it to be visible across the web server's domain, this is how it will look:

*Setcookie ('visitor', 'Job', time () + 60 \*60\*24\*8, '/');*

## Accessing cookies

Reading the value of a cookie is not that hard. You can access a cookie by simply using the $_COOKIE array. For example, if you want to check if the current browser has a cookie with the name a visitor stored, we use the code below:

*If(isset($_COOKIE['visitor'])) $visitor=$_COOKIE['visitor'];*

Remember, you can read a cookie back after you have sent it to the web browser. In other words, if you release a cookie, you won't be able to read it until the browser refreshes the page or another website with access to your cookie happens to return the cookie to your server.

## Destroying a cookie

So far you know how to create, access, and read a cookie. When it comes to destroying a cookie, you need to issue it once more and define a date. It is important that all the previous details of your cookie be the same except the timestamp. If they are not identical, you will not succeed in deleting the cookie. So, if you wanted to delete the cookie which we created previously, this is what you need to do:

*setcookie('visitor', 'Job', time() - 2592000, '/');*

Make sure that the time indicated should be outdated.

## HTTP Authentication

The HTTP authentication also makes use of the web server as a means to control passwords and users of the system. This is appropriate for those web applications which require users to sign in.

For the HTTP authentication to be applicable, PHP has to transfer the header request which will then begin a dialog with the web browser. Now, for this feature to work, it must be on.

## Username and password storage

MySQL is the popular method of storing data such as usernames and passwords. However, as you know, it is not a good thing to store your passwords in a manner in which anyone can easily access it. One of the ways we can avoid this is by using a method called a 'one-way function.'

This is a very easy function, and what it does is that it changes a string of text into a random string. The nature of these functions makes it very difficult for a hacker to reverse it. With the passing of time, we have come to see that the *md5* algorithm can be hacked, the same goes for the *sha1*. Which is why I recommend that you use the PHP hash function. To see how it works, we pass it a *ripemd* version algorithm:

$token = hash ('ripemd128', 'mypassword');

The end result of the token is a random string.

## Salting

However, using hash on its own does not provide enough security for the database password because the chances are that if a hacker uses brute force, he will successfully retrieve the password. So, to solve this problem, we use a method called 'salting' before we finally apply the hashing. Salting is a process where we now add our own text to each parameter so that it can be encrypted. This is how it happens:

$token =hash ('ripemd128', **mysaltstring**mypassword');

In the above example, the *mysaltstring* has been attached to the password.

## Using sessions

You have already used this in the practical example. Sessions help you monitor what your visitors are doing when they move from one page to another.

## Starting a session

To start any session, you must write or put the *session_start* function before the HTML, in the same way, that cookies are set. Now, if you want to save the session variables, you need to allocate them to the $_SESSION array by doing this:

*$_SESSSION ['variable'] = $value;*

If you want to read your session, you can do this:

*$vartable =$_SESSION['vartable'];*

## Ending a session

The function *session_destroy*, will help you end or destroy a session.

# Conclusion

Having read every chapter in this book, now you know how to write PHP code that can connect to the database, you understand the different database concepts, you can build a complete user registration system, and many more. Well, we also believe that you know how to write an innovative PHP code. Remember, PHP is an easy to understand language, and if you can give yourself sufficient time to practice, you will become a professional in PHP.

If you can master the basic fundamentals explained in this book, then you will be ready to start building PHP applications. PHP is an incredibly useful programming language which can help you develop robust applications. To become a great PHP developer, you have to put in a lot of effort. An excellent programmer should stay updated with the latest changes in the world of PHP to learn and understand the vital things that everyone has to know. Most importantly, I will suggest that once you have finished reading this book, the next step is to look for PHP books that have practical tests you can try. Get in-depth PHP books to help you understand the concepts better.

In this book, we have set the path for you continue exploring and learning deeper PHP concepts.

The next step you should take is writing your own PHP code. Practice every day until you master it.

Thank you and good luck!

# JAVA

*Basic Fundamental Guide for Beginners*

# Introduction

Congratulations and thank you for downloading *Java*.

Only a few languages have redefined the way of programming like Java has. Every year, the Java language keeps changing and evolving. One reason to explain this was the culture of innovation and the need for change to fulfill a given desire.

Java comprises of a compiler, Java virtual machine (JVM), libraries, and the language itself. The Java virtual machine is responsible for allowing software developers from different platforms to write code in different languages which will still be executed on the JVM. The design of the Java language was on the basis of the following features:

- Independence of a platform.

- A language which is strongly typed

- An automatic memory management

- An object-oriented language

- A language which is interpreted and compiled.

In this eBook, you will learn and practice the important concepts of the Java programming language. You will learn about the classes, methods and inheritance and many other basic concepts about the Java language. This eBook will help you develop Java programming skills important to start solving real-world problems. You will learn the fundamentals of the Java language and how you can use them in your program. Java is a very popular language and easy to learn. It is a widely used language to develop android apps and web applications. If you are new to programming and want to gain the fundamentals concepts in Java, reading this book will prove a valuable choice for you.

# Chapter 1

# Java Fundamentals

## Java Program and its Development Environment

The invention of the Internet alongside with the World Wide Web redefined the computing sector. Before the advent of the internet, the cyber industry was driven by the stand-alone PCs. Nowadays, about every computer is connected to the internet. The internet has been redefined to the point where it allows the sharing of files and information across multiple devices. Today, it has grown and expanded widely. So, with the above changes. We had new ways which you can code in Java.

Java is a special language which is mostly used on the internet. But, that is not enough. There are so many things which it can help one accomplish. However, it is more than that. We can say that Java redefined the programming sector, it revolutionized the way programmers can think about its function and structure. To become an expert in Java language, you need to do a lot of practice in coding. This chapter will take you through some of the Java fundamentals, we shall teach you the history of Java and some of its important features.

One of the most interesting things about learning to program in any language whether it is python, PHP, etc. is that no element exists on its own. Rather, every component of the language works hand-in-hand with another component. This kind of relationship is dominant in Java. For your information, every time you want to discuss a given concept in Java, most of the time you may need to involve another related topic. This is something that you are going to realize as a means to solve such a problem. We shall give you a briefing about the features of Java programming in this Chapter including a simple Java program. We shall

146

not dig deep into the details, but we shall focus on the general concepts which are prominent in any Java program.

## How Java Started

I know this is something which you would like to know especially if you are just starting out in Java programming. It is important as a new beginner to Java programming to know its origin because everything has its place of origin. Well, you need to know that there are two factors which contribute to language innovation in the computing industry. These two factors include enhancement in the way we program and the modifications in the computing environment. Java is founded based on these two factors. It is built upon the existing foundation of the C and C++ programming languages. In other words, Java improves on the overall aspects of the two programming languages. As a response to the alarming rise of the online presence, the language comes with several features to enhance the level of coding.

Would you want to know the people who invented Java? Of course, you do. James Gosling, Ed Frank, Mike Sheridan, Chris Warth, and Patrick Naughton at Sun Microsystems are behind the invention of the Java language in 1991. Before it was called Java, it was initially referred to as "Oak." The reason behind the invention of Java wasn't the internet, but instead, they wanted a language which could work on many different platforms to help in the creation of software. This software would later be installed in various consumer electronics. As you know, different CPUs types act as computer controllers. The major difficulty was, at that time, the majority of the languages used to program were meant to work on a specific device. For example, C++.

While you could compile a program in C++ for whatever CPU, to achieve this you had to have a complete C++ compiler designed for that specific CPU. The problem has been that compilers are very expensive. Besides that, they are time-consuming to develop. Therefore, in a move to find a much better solution to this problem, James Gosling and his company decided to create a language which was cross-platform and portable. This would then make it possible to run on different CPUs under various environments. It was this effort which resulted in the release of Java.

Coincidentally, while Java was being created, something very important emerged. Later on, it came to be an important factor in the rise of Java programming. Had it not been for the World Wide Web, Java won't have become a very popular programming language applied in consumer electronics. But, the World Wide Web played a key role in the spread of Java programming because Java was a portable language and the Web required programs which were portable.

As a programmer, you have read several programming books or have heard your fellow programmer emphasize the importance of portable programs. Although the demand to have portable programs was an old idea, with the coming of the World Wide Web, this old problem re-emerged in a different manner. The members of the Java design experienced problems with portability. As you can guess, this discovery was what led the design team to shift their attention from the consumer devices to the Internet. In brief, the internet was the sole success for Java program.

## Class Libraries in Java

In Java programming, we have something called class and method. We shall discuss this more in the coming Chapter. So, it is possible to create each method and class to have your Java programs. However, programmers in Java most of the time make use of the existing collection of methods and classes in the Java libraries. These are also known as the Java APIs.

We now want to look at the steps taken to create and execute an application in Java with the help of a Java development environment. To begin with, Java programs usually go through a number of stages. There are five stages involved:

- Edit

- Compile

- Load

- Verify

- Execute

Something else I would want to mention is that you need to have installed the Java environment to help you run the program in Java. That is the JDK on your computer. The JDK is freely provided on the Oracle website.

There are several versions of JDK. Look and choose whichever fits your computer and operating system. Don't forget that the JDK runs in the command prompt platform and makes use of the command-line tools. In addition, there are several IDEs which you can use to run your Java programs. Some of them include Eclipse and NetBeans. Which to choose is up to your choice. Personally, I have worked with NetBeans.

If you visit the main Oracle website, you will read guidelines to help you install JDK on different operating systems.

However, let's assume that you are not using any of the above OS. I will suggest that you take time and read the documentation designed for the Java environment. Or you can find an instructor to help you out.

## Creating a Program with Java

The first program comprises of doing a few edits to a program using the editor program. Most people call it an editor. You will use the editor to write your program and perform several changes. Java programs are saved with the name of the file which will end with the .java. This shows that the file's source code uses the Java programming language.

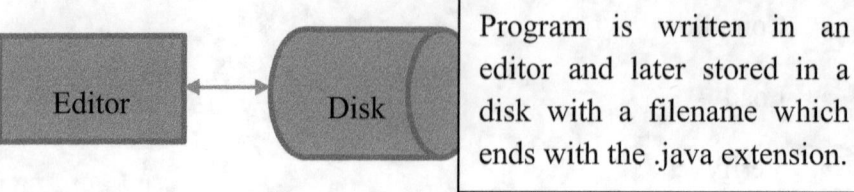

Program is written in an editor and later stored in a disk with a filename which ends with the .java extension.

## Compile a Java program into Bytecodes

Now, in the second stage, the command Javac is used to compile the program. For example, if you want to run a Java program Firstprogram.java, then you must type:

***Javac Firstprogram.java*** into the command window of your computer. In this case, the Command Prompt if you are working on Windows and the shell prompt if you are using Linux. For those using the Mac computers, you can use the Terminal application. If the program compilation succeeds, the compiler will produce a class file called Firstprogram.class.

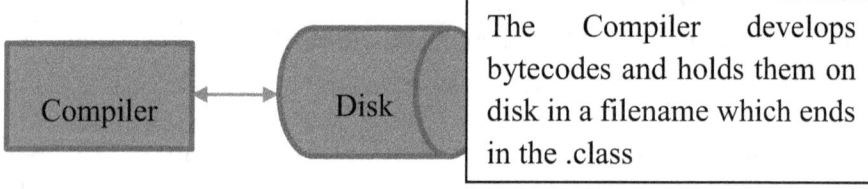

The Compiler develops bytecodes and holds them on disk in a filename which ends in the .class

The Compiler in Java will translate the source code into bytecodes which consist of the operations to be performed in the execution phase. The bytecodes are then executed in the Java Virtual Machine which is part of the JDK and the foundation of the Java platform. The Java Virtual Machine has been widely used as a virtual machine. The Microsoft's .NET applies the same virtual-machine architecture.

Now, unlike the machine language which relies on certain computer hardware, the byte-codes are independent. In other words, byte-codes don't rely on a specific hardware platform. Therefore, the bytecodes of Java are portable. This means that even if you don't recompile the source code, you can still execute the byte-codes on a different platform which has the JVM and can interpret the version of Java which the bytecodes are compiled.

## Load a program into Memory

The virtual machine in Java will load the program for execution. This process is called loading. The class loader of the JVM has the .class files which contain the program's bytecodes and places them in the primary memory. The class loader will also load the .class files produced by the Java program. The .class files can be transferred from the disk on your system over a network.

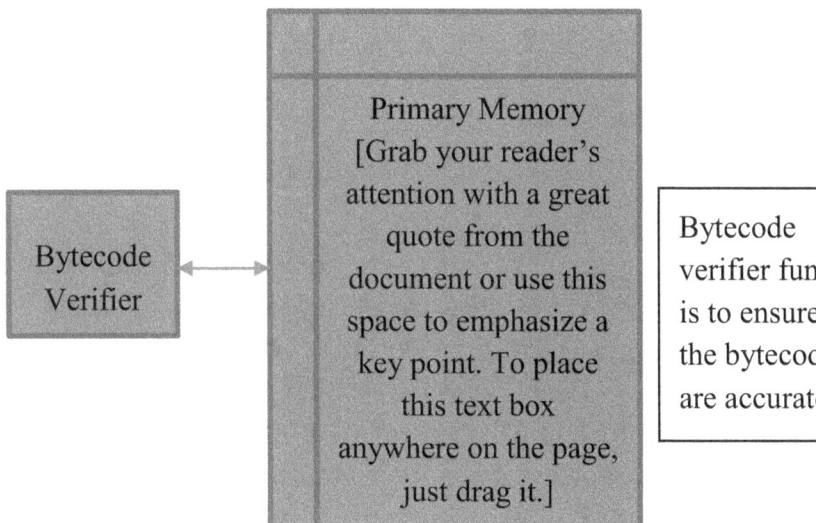

## Execution Phase

The last phase is the execution phase. Here, the JVM has the role to execute the program's bytecodes. In other words, it will be executing problems detailed in the program. The early Java versions, the JVM acted as an interpreter for Java bytecodes. This resulted in slow execution in the majority of the Java programs. The slow execution was as a result of the JVM's need to interpret and execute a single bytecode at a time. However, we have modern computers which can execute different instructions in parallel. In fact, the modern JVMs can execute bytecodes by applying a combination of interpretation and the just-in-time compilation. This process involves the JVM performing bytecodes analysis when they are interpreted and look for hot spots parts in the bytecodes which execute regularly. In such cases, the just-in-time compiler will convert the byte-codes into computer's machine language. So, the next time the JVM comes in contact with the compiled parts, the faster machine language executes. Therefore, programs in Java run through two phases of compilation:

1. The source code is converted into bytecodes for the sake of portability across JVMs.

2. At the time of execution, the bytecodes are converted into machine language for the actual device which the program executes.

## Some of the problems that might happen during the execution time

There are times when programs don't work on the first run. Each of the phases discussed above can fail because of some errors. For instance, a program which is in the process of execution might try to perform a division by zero. This would lead to the Java program to show an error message. If such a problem happens, you will need to go back to the editing phase and make the required corrections. Once you have done the corrections, you can proceed to the next phase to figure out whether the errors have been fixed.

## Your first Java program

So far you have learned on the phases of creating, compiling and executing your Java program. We want to apply the knowledge in creating a simple Java program which prints a short message on your computer screen.

Here is the program you are going to learn how to write:

Example 1: Display message on computer screen.

```
class First {
  public static void main(String[] arguments) {
    System.out.println("Let's do something using Java technology.");
  }
}
```

You will type the above program in your favorite Java IDE. Once you have this program in your editor, it is time to compile and run it. The output should resemble the image below:

## Output of program:

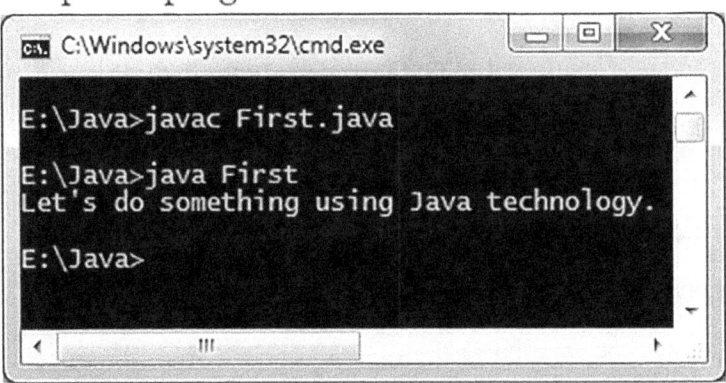

Let's briefly examine the components of the above program:

> *class First {*

This line starts with the keyword *class* as a way to declare the class which is being defined. Class in Java represents the basic unit. In this example, *First* is the class name. Classes in Java begin with { and close with }. Whatever is found inside the curly brace belongs to class members. For now, don't be anxious about the class members, we shall handle that later.

```
public static void main (String args[]) {
```

153

In the code above, we have the *main()* method. All Java programs have the main function. We shall not explain in detail the meaning of the above line because you need to understand other features of Java first. But, because you are going to interact with the majority of the code in Java which uses this approach, we shall look at it in brief.

The name *public* is a keyword access modifier. This means that it determines the way the rest of the other programs will access the members in the class. In Java programming, if you have your class defined with the *public* keyword, members of the class are free to be used by the rest of the code in the program. However, this does not apply to a *private* class. As the name suggests, *private* classes have some restrictions.

The *String args []* are parameters of the main method. To relay information to the main method, we make use of it. In case a method does not have parameters, we use the empty parentheses.

The next line of the code,

*System.out.println("Let's do something using Java technology".);*

This line displays the details of the message you would like to print on the screen. The *println()* method is a built-in method. It always displays a string passed into it. Something you need to note is that the lines of code always end with a semicolon. The semicolon indicates the end of one line of Java code.

# Chapter 2

# Introduction to Java Operators and Data Types

The main stem of a computer language is the aspect of the data types and operators. Java is not an exception to this. If you are starting out in Java programming, you must know the data types and operators in Java. These are the aspects which determine the limit of the language as well as which types of tasks it can perform. Luckily, there is an extensive list of operators and data types in Java. They help one program different types of problems.

As you will realize, data types and operators are an extensive topic. Therefore, we shall only look at the commonly used data types and operators in Java. We shall also discuss something to do with the variables and expression in Java.

## Importance of Data Types

You might be wondering if it is important to discuss data types in Java programming. Well, here is the answer for you: Yes, it is. Why? Java is a strongly typed language. If there are any illegal operations, it won't be compiled. Therefore, this strong typing is important because it helps prevent errors and improves readability. For the strong typing to be successful, all variables, values, and expressions must have a specific type.

# Primitive Type in Java

Built-in data types exist in two types:

- The one which is object-oriented

- The other one which is non-object-oriented

The object-oriented data types in Java are defined by classes. We shall discuss more on classes in the later chapters. At the foundation of Java, there were eight primitives used to demonstrate that these types are non-object-oriented. They were simply normal binary values. One of the reasons why they are not object-oriented is because of issues with efficiency. The following figure shows Java primitive types:

| Type | Meaning |
|------|---------|
| boolean | Represents true/false values |
| byte | 8-bit integer |
| char | Character |
| double | Double-precision floating point |
| float | Single-precision floating point |
| int | Integer |
| long | Long integer |
| short | Short integer |

Java provides a strict specification of the range and attributes of the primitive type. In all those specifications, the Java Virtual Machine has to support them. As a result of the portability aspect, Java cannot be compromised. For instance, an *int* will be the same for all environments. This makes programs be completely portable. It eliminates the requirement to rewrite the code so that it fulfills a given platform.

# Integers

Integers in Java are of four types: *short*, *long*, *int*, and *byte*

| Type | Width in Bits | Range |
|------|---------------|-------|
| byte | 8 | −128 to 127 |
| short | 16 | −32,768 to 32,767 |
| int | 32 | −2,147,483,648 to 2,147,483,647 |
| long | 64 | −9,223,372,036,854,775,808 to 9,223,372,036,854,775,807 |

As you will notice in the above table, the integers have been signed. In Java, it does not provide for unsigned integers. Majority of languages have unsigned and signed integers. The designers behind the Java language felt this was going to be unnecessary.

## N/B

The Java runtime has the ability to make use of whichever size to contain the primitive. However, most of the time, the types should behave according to the way they have been outlined. The most common used integer in Java is the *int*.

When we have an integer whose range is beyond the *int*, we use the *long*. For example, if we have a program which computes a result such as 5280 * 13

The result of this operation can't be stored in an *int* variable. We use a long integer type. The smallest type of integer is the byte. Bytes are excellent when you have data in binary form. The short type often creates the short integer. Short variables are excellent when you don't want bigger values you get from *int*.

## Floating point types

The floating type represents fractional numbers. The floating types exist in two types, the double and float. The double represents the double precision numbers while the float represents the single precision numbers.

The double is applied frequently since functions of mathematics use double value. For instance, sqrt() will output a double. You can check its application in the code below. In this example, sqrt() has been applied to calculate the longest side of a triangle when the length of the other sides has been provided.

```
/*
    Use the Pythagorean theorem to
    find the length of the hypotenuse
    given the lengths of the two opposing
    sides.
*/
class Hypot {
  public static void main(String args[]) {
    double x, y, z;

    x = 3;
    y = 4;                      Notice how sqrt( ) is called. It is preceded by
                                the name of the class of which it is a member.
    z = Math.sqrt(x*x + y*y);

    System.out.println("Hypotenuse is " +z);
  }
}
```

The output from the program is shown here:

```
Hypotenuse is 5.0
```

We need to notice in the example above that *sqrt()* belongs to the *Math* class. But, notice the way the *sqrt()* has been used: first, it has been preceded by the *Math* name. If you can recall the example we used in the first Java program in Chapter 1, we used *System.out* before the *println()* method. Now, for *sqrt()*, it is similar.

## Characters

If you have programmed in another language, you might be thinking that characters in Java are 8. No! Java has Unicode. What a Unicode does is to define a set of characters which represents characters existing in the human languages. The example below demonstrates:

*Char th;*

*th = 'Y';*

Still, if you want to display a char value by applying the *println()* statement. This example will show you how to do it:

```
System.out.println("This is th: "+ th);
Given that the char is unsigned 16-bit type, you can do some arithmetic operations
in the char variable. For instance, look at the program below:

Class CharArith {
Public static void main (String args []) {
Char th;
th = 'X';
System.out.println("th has "+ th);
th++; // we increment the th, it is possible to increment a char
System.out.println("th is now "+ th);
th = 90; // we assign th the value Z
System.out.println("th is now "+ th);
}
}
Here is the output of the above program:
"th has X"
"th is now Y"
"th is now Z"
```

This program assigns variable *th* the value *'X'*. Then, it is incremented to *Y*, which is the next character in the Unicode sequence.

## The Boolean Type

In Java, the Boolean type refers to false or true values. Java finds out if it is true or false using the reserved keywords. Therefore, an expression Boolean type will assume one of these values. An example to demonstrate include:

```
class BoolPro {
public static void main (String args []) {
  boolean q;
  q = false;
  System.out.println ("q is "+ q);
  q= true;
  System.out.println("q is "+ q);
  // a boolean value can also control the if statement
  If(q)
  System.out.println("This is executed.");
  q = false;
  if(q)
  System.out.println("This is not executed");
  // Describe the results of the relational operator
  System.out.println("11 > 8 is "+ (10 > 8));
  }
}
```
The output:
q is false
q is true
This is executed
11 > 8 is true

There are a few things to note about this program. First, the *println()*, displays a boolean value. Secondly, the boolean values control the flow of an if statement. You don't need to go the long way in writing the boolean type this way: *if (b == true)*

The result shown by the operator such as < is boolean. It is one of the reasons why we have the expression *11 > 8* showing the value *true*. In addition, the other pair of parentheses near the *11 > 8* is important since plus comes before the >.

## Literals

When it comes to literals in Java, we mean the fixed values which appear in the form in which human beings can read. We can say the number 200 is a literal. Most of the time, literals can be constants. Literals are important in a program. In fact, most Java programs use literals. Some of the programs we have already discussed in this book use literals.

Literals in Java can fall on various primitive data types. The manner in which every literal is shown is determined by its type. Like it was mentioned some time back, we enclose character constants in single quotes such as *'c'* and *'%'*.

We define literals in integers without involving the fractional part. For instance, 12 and -30 are integer literals. A floating point literal should contain the decimal point plus the fractional part. 12.389 is a floating literal. Java further permits for one to apply the scientific notation for the floating point literals. Integer literals contain int value and anyone can initialize them with a variable of *short*, *byte*, and *char*.

## Hexadecimal, Binary, and Octal literals

A base-8 number system is octal, and it has 0 to 7 digits. In the octal number system, 10 is equivalent to 8 in decimal. The 16-base number system is referred to as hexadecimal and has the digits running from 0 to 9 together with the letters A to F.

## Character Escape Sequences

Surrounding them with single quotes works for the majority of printing characters. However, there are certain characters which have a problem with the text editor. Furthermore, double and single quotes tend to have a unique meaning to Java. This means you cannot just use them directly. Now, because of the above reason, Java has specific escape sequences, sometimes it is called a *backslash character constant*. This table illustrates:

| Escape Sequence | Description |
| --- | --- |
| \' | Single quote |
| \" | Double quote |
| \\ | Backslash |
| \r | Carriage return |
| \n | New line |
| \f | Form feed |
| \t | Horizontal tab |
| \b | Backspace |
| \ddd | Octal constant (where *ddd* is an octal constant) |
| \uxxxx | Hexadecimal constant (where xxxx is a hexadecimal constant) |

For example, *th* is assigned the tab character below:

th = '\t';
Next example, we assign a single quote to th
Th = '\'';

## String Literals

Java further supports other types of literal such as the string. These characters lie inside the double quotes. Take for example:

*"come here"* is a string. In the preceding Java programs, you must come across *println()* method. Besides the normal characters, it is possible for the string literal to have more than one escape sequences. Here is an example of what I am talking about,

```
// Demonstrate escape sequences in strings.
class StrDemo {
  public static void main(String args[]) {
    System.out.println("First line\nSecond line");
    System.out.println("A\tB\tC");
    System.out.println("D\tE\tF") ;
  }
}
```

Use \n to generate a new line.

Use tabs to align output.

The output is shown here:

```
First line
Second line
A         B         C
D         E         F
```

You should be able to recognize the \n escape sequence which has been applied in creating a new line. It is not a must to use the *println()* statements to receive the multiline output. You can get it by embedding the \n in the longer string where you want the new lines to appear.

## Let's turn to variables

Variables in Java are declared using this syntax:

*Type var-name;*

A variable can be declared of any type. This also includes the simple types and each variable will have a type. In other words, what a variable can do will be resolved by its type. For instance, a variable of *boolean* type can never be applied in storing a floating point value. In addition, the type of variable remains throughout its lifetime. For example, a floating variable will forever remain a floating variable. At no point will it change to become an int variable or character variable.

You need to also know that variable declaration is done before you can proceed to use it. This is crucial since the compiler has to know the data types which a variable contains before it does the compilation of a statement applied by the variable. This will also enhance strict type checking.

163

## Variable Initializing

At a certain point in this chapter, I mentioned something about initializing. Well, if you didn't understand what I meant by variable initialization, it's time to understand. Generally, it is a requirement to have your variable store some value before we can use them. One of the easiest ways you can ensure that your variable has some value is using the assignment statement, which I believe you have seen in some examples. Another way you can do it is by assigning your variable an initial name before you proceed to use it. To achieve this, you use the equal sign and the value you would like to assign to the variable. In general, the syntax to follow for variable initialization is:

*Type var = value;*

In this, the value represents the value you would like to assign to the variable at the time of creation. It is important for the value to be compatible with the type of variable. You can look at some examples below:

*int Sum = 12;*

*char th = 'T';*

*float f = 3.2 F // f has been initialized with the 3.2*

*Whenever you are declaring more than two variables of the same type by separating them with a comma, it is important to assign one with an initial value. Here is an example,*

*int x, y = 8, c = 11, d; // Y and c have been initialized with some values*

## Dynamic initialization

While in the previous examples, we have only made use of the constants in the initialization, Java will permit variable initialization dynamically on any valid expression at the time of declaration. For example,

You can have a look at this program which will calculate the volume of a cylinder when the radius and base have been provided:

```
Class DymVolume {
Public static void main (String args []) {
Double radius = 4, height 5;
double volume = 3.1416 * radius * radius * height;
System.out.println("Volume is "+ volume);
}
}
```

## The scope and variable lifetime

So far, you have realized that all variable declaration happens at the main method when it starts.

However, Java will allow variable declaration in any block. A block will define the variable scope. In other words, when a new block begins, a new scope is created. A scope defines objects which will be accessible by the program. It also defines the lifetime of objects.

If it is not your first time to learn a computer language, then you must have come across other computer programming languages which tend to define two type of scopes, the global and local. While they are still supported in Java, this is not the right way to categorize scope in Java. The main scopes in Java as you will see are the ones defined by both the method and class.

In general, variables which have been declared within the scope aren't visible to the code which has been defined beyond the limits of the scope. Now, whenever you define a variable within a scope, you make that variable available as a local variable and safeguard it against unauthorized use. In other words, the rules of scope set precedence for encapsulation.

Something else which you need to know as a new beginner to Java programming is that you can have a nested scope. For you to understand this concept, study the code below:

```
// we are showing block scope
class ScopeShow {
int x; // this is accessible to all the code found in Main function
x = 12;
if (x == 12) {// we start a new scope
int y = 20; // only accessible to this block
// x and y are known here
System.out.println ("x and y: "+ X + ""+ y);
X = y* 2;
}
// y = 100; // an error is here, y is not known here, because it is found outside the
scope
// x is still visible here
System.out.println("x is "+ x);
}
}
```

The declaration of *x* happens at the start of the main method. This means that it is only visible to the part of code enclosed in the main method. Inside the if statement, we have the *y* variable declared. Given that a block will define the scope, *y* is accessible only to the part of the code inside the block. Again, inside the if block, we can use *x* because it is inside a nested scope.

One last point you should remember is variable are created when you enter the scope and ends when you exit scope. What this means is once we are out of the scope, the variable will not store its value.

## Operators

Java has an extensive list of operator environment. If you are wondering what an operator is, you can look at it as a symbol which conveys a specific message to the compiler to carry out a logical or mathematical operation. In Java, you will interact with four classes of operators. The four classes include:

- Logical operator

- Bitwise operator

- Relational operator

- Arithmetic operator

166

Like other computer languages, Java has a defined list of additional operators to take care of certain specific scenarios.

## Arithmetic operators

Arithmetic operators in Java include:

- \+ represents addition

- \- represents subtraction

- \* represents multiplication

- / represents division

- % represents modulus

- ++ represents increment

- -- represents decrement

Operators such as +, -, *, and / all perform the same function just like the rest of other languages.

# Chapter 3

# Java Program Control Statements

In Java, we have three types of program control statements. That includes the **selection** statements which consist of the *switch* and *if*; **iteration** statements contain the *do-while, while,* and *for* loops. The **statement jump** consists of the *return, break*, and *continue*. Besides the return statement, the remaining control statements you are going to learn more about here.

## The if control statement

In the previous chapter, you have briefly interacted with the structure of an if statement. It takes the following construct:

> *if(condition) {*
>
> > *//sequence statement*
>
> *}*
>
> > *else*
> >
> > *{*
> >
> > *//sequence statement*
> >
> > *}*

This is one of the simplest forms of the if statement. It is straightforward to understand. At no point will all the sequence statements be executed at the same time. What you should realize in the above if statement is that the condition expression which controls the flow of the if statement has to produce a true or false value. True or false is a boolean type. We want to see how an if statement works in a program. Before we look at the program, you need to notice that this program requires one to input a character with their keyboard. The Java method for this is the *System.in.read()*.

Here's a program similar to the guessing letter game:

```
// we are showing block scope
class ScopeShow {
int x; // this is accessible to all the code found in Main function
x = 12;
if (x == 12) {// we start a new scope
int y = 20; // only accessible to this block
// x and y are known here
System.out.println ("x and y: "+ X + ""+ y);
X = y* 2;
}
// y = 100; // an error is here, y is not known here, because it is found outside the scope
// x is still visible here
System.out.println("x is "+ x);
}
}
```

In this program, the user is prompted to key in a character from the keyboard. Then the if statement will compare if the character entered is correct with the answer. A correct answer will result in a message shown on the screen. Otherwise, a different message is shown to the user to tell him or her they are wrong.

## Nested ifs

We have previously looked at nested scopes; now we want to look at nested ifs. You will interact most of the time with a nested if. The greatest lesson to learn is nested ifs point to the block of code with the else.

Read the following example:

```
If( i ==10) {
If ( j < 20) a = b;
If (k > 100) c = d;
else a – c; // this else will point to the if (k > 100)
}
else a = d; //this else will point to the if (i ==10)
|
```

You should be able to note that the last else has not been associated with if(j<20), but associated with the if(i==10).

## if-else-if Ladder

This is a common programming syntax which depends on the nested if. It picks the following construct:

```
If(condition)

Statement

else if (condition)

statement

else if (condition)

statement

else

statement
```

In this syntax, the conditional expressions are tested from top to bottom. The moment a true condition is evaluated, the statement which is linked to it gets executed while the remaining sections are skipped. Supposing all conditions evaluated to be untrue, the last else statement runs. In this type of else statement, the final else is considered the default condition. If you fail to include the final else, no action will happen.

This program shows the if-else-if ladder:

```
// Demonstrate an if-else-if ladder.
class Ladder {
  public static void main(String args[]) {
    int x;

    for(x=0; x<6; x++) {
      if (x==1)
        System.out.println("x is one");
      else if(x==2)
        System.out.println("x is two");
      else if(x==3)
        System.out.println("x is three");
      else if(x==4)
        System.out.println("x is four");
      else
        System.out.println("x is not between 1 and 4");  ◄──── This is the
    }                                                           default statement.
  }
}
```

The program produces the following output:

```
x is not between 1 and 4
x is one
x is two
x is three
x is four
x is not between 1 and 4
```

From this program, you should be able to realize that *else* statement is only executed when there is no *if* statement which is true.

## The Switch Statement

The next of Java's selection statement you will learn is the *switch*. The switch statement will allow a program to pick from various choices available. The switch involves testing an expression value with constants. If it matches any of the choices, the following statements associated with it are run. Switch uses the following syntax:

```
switch(expression) {
  case constant1:
    statement sequence
    break;
  case constant2:
    statement sequence
    break;
  case constant3:
    statement sequence
    break;

  .

  .

  .

  default:
    statement sequence
}
```

The *default* statement will be executed when none of the case constant match the expression. It is an optional choice.

Here is a program which illustrates the switch statement:

```java
// Demonstrate the switch.
class SwitchDemo {
  public static void main(String args[]) {
    int i;

    for(i=0; i<10; i++)
      switch(i) {
        case 0:
          System.out.println("i is zero");
          break;
        case 1:
          System.out.println("i is one");
          break;
        case 2:
          System.out.println("i is two");
          break;
        case 3:
          System.out.println("i is three");
          break;
        case 4:
          System.out.println("i is four");
          break;
        default:
          System.out.println("i is five or more");
      }
  }
}
```

The output produced by this program is shown here:

```
i is zero
i is one
i is two
i is three
i is four
i is five or more
i is five or more
i is five or more
i is five or more
i is five or more
```

You can see in the above example that whenever the loop iterates, the statement linked to the case statement with it gets executed while the rest are skipped. If i is >= 5, we have no case statement to match that, so the default case has to be executed. The break statement is optional, but a lot of switch statements still use it.

## Nested switch statements

The same way we have nested ifs, we can also have nested switch statements. You can see this example:

```
switch(ch1) {
  case 'A': System.out.println("This A is part of outer switch.");
    switch(ch2) {
      case 'A':
        System.out.println("This A is part of inner switch');
        break;
      case 'B': // ...
    } // end of inner switch
    break;
  case 'B': // ...
```

## The for loop

Since the start of Chapter one, you have been making use of the *for* loop. You will be surprised to learn that the for loop is efficient and flexible. Here is the basic syntax for of a for loop:

for(*initialization; condition; iteration*) *statement;*

For repeating a block, the general form is

for(*initialization; condition; iteration*)
{
  *statement sequence*
}

The *condition* has a true or false expression which will define if the for loop can make another cycle. The iteration expression determines the number of times the loop repeats. Here you should see that we have separated all the three parts of the loop by semicolons.

The for loop will progress with the execution if the condition is always found to be true. If the condition is evaluated to be false, the program exits and executes the next line of code of the program.

This program below demonstrates the use of a for loop:
```
//1-99 and the rounding error
Class SqrRoot {
public static void main (String args []) {
double number, sroot,rerr;
for (number = 1.0; number < 100.0; number++) {
sroot = Math.sqrt(number);
System.out.println("Square root of "+ number + "is "+ sroot);
// compute the error
rerr = number – (sroot * sroot);
System.out.println("Rounding error is "+ rerr);
System.out.println();
}
}
}
```

You should realize that to compute the rounding error, we square the square root of every number. Later, subtract the outcome from the previous number.

## The While loop

The general structure of a while loop includes:

*while(condition) {*

*//sequence*

*}*

In the while loop, the loop will repeat as long as the condition is true. A false condition will result in the program exiting the loop. To demonstrate the while loop, below is a program:

```java
// while loop in java
class WhileDem {
public static void main (String args []) {
char ch;
// print using the while loop
ch = "b";
while (ch < = 'z') {
System.out.println(ch);
ch++;
}
}
}
```

In this example, we have initialized *ch* and assigned the value *"b"*. Every time the loop runs, *ch* is displayed then incremented. The process will proceed until the time we have the value of ch higher than *z*.

## The do-while loop

It is the last type of loop in Java. When it comes to *do-while* loop, it is different compared to the while and for loops. The do-while loop will run the code inside it at least once before it tests the condition. Here is the syntax of a do-while loop:

>*do*
>
>*{*
>
>*statements;*
>
>*}*
>
>*While (condition);*

Even though it is not important to have the braces, they are placed there to improve the readability so that we do not confuse it with the while loop. In this program, we implement with the do-while loop:

```
// Demonstrate the do-while loop.
class DWDemo {
  public static void main(String args[])
    throws java.io.IOException {

    char ch;

    do {
      System.out.print("Press a key followed by ENTER: ");
      ch = (char) System.in.read(); // get a char
    } while(ch != 'q');
  }
}
```

## Break to exit a loop

Sometimes you might want to exit a loop even if it has not run to completion. You may have achieved what you wanted and you don't see the need to continue running the loop. This is the time when the *break* statement becomes important. A *break* statement placed in a loop forces the loop to terminate. This makes the program to resume executing the subsequent lines.

176

Look at this example:

```
// Using break to exit a loop.
class BreakDemo {
  public static void main(String args[]) {
    int num;

    num = 100;

    // loop while i-squared is less than num
    for(int i=0; i < num; i++) {
      if(i*i >= num) break; // terminate loop if i*i >= 100
      System.out.print(i + " ");
    }
    System.out.println("Loop complete.");
  }
}
```

This program generates the following output:

```
0 1 2 3 4 5 6 7 8 9 Loop complete.
```

The *break* statement in this example has been used to terminate the loop. The *break* statement can be freely applied in whichever type of loop in Java language.

## The use of continue

While you can terminate the execution of a loop, it is also possible to skip the normal control structure of a loop. The *continue* statement will help you achieve this.

```
// Use continue.
class ContDemo {
  public static void main(String args[]) {
    int i;

    // print even numbers between 0 and 100
    for(i = 0; i<=100; i++) {
      if((i%2) != 0) continue; // iterate
      System.out.println(i);
    }
  }
}
```

# Chapter 4

# Starting Out with Classes in Java, Objects, and Methods

To become a professional Java programmer, you must understand the concept of classes in Java. The class is the main part of any Java program. In other words, it is the basis on which the whole Java language is created, and one reason for this is that the class holds the features of an object.

Inside a class, you will find data defined as well as the code which executes the data. The code exists in the methods. This chapter will take you through a brief understanding of the classes, methods, and objects in Java. It is crucial that you have a basic foundation of the above features so that you can know how to write complicated Java programs.

## The fundamentals of Class

Since the start of this book, we have been using Java class. You should have noticed that every Java program has a class. Although we have been using Java classes, the classes were simple and we did not take advantage of the many features which a class comes with. Soon you will discover that the Java class is even more efficient than what we have used previously in the different programs.

So, let's start by looking at the basics of a class in Java. We can look at a class as a blueprint which determines the object properties. It defines in detail the program data and code. And so, a class is like a template which describes how you can create an object. It is vital to be elaborate about a class; it is a logical abstraction. Methods and variable of a class are referred to as members.

## The basic style of a class

Whenever you describe a class, you will be declaring its nature and form. To declare a class involves making a specification of its instance variables as well as the methods of the class. While simple classes may only have methods or some might have instance variables alone, the majority of the real-world classes have both the class and instance variables.

The keyword class is used in declaring a class. Here is an easy class definition:

```
class classname {
    // declare instance variables
    type var1;
    type var2;
    // ...
    type varN;

    // declare methods
    type method1(parameters) {
        // body of method
    }
    type method2(parameters) {
        // body of method
    }
    // ...
    type methodN(parameters) {
        // body of method
    }
}
```

A class defined clearly should have a logical entity. For instance, if we have a class which holds telephone numbers and names of people, it will never hold other unrelated information such as average rainfall. The point to note here is that a class which is well-designed will store information that is logically connected. If you store information which is unrelated to the class, it will destroy the structure of your code.

So far, we have used classes which come with a single *main()* method. Soon you will learn how to build other methods, but I want you to know that the basic style of a class is not the way the *main()* method is defined.

We only need the *main()* method in case our class as it is the beginning point of our program. In addition, certain types of Java applications don't need the *main()* method.

## Definition of a class

To reveal the concept of Java classes, we shall create a class which will store information about vehicles. The class is called *Vehicle*. This class will have information such as the number of passengers, the capacity of the fuel, as well as the average fuel consumption. In this class, we have three instance variables defined: fuel cap, passengers, and mpg. You should be keen to realize that the class Vehicle is without a method. At the moment, we consider it a data class.

```
class Vehicle {
  int passengers; // number of passengers
  int fuelcap;    // fuel capacity in gallons
  int mpg;        // fuel consumption in miles per gallon
}
```

By defining a class, it has to create a new data type.

Don't forget that class declaration involves only specifying the type description. No actual object is created. Therefore, the previous example will not enforce the objects of type vehicle to become active.

This statement helps one create an object which belongs to the Vehicle class.

*Vehicle minisalon = new Vehicle(); // we have created a variable object called minisalon*

When this statement is executed, *minisalon* becomes an instance of the class *Vehicle*. Now, it will be said to have a physical reality. To access any member of a class, the dot operator helps you achieve that:

*Object.Member*

Take, for instance, we want our *minisalon* to hold the value 12. This is how it is done:

*minisalon.fuelcap = 12;*

Overall, the dot operator allows you to access the methods and instance variables. You can take a look at this entire program which uses the Vehicle class:

```
/* A program that uses the Vehicle class.

   Call this file VehicleDemo.java
*/
class Vehicle {
   int passengers; // number of passengers
   int fuelcap;    // fuel capacity in gallons
   int mpg;        // fuel consumption in miles per gallon
}
// This class declares an object of type Vehicle.
class VehicleDemo {
   public static void main(String args[]) {
      Vehicle minivan = new Vehicle();
      int range;

      // assign values to fields in minivan
      minivan.passengers = 7;
      minivan.fuelcap = 16;  ←————— Notice the use of the dot
      minivan.mpg = 21;                 operator to access a member

      // compute the range assuming a full tank of gas
      range = minivan.fuelcap * minivan.mpg;
      System.out.println("Minivan can carry " + minivan.passengers +
                     " with a range of " + range);
   }
}
```

If you want to run this program, you need to run the file with the name *Vehicle.Demo.java*. The main method is found in that class. This program will display:

```
Minivan can carry 7 with a range of 336
```

## Reference variables and assignment

When handling the assignment operation in Java, you should underline that the object reference behaves differently from primitive variables. In this case, if you will assign a primitive type variable to another, it is simple. In simple terms, what the left variable does is to store what is held in the variable at right. However, if you choose that you will allot a single object reference variable to the other, the scenario becomes complicated. Why? You will be modifying the object which the reference variable refers to. Here is an example:

```
Vehicle car1 = new Vehicle ();
Vehicle car2 = car1;
```

By looking at the above code snippet, you might reason that both objects point to separate objects, however, that is not true. In this code, both car1 and car2 point to the same object. Something I would like you to learn here is that even though we have car1 and car2 pointing to the same object. They aren't related.

## Methods

As we had said before, methods are members of the classes. At the moment, our Vehicle class has data, but no methods. While having a class which contains data alone is valid, the majority of the classes will have methods. Methods act upon the data which has been defined in the class, and most of the time it offers access to the data.

A method can carry at least one statement. A fully written Java code will contain a method which acts only on one particular task. Every method must be given a name. The name of the method helps one use the method in the code. You can choose to give your method whichever name you want, but note that the *main()* method is meant for the method which will start your program execution. Another important point is that you should never use Java keywords as part of your method name. The syntax for Java methods includes:

*Type Your_methodname (parameter-list) {*

*//the body*

*}*

In the above example, the *type* represents the type of data you would want your method to return. A *void* method is one which does not return data. We specify method name by *your_methodname*. The *parameter-list* refers to a series of type and identifier differentiated using commas. Parameters point to variables which are going to acquire the arguments which have been passed to the method after it has been called.

## We give a method the Java vehicle class

To add a method to the Vehicle class, we will state it in the Vehicle's declaration. In this example, the Vehicle has a method called *range()* which output several types of vehicle:

```
// Add range to Vehicle.

class Vehicle {
    int passengers; // number of passengers
    int fuelcap;    // fuel capacity in gallons
    int mpg;        // fuel consumption in miles per gallon

    // Display the range.
    void range () {  ◄——— The range() method is contained within the Vehicle class.
        System.out.println('Range is " + fuelcap * mpg);
    }                                        ▲          ▲
}                                            └────┬─────┘
                    Notice that fuelcap and mpg are used directly, without the dot operator.
class AddMeth {
    public static void main(String args[]) {
        Vehicle minivan = new Vehicle();
        Vehicle sportscar = new Vehicle();

        int range1, range2;

        // assign values to fields in minivan
        minivan.passengers = 7;
        minivan.fuelcap = 16;
        minivan.mpg = 21;
```

```
// assign values to fields in sportscar
sportscar.passengers = 2;
sportscar.fuelcap = 14;
sportscar.mpg = 12;


System.out.print("Minivan can carry " + minivan.passengers +
                 ". ");

minivan.range(); // display range of minivan

System.out.print("Sportscar can carry " + sportscar.passengers +
                 ". ");

sportscar.range(); // display range of sportscar.
    }
}
```

This program will show the following output:

```
Minivan can carry 7. Range is 336
Sportscar can carry 2. Range is 168
```

We now want to review this program by starting with the method range(). Here is the first line:

*Void range() {*

What happens here is that we have declared a method whose name is *range*, and it has no parameter. The body of the method has the *System.out.println("……");* construct which will display the range of the vehicle after performing a few calculations. The method *range()* closes when it encounters the closing curly brace. This leads to the main program control to switch to the original caller. Well, let's review the code starting from the main method:

## Minivan.range();

What is happening here is that the *range()* method is called by using the object variable minivan. Calling a program causes the program control to migrate to the method. And so, if the method execution comes to an end, control is relayed to the caller, and the program execution resumes

184

from the following code. If we consider the above example, the method *range* here is going to display all the variation of vehicles defined by the minivan, similar to a call done by *sportscar*. Whenever you call *range()*, it will output the range listed by the object.

There is one particular thing you should discover about the method *range()*. Some of the instance variables have been addressed directly using the . operator.

## Returning to a method

Generally, we have only two conditions which result in a method returning a value. First, the closing curly brace interacts with the method—this is clear in the method *range()*. The second condition for a method to return happens when a *return* statement gets executed. Don't forget that there are two types of return: the *void* method and the other one which returns values. We shall look at the first form here:

In a void method, it is possible to enforce an immediate termination by applying the *return* statement.

When the return statement is executed, the program control will get back to the caller by jumping all the rest of the code in a method. Consider the following example:

```
type-specifier array_name[ ] [ ] = {
    { val, val, val, ...., val },
    { val, val, val, ...., val },

    .

    .

    .

    { val, val, val, ...., val }
};
```

In this case, the for loop will execute from 0–5 because when it reaches 5, the method is enforced to return a value. You can still develop many return statements in one Java method, especially when you have two pathways.

## Returning a Value

While it is rare for a void method to return a value, there are specific methods which return a value. The potential for the method to have a return is an important property of a method. You have perhaps seen an example in the square root function to find the square root. Return value is important in programming to show a given result of a calculation like in the *sqrt()* function.

Sometimes, the return value proves the success or failure of a given method. The syntax used for a method with a return value is:

    *return* *value;*

# Chapter 5

# In-depth look at Data types and Operators

I n this chapter, we are going to discuss arrays, the bitwise operators, string types, and the ternary operator.

## Arrays

We haven't covered anything about arrays in the previous chapter. However, what you should note is that arrays are simply a collection of variables of a similar type. Java arrays can take more than one form and dimension, even though you will discover that the one-dimension type of array is popular. Arrays are applied in programming to accomplish several tasks because they are the best for handling many related items.

The greatest benefit of arrays is that it arranges the data in a manner which is easy to modify. For instance, let's say you have an array which has the salary for different people. It becomes easy to calculate the total of the salary or even the average of the salary. Arrays will also organize the data in a manner which will make everything simple to sort.

While Java arrays can still be used the way we do in other languages, they have a unique feature: you implement them using objects. Implementing arrays as objects gives several advantages.

### The one-dimensional arrays

When we talk about a one-dimensional array, we are referring to variables in a list that have a certain relation. These lists are very popular in the programming languages. A one-dimensional array is declared in the following way:

*Type array-name [] = new type [size];*

In this case, the type of array shows which type the array is while the number of items the array can hold is defined by the array size. When you implement arrays as objects, it has two procedures to adhere to. First, declare the array reference variable, then finalize by setting aside the memory for the array. You can look at this example:

*Int team [] = new int [11];*

As you can notice, array declaration will work the same way we do when you want to initialize an object. The *team* variable will store an address to the memory which has been assigned by *new*. However, for objects, we can break the above example into two:

*int team [];*

*team = new int [11];*

In the above example, when *team* is created, it has no physical object related to it, but when the following statement gets executed, *team* is associated with the array.

An index helps one access individual elements in an array. It specifies the correct position of each element stored in the array. Java arrays begin at 0. Since the array *team* has 11 elements, its index is from 0 to 10. If you want to perform array indexing, you must delineate every element which you want using square brackets. We use arrays in programming because they will help one handle a large number of associated variables. An example of a program which uses an array:

```
// Find the minimum and maximum values in an array.
class MinMax {
  public static void main(String args[]) {
    int nums[] = new int[10];
    int min, max;

    nums[0] = 99;
    nums[1] = -10;
    nums[2] = 100123;
    nums[3] = 18;
    nums[4] = -978;
    nums[5] = 5623;
    nums[6] = 463;
    nums[7] = -9;
    nums[8] = 287;
    nums[9] = 49;
    min = max = nums[0];
    for(int i=1; i < 10; i++) {
      if(nums[i] < min) min = nums[i];
      if(nums[i] > max) max = nums[i];
    }
    System.out.println("min and max: " + min + " " + max);
  }
}
```

The output from the program is shown here:

```
min and max: -978 100123
```

## Two-dimensional array

This is among the easiest type of multidimensional array. You declare it as shown below:

*Int table [] [] = new int [10] [30];*

In this example, we have a two-dimensional array:

```
// Demonstrate a two-dimensional array.
class TwoD {
  public static void main(String args[]) {
    int t, i;
    int table[][] = new int[3][4];

    for(t=0; t < 3; ++t) {
      for(i=0; i < 4; ++i) {
        table[t][i] = (t*4)+i+1;
        System.out.print(table[t][i] + " ");
      }
      System.out.println();
    }
  }
}
```

189

## Three or more dimensional arrays

Java still has arrays of more than two dimensions. Here is how it is declared:

*type name*[ ][ ]...[ ] = new *type*[*size1*][*size2*]...[*sizeN*];

## How to initialize multi-dimensional arrays

To initialize a multi-dimensional array, you have to enclose every dimension using specific curly braces. For instance, the general style to apply when you want to initialize a two-dimensional array includes:

```
type-specifier array_name[ ][ ] = {
    { val, val, val, ..., val },
    { val, val, val, ..., val },

    .

    .

    { val, val, val, ..., val }
};
```

In this example, *val* is the variable which is applied in the initialization. For each block inside the curly braces, it represents a specific row. For every row, it will hold the first value of the subarray. When we review the second value, it will take the second position, and the cycle continues. You must realize we are using commas to delineate the semicolon and the variable for initialization. The program below, the array *sqrs* is initialized with numbers between 1 to 10 together with their squares.

```
// Initialize a two-dimensional array.
class Squares {
  public static void main(String args[]) {
    int sqrs[][] = {
      { 1,   1 },
      { 2,   4 },
      { 3,   9 },
      { 4,  16 },
      { 5,  25 },          Notice how each row has
      { 6,  36 },          its own set of initializers.
      { 7,  49 },
      { 8,  64 },
      { 9,  81 },
      { 10, 100 }
    };
    int i, j;

    for(i=0; i < 10; i++) {
      for(j=0; j < 2; j++)
        System.out.print(sqrs[i][j] + " ");
      System.out.println();
    }
  }
}
```

## Assigning array references

Similar to other objects, when you chose to earmark an array a reference variable to another, you will be shifting the object which the variable points to. You will not be leading to a copy of an array to make any changes to the details stored in the array.

You can consider this example:

191

```
// Assigning array reference variables.
class AssignARef {
  public static void main(String args[]) {
    int i;

    int nums1[] = new int[10];
    int nums2[] = new int[10];

    for(i=0; i < 10; i++)
      nums1[i] = i;

    for(i=0; i < 10; i++)
      nums2[i] = -i;
    System.out.print("Here is nums1: ");
    for(i=0; i < 10; i++)
      System.out.print(nums1[i] + " ");
    System.out.println();

    System.out.print("Here is nums2: ");
    for(i=0; i < 10; i++)
      System.out.print(nums2[i] + " ");
    System.out.println();

    nums2 = nums1; // now nums2 refers to nums1  ◄——Assign an array reference.

    System.out.print("Here is nums2 after assignment: ");
    for(i=0; i < 10; i++)
      System.out.print(nums2[i] + " ");
    System.out.println();

    // now operate on nums1 array through nums2
    nums2[3] = 99;

    System.out.print("Here is nums1 after change through nums2: ");
    for(i=0; i < 10; i++)
      System.out.print(nums1[i] + " ");
    System.out.println();
  }
}
```

The output from the program is shown here:

```
Here is nums1: 0 1 2 3 4 5 6 7 8 9
Here is nums2: 0 -1 -2 -3 -4 -5 -6 -7 -8 -9
Here is nums2 after assignment: 0 1 2 3 4 5 6 7 8 9
Here is nums1 after change through nums2: 0 1 2 99 4 5 6 7 8 9
```

## The for-each loop

Sometimes situations arise in dealing with arrays where it is a requirement to go through every element in the array. Such situations are many, like if you want to perform an average operation or do a sum calculation. You will have to add every value stored in the array. The procedure of individually adding each element before you can perform the average is tiresome.

This type of for loop we will discuss is *for-each*. A for loop will go around a collection of objects in a sequential style from the start to the end. The general syntax of a for-each loop is:

for(*type itr-var : collection*) *statement-block*

## Strings

*String* is also another crucial element of the Java data type. A string will define and support the character string. In many programming languages, a string is an array of characters. But, Java is a bit different. Instead, strings are considered objects.

For your information, we have used the string class from the time this book started, but you never realized that. Any time you decide to declare a string literal, you will simply be creating an object of String. For instance, the statement:

*System.out.println("Strings are objects in Java");*

"Strings are objects in Java" is automatically defined into a string object by Java.

## Constructing a string

To declare a string, you do it the same way you can declare other objects:

*String play = new String ("how are you");*

This code will generate a String object called *play* which has the character string *"how are you"*. It is still possible to generate a string with the help of a different String. Take this example:

193

```
String play = new String ("How are you");
String play1 = new String (play);
```

When the code executes, play1 will also contain the string "How are you".

What you need to know is that the moment you create your string object, you can really make use of it any place where quoted strings are permitted. For instance, you may use it in *println()*, this is provided in the example below:

```
// Introduce String.
class StringDemo {
  public static void main(String args[]) {
    // declare strings in various ways
    String str1 = new String("Java strings are objects.");
    String str2 = "They are constructed various ways.";
    String str3 = new String(str2);

    System.out.println(str1);
    System.out.println(str2);
    System.out.println(str3);
  }
}
```

The output from the program is shown here:

```
Java strings are objects.
They are constructed various ways.
They are constructed various ways.
```

## How to operate on Strings

The class string has different methods which work on strings. You can look at them in the table below:

| | |
|---|---|
| boolean equals(*str*) | Returns true if the invoking string contains the same character sequence as *str*. |
| int length( ) | Obtains the length of a string. |
| char charAt(*index*) | Obtains the character at the index specified by *index*. |
| int compareTo(*str*) | Returns less than zero if the invoking string is less than *str*, greater than zero if the invoking string is greater than *str*, and zero if the strings are equal. |
| int indexOf(*str*) | Searches the invoking string for the substring specified by *str*. Returns the index of the first match or −1 on failure. |
| int lastIndexOf(*str*) | Searches the invoking string for the substring specified by str. Returns the index of the last match or −1 on failure. |

If you would like to see a program which uses the above methods. Here is an example

```
// Some String operations.
class StrOps {
  public static void main(String args[]) {
    String str1 =
      "When it comes to Web programming, Java is #1.";
    String str2 = new String(str1);
    String str3 = "Java strings are powerful.";
    int result, idx;
    char ch;

    System.out.println("Length of str1: " +
                         str1.length());

    // display str1, one char at a time.
    for(int i=0; i < str1.length(); i++)
      System.out.print(str1.charAt(i));
    System.out.println();
    if(str1.equals(str2))
      System.out.println("str1 equals str2");
    else
      System.out.println("str1 does not equal str2");

    if(str1.equals(str3))
      System.out.println("str1 equals str3");
    else
      System.out.println("str1 does not equal str3");

    result = str1.compareTo(str3);
    if(result == 0)
      System.out.println("str1 and str3 are equal");
    else if(result < 0)
      System.out.println("str1 is less than str3");
    else
      System.out.println("str1 is greater than str3");

    // assign a new string to str2
    str2 = "One Two Three One";

    idx = str2.indexOf("One");
    System.out.println("Index of first occurrence of One: " + idx);
    idx = str2.lastIndexOf("One");
    System.out.println("Index of last occurrence of One: " + idx);
  }
}
```

This program generates the following output:

```
Length of str1: 45
When it comes to Web programming, Java is #1.
str1 equals str2
str1 does not equal str3
str1 is greater than str3
Index of first occurrence of One: 0
Index of last occurrence of One: 14
```

Just like any other data type, it is possible to assemble strings like arrays. For instance:

```
// Demonstrate String arrays.
class StringArrays {
  public static void main(String args[]) {
    String strs[] = { "This", "is", "a", "test." };

    System.out.println("Original array: ");
    for(String s : strs)
      System.out.print(s + " ");
    System.out.println("\n");

    // change a string
    strs[1] = "was";
    strs[3] = "test, too!";

    System.out.println("Modified array: ");
    for(String s : strs)
      System.out.print(s + " ");
  }
}
```

## "Strings are immutable"

What this means is that once you have the strings created, you can't modify the character sequence of the string. This type of limit permits Java to implement strings in an efficient way. While this might sound like a big disadvantage, it is not. If you want a string which is a modification of the one you already have, just create the string which has the desired modifications.

196

## Use a string to control the switch statement

In the previous chapter, we saw that the switch control statement had to be an integer type like *char* or *int*. Today, we can apply a string as the control of a switch. This will lead to a code which is readable and efficient in most situations.

This example will illustrate how to control a switch with a String.

```java
// Use a string to control a switch statement.

class StringSwitch {
  public static void main(String args[]) {

    String command = "cancel";

    switch(command) {
      case "connect":
        System.out.println("Connecting");
        break;
      case "cancel":
        System.out.println("Canceling");
        break;
      case "disconnect":
        System.out.println("Disconnecting");
        break;
      default:
        System.out.println("Command Error!");
        break;
    }
  }
}
```

This program will display the output: Cancelling

## Bitwise Operators

While in the opening chapters we learned the logical, relational and arithmetic operators, Java still has other operators which cover different types of problems. These are the bitwise operators. You can use the bitwise operators on *short, long, byte* or *int* values. However, we can't apply operations of this type of operator on *float, double* and *boolean* or even class types. We call them bitwise operators because of their

197

operation: they alter the bits that produce a value. This table shows some of the bitwise operators:

| Operator | Result |
| --- | --- |
| & | Bitwise AND |
| \| | Bitwise OR |
| ^ | Bitwise exclusive OR |
| >> | Shift right |
| >>> | Unsigned shift right |
| << | Shift left |
| ~ | One's complement (unary NOT) |

## The ? Operator

This is the most interesting thing about Java operators. Often, the ? Replaces most used if-else:

```
|
If(condition)
Var = expression1;
Else
Var = expression2;
```

The ? is the ternary operator. Its syntax is:

Exp1? Exp2: Exp3:

The first expression is the Boolean type, while the second and third expression can be any type of expression. Make sure you note the placement of the colon.

This is how the ternary works: exp1 is tested, then if true, exp2 is taken to be the value of the whole expression tested. However, when it happens that exp1 is not true, exp3 will automatically be the current value of the expression.

Below is an example of the ? operator:

```
// Prevent a division by zero using the ?.
class NoZeroDiv {
  public static void main(String args[]) {
  int result;

  for(int i = -5; i < 6; i++) {
    result = i != 0 ? 100 / i : 0;  ◄——————— This prevents a divide-by-zero.
    if(i != 0)
      System.out.println("100 / " + i + " is " + result);
    }
  }
}
```

The output from the program is shown here:

```
100 / -5 is -20
100 / -4 is -25
100 / -3 is -33
100 / -2 is -50
100 / -1 is -100
100 / 1 is 100
100 / 2 is 50
100 / 3 is 33
100 / 4 is 25
100 / 5 is 20
```

# Chapter 6

# Inheritance in Java

This chapter will proceed with the objected-oriented programming in Java. In this chapter, we discuss inheritance in Java. Inheritance is another way of software reuse. It involves creating a new software by making use of existing class members. Inheritance will allow you to save time during the process of program development by creating new classes on existing classes. Inheritance further provides for the chance that a system will be developed and maintained effectively.

An existing class in Java is called the superclass while a new class declared is called the subclass. In the C++ programming language, the superclass is the base class while the subclass is the derived class. Every subclass may become a superclass for the later subclasses.

A subclass can later create its own methods and classes. This means a subclass is specific compared to the superclass and it represents a specialized group of objects.

In Java, the class inheritance will start with the class object. Java has only single inheritance. This is where each class is extracted from one direct superclass.

## Superclass and Subclasses
Usually, an object which belongs to one class is an object of another class too. You can take a look at the superclasses and subclasses below:

| Superclass | Subclasses |
|---|---|
| Student | GraduateStudent, UndergraduateStudent |
| Shape | Circle, Triangle, Rectangle, Sphere, Cube |
| Loan | CarLoan, HomeImprovementLoan, MortgageLoan |
| Employee | Faculty, Staff |
| BankAccount | CheckingAccount, SavingsAccount |

Taking one example above, we can say CheckingAccount inherits from the class BankAccount. In other words, CheckingAccount is a subclass and BankAccount is the class. Since each subclass belongs to a superclass, and it is possible to have a single superclass with many subclasses, we can say that a superclass represents a large set of objects compared to what a subclass can represent. For instance, the superclass shape will represent all types of shapes, but the subclass circle will represent specific types of circles.

## Member hierarchy in a university community

The inheritance relationship builds a specific tree-like structure. The superclass at the top while the subclass comes below the superclass. We want to build an inheritance hierarchy of a university community. You know well that a university has thousands of people including students, alumni, professors, and employees. The employees can still be for the staff or faculty members. The faculty members can further be administrators such as chairpersons or lecturers. The hierarchy could have a lot of classes. For instance, we can have students who are undergraduate and graduate. The undergraduates can further be categorized into freshmen, juniors, sophomores, and seniors.

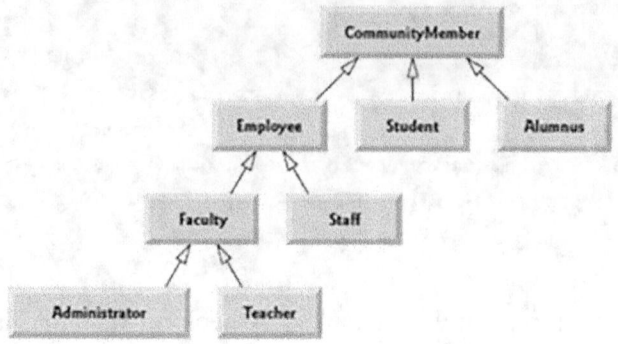

Every arrow in the above hierarchy indicates an is-a relationship.

## The shape hierarchy

Let's now look at the shape hierarchy. This hierarchy will start with a super-class *Shape*. The superclass *Shape* is extended by *ThreeDimensionalShape* and *TwoDimensionalShape*. The third level in the shape hierarchy has specific types of *TwoDimensionalShape* as well as *ThreeDimensionalShape*. The same way we did for the University hierarchy, we can apply the same in the shape hierarchy. Find out how many relationships do we have. This shape hierarchy could have as many classes as possible.

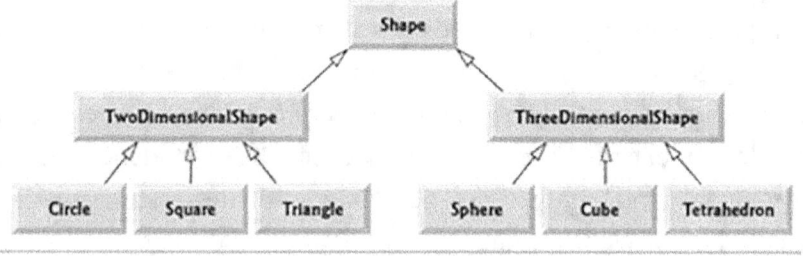

Something which you need to note is that not every class relationship can be an inheritance relationship.

## Protected Members

At one point in this book, we discussed briefly the *public* and *private* modifiers. Public members are free to be accessed at any time but not the same case as protected members.

Now we want to look at an example:

We know that Java will support inheritance by providing for inclusion of one class into another one in the declaration. You achieve this with the keyword *extends*. Therefore, the subclass will extend to the superclass. Here is an example which demonstrates some dominant features of inheritance as discussed previously. The superclass in this program is *TwoDShape*. It holds both the dimensions of a 2-D object and a subclass referred to as *Triangle*. You should note the way the keyword *extends* has been used to develop the subclass.

```
// A simple class hierarchy.

// A class for two-dimensional objects.
class TwoDShape {
```

```java
    double width;
    double height;

    void showDim() {
      System.out.println("Width and height are " +
                         width + " and " + height);
    }
}

// A subclass of TwoDShape for triangles.
class Triangle extends TwoDShape {
    String style;                              ← Triangle inherits TwoDShape.

    double area() {
      return width * height / 2;    ←——— Triangle can refer to the members of TwoDShape
    }                                          as if they were part of Triangle.

    void showStyle() {
      System.out.println("Triangle is " + style);
    }
}

class Shapes {
    public static void main(String args[]) {
      Triangle t1 = new Triangle();
      Triangle t2 = new Triangle();

      t1.width = 4.0;
      t1.height = 4.0;   ←——— All members of Triangle are available to Triangle
      t1.style = "filled";        objects, even those inherited from TwoDShape.

      t2.width = 8.0;
      t2.height = 12.0;
      t2.style = "outlined";

      System.out.println("Info for t1: ");
      t1.showStyle();
      t1.showDim();
      System.out.println("Area is " + t1.area());

      System.out.println();


      System.out.println("Info for t2: ");
      t2.showStyle();
      t2.showDim();
      System.out.println("Area is " + t2.area());
    }
}
```

The output of the above program is:

```
Info for t1:
Triangle is filled
Width and height are 4.0 and 4.0
Area is 8.0

Info for t2:
Triangle is outlined
Width and height are 8.0 and 12.0
Area is 48.0
```

In the above program, *TwoDShape* describes the features of the common two-dimensional shape. The class *Triangle* will create a precise category for a triangle in the *TwoDShape* class. The style of the triangle is kept in the style which can also have any string which defines more about the triangle. The method *area()* will calculate triangle area, while *showStyle()* output the shape of the triangle.

While *TwoDShape* is a superclass of the *Triangle*, it is still an independent class. Since it is a superclass for the subclass, that does not nullify it from getting used by its own. For instance, this is accepted:

```
TwoDShape shape = new TwoDShape ();
shape. width = 10;
shape. height = 30;
shape. showDim ();
```

The general nature of a class declaration takes a superclass like the way is indicated here:

```
class subclass-name extends superclass-name {
   // body of class
}
```

In Java, only a single superclass is permitted for a single subclass. This means you can't have multiple superclass inheritance.

## Constructors and inheritance

In the hierarchy, we can have the superclass and subclasses having their own constructors. This brings up a very crucial issue on the role of a constructor in developing an object and subclass. Do we go with the one in the superclass or subclass? However, if you have experienced this problem, this is what you need to learn today: a superclass's constructor will have its own object, and the subclass's constructor will also have its own object. In the previous example, we have depended upon the default constructor built by Java. Now, this wasn't a problem. But, in the majority of the Java inheritance examples, there will be an explicit constructor. For instance, below is a modified example of the *Triangle* which defines the constructor:

```
// Add a constructor to Triangle.

// A class for two-dimensional objects.
class TwoDShape {
  private double width; // these are
  private double height; // now private

  // Accessor methods for width and height.
  double getWidth() { return width; }
  double getHeight() { return height; }
  void setWidth(double w) { width = w; }
  void setHeight(double h) { height = h; }

  void showDim() {
    System.out.println("Width and height are " +
                       width + " and " + height);
  }
}
```

```
// A subclass of TwoDShape for triangles.
class Triangle extends TwoDShape {
  private String style;

  // Constructor
  Triangle(String s, double w, double h) {
    setWidth(w);
    setHeight(h);  ◄───────────────────────────── Initialize TwoDShape
                                                    portion of object.
    style = s;
  }

  double area() {
    return getWidth() * getHeight() / 2;
  }

  void showStyle() {
    System.out.println("Triangle is " + style);
  }
}

class Shapes3 {
  public static void main(String args[]) {
    Triangle t1 = new Triangle("filled", 4.0, 4.0);
    Triangle t2 = new Triangle("outlined", 8.0, 12.0);

    System.out.println("Info for t1: ");
    t1.showStyle();
    t1.showDim();
    System.out.println("Area is " + t1.area());

    System.out.println();


    System.out.println();

    System.out.println("Info for t2: ");
    t2.showStyle();
    t2.showDim();
    System.out.println("Area is " + t2.area());
  }
}
```

In this example, the *Triangle* constructor will initialize the members of the TwoDClass which have its own field. When we have both the "superclass and subclass" describe a constructor, the situation is much difficult since the all the superclass and subclass have to be executed. In such a scenario, you need to use the Java *super* keyword which takes two forms:

- Superclass constructor

- Access member of the superclass

## Super calling the Superclass Constructors

It is possible for, let's say a subclass, to make a call to a constructor which is well-defined by the superclass. This is how it is defined:

*super(parameter-list);*

In the above syntax, the *parameter-list* refers to the parameters required by the constructor in the superclass. If you want to see how you can use *super()*, here is an example for you:

```
// Add constructors to TwoDShape.
class TwoDShape {
  private double width;
  private double height;

  // Parameterized constructor.
  TwoDShape(double w, double h) {        <——————— A constructor for TwoDShape
    width = w;
    height = h;
  }

  // Accessor methods for width and height.
  double getWidth() { return width; }
  double getHeight() { return height; }
  void setWidth(double w) { width = w; }
  void setHeight(double h) { height = h; }

  void showDim() {
    System.out.println("Width and height are " +
                        width + " and " + height);
  }
}

// A subclass of TwoDShape for triangles.
class Triangle extends TwoDShape {
  private String style;

  Triangle(String s, double w, double h) {
    super(w, h); // call superclass constructor
    style = s;
  }
}
```

Use super() to execute the TwoDShape constructor.

208

```
  double area () {
    return getWidth() * getHeight () / 2;
  }

  void showStyle () {
    System.out.println("Triangle is " + style);
  }
}

class Shapes4 {
  public static void main(String args[]) {
    Triangle t1 = new Triangle("filled", 4.0, 4.0);
    Triangle t2 = new Triangle("outlined", 8.0, 12.0);

    System.out.println("Info for t1: ");
    t1.showStyle();
    t1.showDim();
    System.out.println("Area is " + t1.area());

    System.out.println();

    System.out.println("Info for t2: ");
    t2.showStyle();
    t2.showDim();
    System.out.println("Area is " + t2.area());
  }
}
```

In this code, the *Triangle()* method will call the *super()* together with its
parameters. This will result in the *TwoDShape()* constructor getting
called. It then assigns the *height* and *width*. The *Triangle* will no longer
initialize the above values by itself. This would make *TwoDShape* build
its own smaller object in whichever way it selects. In addition,
*TwoDShape* can extend the number of operations to be performed on the
subclasses of which we have no knowledge. This prevents the current
program from failing.

## Overriding a method

Calling a method overridden inside a subclass will refer to the type of
the method declared in the subclass.

209

```
// Method overriding.
class A {
   int i, j;
   A(int a, int b) {
      i = a;
      j = b;
   }

   // display i and j
   void show() {
      System.out.println("i and j: " + i + " " + j);
   }
}

class B extends A {
   int k;

   B(int a, int b, int c) {
      super(a, b);
      k = c;
   }

   // display k - this overrides show() in A
   void show() {                                      This show() in B overrides
      System.out.println("k: " + k);                  the one defined by A.
   }
}

class Override {
   public static void main(String args[]) {
      B subOb = new B(1, 2, 3);

      subOb.show(); // this calls show() in B
   }
}
```

The output:

> *K: 3*

When you call *show()* on type *B* object, the method *show()* declared inside *B* is executed. This means this method *show()* within the B will override the one stated in *A*.

## Tips while starting out in Java

If you want to have a successful career in Java programming, perhaps these tips will help you. They will help you attain your goals in programming. You can apply them still in any other programming language.

## Master the basics

The basics of any language are important in helping you master the rest of the language. This book has given you the basics which can drive you to become a pro in Java. You can begin right away and read this book then master the highlighted basics of this language. It will help you begin your Java programming career at a much better level. Like all other things, if you are a complete beginner, you might look at code and think as if is a collection of letters and numbers. Just note that everyone started at that point. If you can withstand it, your future is going to be bright.

## Practice to program frequently

Have you heard of the old cliché, "practice makes perfect?" Yes! It still applies in programming. If you are not ready to put in your sweat to learn the basics and the syntax of the language, you will not become the best or even a pro in Java. The best thing you have for you is that it is possible to practice coding wherever you are as long as you have a laptop. Once you get competent with the basics of the language, make it a hobby to spend most of your time trying to code in Java as well as understanding the different concepts of the language.

## Set algorithm

This is where you put yourself in a trial test. You can't set your algorithm if you don't know the basics of the language. You will need to look for a problem or even create a problem for yourself and provide a solution for it. This is one of the steps in the learning curve. If you can solve as many questions as you can, the better you will become. Algorithms will play an important role in your entire life as a programmer because they direct your computer to know exactly what to do to solve a given problem. Before you can set your own algorithm, it is important to have some trials.

## Look for more sources in Java

Best Java developers don't read one book about Java. Instead, they have as many books on their shelf to read about it. You need to pump your head with enough knowledge in Java so that you can easily know how to code and improve your problem-solving skills. Remember, most resources of Java are available online. You can spare time to browse the internet and find the recent information about the language. Regardless of your level of experience in Java, reading extra sources will be invaluable. I will still recommend that you become a member of an active forum online. Forums have people who ask questions in a given topic then experts come in and give a response. Quora could be a wonderful place to start, but there are still many forums which you can join.

## Try and trace your code on paper

Do you know what that means? It would be great for you if you are just beginning.

## Don't be afraid to request help when you need

This is the reason why it is important to join an online forum. If you know an answer to a solution, provide the answer. The best way to learn is to teach someone who does not know. It will help you master the concept and even understand it on a deeper level.

## Stick to one kind of task

As a beginner in Java, you don't want to switch from one area to another. Remember, Java programming fits in many fields. You can focus on web programming with Java or create desktop applications in Java. Stick to one particular area so that you don't end up getting confused in the process.

# Conclusion

Thank for making it through to the end of *Java: Basic Fundamental Guide for Beginners*. Let's hope it was informative and able to provide you with all of the tools you need to achieve your goals whatever they may be.

This book has taken you through the core fundamentals of Java to help you develop the right foundation to explore deeper concepts in Java. It is important for you to understand the various data types in Java: the variables, strings, and arrays. In addition, mastering the method, classes, and inheritance is crucial. Remember. Java is an object-oriented language. This means that having a deep understanding of the topic of classes, methods, and inheritance is fundamental.

Java is a very powerful language, it powers the majority of enterprises and organizations. It is one of the best languages for developers when they want to implement internet-based applications. Furthermore, software devices which must cross communicate over a given network are developed with the help of Java. Many devices today use Java. This shows how Java is an important computer programming language. While this book has tried to present you with the basics skills of programming in Java, it is highly important to emphasize that it is just a starting point. Java goes beyond the elements which determine the language. For you to become an excellent Java programmer, you need to take time to read deep and master the concepts in Java. Luckily, this book helps you develop the right knowledge to expand more on other areas of Java. Therefore, the next step for you to take after reading this book is to look for a comprehensive Java textbook to read.

Finally, if you found this book useful in any way, a review on Amazon is always appreciated!

# JavaScript

*Basic Fundamental Guide for Beginners*

# Introduction

Congratulations on purchasing *JavaScript : Basic Fundamental Guide for Beginners* and thank you for doing so.

The following chapters will discuss how to program using JavaScript. We're going to start from the very beginning and explain program logic as we make our way through this broad topic and try to uncover everything as possible.

JavaScript is immensely popular. Therefore, you're doing the right thing by trying to learn it. My goal is to give you all of the tools and information you need to become a fantastic JavaScript programmer in no time at all.

There are plenty of books on this subject on the market. Thanks again for choosing this one! Every effort was made to ensure that this book is packed with useful information. Please enjoy!

# Chapter 1

# History of JavaScript

This book is going to tackle a couple of hefty questions and also assume that you've got little to no practical programming experience. The reason for this is that, for a lot of people, JavaScript is their first language. Many people start out with something like web development or perhaps with a recommendation from a friend and find that JavaScript is one of the "easiest" languages to learn.

This is a bit of a misnomer of course; I've helped a lot of people learn to program. Some benefit more from a language that is more abstract and easier to understand, such as JavaScript. Others still benefit more from languages where everything is a concept and put right in front of them to toy with, because the verbosity helps them to understand what they're working within a better sense, such as Java or C++.

Regardless of these, I'm going to assume, since you're here, that you're in the first camp, as well as explain things with enough rigor so that you'll still understand the language well if you're already in the second camp. JavaScript is not a difficult first language. Actually, it's far from it. It's easy to understand, abstract, and master. However, there is a definite degree of challenge that comes with, such as getting out of your comfort zone and learning all of the little concepts related to programming itself.

Therefore, let's think for a second. What is JavaScript? JavaScript is a programming language. A programming language is basically something that allows you to talk to computers and instruct them on what to do. We know for a fact that computers don't understand English. In fact, they don't even understand programming languages. When you break it down, you'll find that computers only really understand things in terms of binary codes - a sequence of ones and zeroes. This is where the name of the computer comes from a *computer*.

The computer makes millions of tiny computations that you can't see every single second. All of these computations are performed using these ones and zeroes that are present at the very smallest level of the computer that you can't see. Knowing this, we've figured out over the years that these ones and zeroes could be controlled and manipulated, first, through the development of languages that work with the processor of the computer itself (assembly) and, second, through the development of languages that serve as the connection between the complex zeroes and ones and the programmer.

As computers have gotten more popular and stronger these days, people who are interested in programming want to learn languages that aren't absurdly difficult to use and understand. As a result, over time, programming languages too have become much simpler as more people started programming as a hobby. The increased processing power of computers over the years and the standardization of an object-oriented paradigm have led to the development of far simpler languages.

In order to understand JavaScript itself, we have to first learn it's history. In the 1970s, there was a place called Bell Labs, a research lab owned and managed by AT&T. A lot of important technological advances originated from Bell Labs. One of the most important ones that you've probably heard before is the *Unix* system.

Unix was a landmark. It was an open-source and simple operating system that was intuitive enough that it could easily be marketed to businesses, developers, and universities all in tandem with one another without encroaching on each other's markets. This was spurred by the development of the C programming language.

The C programming language itself has it's long line of history, but essentially it was the first simple and intuitive language that almost anybody can figure out. It offers a layer of abstraction from the system itself and also offers the programmer the ability to scrutinize the system buildup and therefore understand the computer much better. This allows the programmer to directly manage things, such as memory allocation, or the amount of memory being used by the program in order to perform certain processes. In short, C allows programmers to better understand the system. However, they are expected to handle a great amount of difficult information and are prone to manipulate, for example, the computer's processing capabilities.

Unix would eventually be rewritten in C instead of the standard Assembly code. This is part of the reason why C became so famous. This was a huge deal because it means that any processor that can run a C compiler, that is, the program which converts human-readable programming code to Assembly code that the computer can understand can run Unix as well. Now, this program can be compiled in any system that has a C compiler. This made the program extremely popular worldwide.

Moreover, since C is open source, universities often teach their students the language so that even if they cannot immediately compile Unix for their computers, they can at least modify the code so that they *can* run Unix on them. In addition, Unix is beneficial to C and vice versa because, first, C is being taught in universities to allow students to gain experience first before handling their Unix courses and, second, because Unix comes with a C compiler which makes it even easier for people to write and run codes on Unix systems.

This may seem like an irrelevant detail, but it's a pretty important factor in the overall development of JavaScript and is a key part in the development of modern programming languages in general. This is because these languages can inspire a ton of different languages. For example, the extremely popular languages Java, Python, and C++ all have been – to one extent or another – inspired by C.

JavaScript is no exception. However, with that context, let's think back what the computing landscape was like in the late 80s and early 90s. The general population was slowly being introduced with computers because of the popularity of both C and Unix. The combined popularity and accessibility of these mean that a lot of applications are being built for a lot of computers, approximately exponentially more every year.

However, the Internet was still in its infancy in many ways. Web browsers, for example, were unpopular and nowhere near their technological peak. Web browsers were, in many ways, much more simple and unsophisticated as were web pages themselves.

Currently, web pages primarily consist of just basic text markup rendered through HTML. This book isn't going to tackle HTML except when it's necessary. Therefore, a working knowledge about it is assumed. JavaScript is, after all, one of the three core web development languages alongside HTML and CSS. So, it's worthwhile to learn HTML and CSS as well.

Anyhow, early web browsers were known as *static web pages*. Static web pages are the opposite of *dynamic* web pages, which are web pages that are designed to reflect and render text and images only. Basically, once a static web page is loaded, it cannot be changed from within the page without changing and the reloading the *web file*.

Dynamic web pages – or pages that can be changed in real-time without altering the web file itself – are implemented through what is called *client-side scripting*. Client-side scripting is about allowing changes to happen on a web page exclusively on the browser side. That is, client-side scripting allows sophisticated logic and dynamic changes to run within the context of the user's web browser. Any changes are made their machine and within their browser and don't necessarily indicate the transfer of information to a server.

Essentially, JavaScript and all related languages are about giving life to web pages. It's about taking web pages and making them able to do things instead of just be still. This functionality was, for a long time, just a glimmer in the eye of people who were looking forward to web development. However, this doesn't mean that scripting didn't exist way before. There was early support for technologies designed to allow web pages to interact more. However, these were very rudimentary. The early graphical web browsers were capable of scripting even during its infancy.

This resulted in the creation of another browser, *Mozilla* which inspired the development of Firefox. Currently, however, Firefox was far from being a factor. Officially, the browser was released as *Netscape*, which was known by many as being among the most popular browsers in the 90s, and if you used a computer in the 90s, then you probably were using Netscape.

In the mid-90s, the idea of embedded codes in web pages – that is, codes written in other programming languages that can be inserted directly into and run from a web page – started becoming even more popular. However, there still wasn't enough information regarding the process of practical embedded languages. Java did somewhat serve the purpose, but it wasn't simple. In fact, it died out because it entails a great amount of raw computing power for it to be used. A better alternative was needed, something that can be directly embedded into and alter the web page. Such a thing didn't exist.

Netscape decided to create a scripting language that can run within HTML documents and be easily embedded and interpreted within the browser itself. The language was supposed to display a similar syntax to Java and C++. This was to differentiate it from other popular scripting languages at that time, such as Perl, Python, and Lisp. Believe it or not, a C-inspired scripting language was relatively nouveau at the time.

The language was first released as LiveScript and then later was changed to *JavaScript*. JavaScript became the final name of the language from that on, most likely as an attempt by Netscape to capitalize the success of the Java programming language that was extremely popular at the time, even though JavaScript wasn't particularly related to Java except in its syntactic in some places.

JavaScript was initially only implemented for client-side scripting or the creation of dynamic web pages (as we've already discussed). The first server-side implementation of JavaScript appeared a year or so after the initial release of JavaScript. Today, the server-side JavaScript is still being implemented even though its implementations are far less common than those of the client-side.

The mid-90s showed the development of many now-important web technologies and also browser wars. JavaScript plays an important part in the browser wars, which gained popularity pretty quickly and was implemented by Netscape in their browser. However, Netscape's primary opponent during that time, Internet Explorer, didn't have a support for JavaScript.

This started to change in late 1996. It was clear that some kind of business-wide standard for JavaScript was needed in order for the World Wide Web to be accessed by all browsers. In order to do this, Netscape sent their language into a standards board in order for the language to be reviewed and standardized. The language standard was called ECMAScript, which was published in 1997. This standardization became the starting point for many different languages and is a language in its own right. It's the *standard* of a language, upon which other languages are derived from. All of these different derivations are referred to as *implementations* of the standard. JavaScript is the most popular one, but there were a few others that transpired, such as ActionScript designed for Flash coding.

With the standardization of ECMAScript, JavaScript was finally being used by other browsers and not just Netscape. JavaScript was an ambition in the mid-2000s. During this time, JavaScript and the things for which it could be used were becoming popular to the public (especially the developers) after the development of a white paper wherein Ajax was defined, basically promising the development of extremely dynamic web pages as opposed to the static pages prior. This resulted in the development of many more technologies that can be used alongside JavaScript, such as jQuery, which remained until 2015 or 2016.

A little later in the Oughts, there was at last cohesive work done in order to push the status of the JavaScript language forward and force new standards fit for new technologies. Since then, newer implementations and constant unified updates have been created to develop a unified version of ECMAScript. Therefore, all implementations of ECMA, including JavaScript, resulted in the development of more technical possibilities.

For the last few years, new standards of ECMAScript have been released every year.

The major breakthrough of JavaScript must have been Ajax when developers began to take interest and supported the language. Today, there is an even greater need for an extensive browser support, and JavaScript began to push for that spotlight. Since then, it has become the most widely used web scripting language.

The history of JavaScript shows that it has undergone challenges to become what it is today. I hope that you appreciated the path that it has taken. In the following chapter, we're going to discuss exactly where we *are* at today and all of the different things that JavaScript can be used for.

# Chapter 2

# How JavaScript is Used

Currently, JavaScript is used for a number of different uses in the mainstream web framework. It is implemented through a number of different layers like *React.js* or *Bootstrap.js*.

Raw JavaScript is fairly uncommon today and is used only to build bigger projects and APIs. Many of these are open source, and you will encounter raw JavaScript generally whenever you're working with these open source projects and not so often in your raw code.

For a long time – though not so often now – jQuery was one of the most popular JavaScript libraries, if not the most popular. You can still sometimes find it lingering around, but it has largely been outpaced by other more popular web frameworks.

This introduces the most popular use of JavaScript, its implementation among other Ajax interfaces and various different web-based frameworks which allow you to create stunning and dynamic web pages. Raw JavaScript, as I said, isn't terribly popular, but you're going to encounter a lot of challenges when using this.

JavaScript is also commonly used with HTML5 and CSS3 to create browser-based games. These are becoming more popular as web pages are becoming increasingly capable of running complex animations. JavaScript offers a fantastic catalyst to all of these because it allows the formation of client-side scripts.

Don't misunderstand; knowing how JavaScript works is extremely useful. You can use this knowledge as a catalyst to other things. Once you're finished with this book, I'd recommend that you start looking into the various web frameworks that use JavaScript. There are numerous.

React.JS, Meteor.JS, Mithril.JS, and Vue.JS are all extremely popular because they allow you to easily build interactive and dynamic web pages. In the modern day, this is an extremely important utility and will greatly benefit you as a programmer.

You'll also find that Node.JS offers a solid server-side scripting implementation. It can stand against PHP as one of the more popular web-based server-side technologies, even though it's much younger than PHP. If you're interested in running your servers and queries efficiently and building generally broad web-based applications, then Node.JS is preferred.

Now, we're going to discuss how to program in raw JavaScript, which will prepare you for using any of these. Having a foundation in programming is incredibly important.

# Chapter 3

# How to Program in JavaScript

In this chapter, we're going to start diving into how one can program in JavaScript. There is a lot to cover in this chapter. So, we're going to start from the basics and work our way up as we cover all of the different topics and try to build a finite idea of what this language is capable of. By the end of this chapter, you're going to understand a plethora of different concepts related to programming. Strap in tight because this is where the bulk of the book is going to come in.

## Setting Up

Setting up JavaScript is incredibly easy. If you have a web browser, then you have JavaScript. It's as simple as that. Web browsers have built-in implementation engines for JavaScript, as does any other programs that purport to run JavaScript, such as the game engines that we mentioned.

This means that running JavaScript doesn't entail you to do much. However, there is one thing that we need to take note of before we continue. While normally you can save JavaScript files on their own and work on them in that way, you can't debug them in a browser like this. In order to use your JavaScript in your browser and have your scripts run, you need to call those scripts in one way or another. In order to simplify this, we're going to create an HTML document using the script tags. Write the following code in a new file called first.htm:

```html
<html>
<head>
  <script>
          document.write("Hello world!\n");
  </script>
</head>
<body>
</body>
</html>
```

Go ahead and save this file and then open it in the web browser of your choice. You'll see the following:

Hello world!

With this, bravo! You've written your first JavaScript script. So, you may be wondering, what is the essential difference between putting data within your file's head tags and your file's body tags?

The head tag is usually reserved for any programmatic logic in HTML. You can put the script in your body tag, and it will work equally well. However, most of the time, the JavaScript would be saved to a *different* file and then from there be loaded into the web page rather than all of it being confined in the same HTML document. This is the simplest way of emulating this sort of functionality within the confines that we've currently developed.

## Data and Variables

At this point, we will talk about a concept that's a little bit heftier: the concept of *data*, *value*, and *variables*. You're going to see these all the time in programming. So, it's important that we start to talk about it a little bit. Depending on how and why you're going to use JavaScript, this may not come up so much. It will still come up, for example, if you're going to focus primarily on modern web development but often in a more abstracted way. However, nonetheless, it's important that we cover this concept because it's foundational to pretty much in all programming, in addition to the fact that this concept is instrumental in understanding some of the later concepts that we're going to be covering. For this reason, we're going to go ahead and just assume that we need to learn it and do that.

So, let's start with a simpler quest before anything else: what is a value? In order to understand the other concepts here, you need to understand how computers process data. As we said in the very first chapter, computers don't understand things like humans do. Ultimately, they process things in a series of mathematical equations, after things have been abstracted into things that resemble nothing like the value which we gave. For example, the bitwise representation of any given number won't really resemble the number that was passed in. Likewise, when you're trying to work with characters and text on-screen, computers have no innate bearing on what any of this is or how it can be used; they don't have the innate capacity for language that we do. All they understand is calculations. So, they need a method by which they can take these abstract human concepts and convert them into smaller numbers that *they* can work with.

However, that doesn't really answer or question. It only gives an entry point. The point that I'm trying to make is that in the end, computers understand all different representations of ideas in different ways, whether those ideas are numbers, letters, or any other thing that you can form some kind of abstract idea out of.

All of these abstract ideas form the nucleus of an idea that is a little bigger – the idea of the *value*. A value is any given abstract representation of some idea. That value could be a number, a character, a set of characters, or none of the above. A value is the communication of an abstract idea that can *be* communicated.

Computers understand these values according to the *type* of value they are. Computers need different types because, again, all of the values that a computer can understand need to be converted from our abstract idea of these values into something that the computer can work with, that is, ones and zeroes. These separate kinds of data can be referred to succinctly as *data types*.

There are numerous different data types in JavaScript, and there even exists the ability to create your own. However, data types are a little bit like atoms; there comes a point where if you break a molecule down that is composed of different atoms, then eventually you just get singular atoms and can't go any further without getting to the subatomic level and dealing with things like particles and quarks and so forth.

Data types in JavaScript and programming, in general, are a bit the same. Every programming language has these nucleic data types that form the basis for all other kinds of data in the programming language. These types that can't be broken down any further are called *primitive* types, and every language has their own primitive types.

JavaScript specifically has six different primitive types, each with their own use cases and definitions. Here, we're going to talk about what these different primitive types are so that you will know what these primitive types can *do* and what different kinds of data you can store and manipulate in JavaScript.

**string** – String denotes a data type which is necessarily composed of just characters. Character here refers to anything that is alphanumeric or symbolic. Basically, character is any text which may be represented on a screen in a computer. String refers explicitly to the idea of these characters and not necessarily to the characters themselves. For example, if you have a string value that hold numbers, then you cannot add a given number to it, because the string numeric value will not be understood by the system as numbers themselves but just as a set of characters which represent numbers. This idea will make a bit more sense later on when we start discussing the idea of arrays.

**number** – Number denotes a data type that uses *any* number, whether those are whole, decimal, or any other kind of number. This slightly separates JavaScript from other programming languages. We'll talk about this more in-depth a little bit later on, but it's a pretty easy concept to grasp, so don't stress about it too much.

**undefined** – Undefined is the data type which belongs to any variable (which we'll discuss in a second) that doesn't have a value set to it just yet. *undefined* can also be returned in a given function, but we'll talk about that later as well when we start talking about functions in general.

**null** – Null in computer science refers to any number which doesn't *have* a value. Null is different from undefined because undefined values simply generally haven't had a value ascribed to them yet, whereas null finitely doesn't have a value affixed.

**boolean** – Booleans are another concept that will make more sense later on but for right now just understand booleans as pertaining to the idea of true or false. Booleans are thereby a little bit of a rougher concept to really completely understand, even if they appear incredibly simple.

**symbol** – Symbols are the hardest primitive to understand for a beginner, and, frankly, as a beginner, you aren't really going to need to know about them. So you can just forget about them for the time being. However, for necessity's sake, we needed to cover it.

All of these also have *object* wrappers, which are another concept we'll talk about later in the chapter. I know, I know, it seems like I'm introducing a whole lot of ideas without talking about them at all, but don't worry. I promise we'll get to *all* of this in due time.

So why is this information important? What can one do with this knowledge? Well, you can do a whole lot. For example, let's change the code that we had so that the document.write line reads like the following:

document.write(4 + 3);

Save your file and refresh the page. You should be seeing the following:

7

See how intuitive that is? You can manipulate these pieces of data. We'll get to that in just a second after we talk about *variables*. Now that you know how data works, you're somewhat prepared to start working with this next concept. See, sometimes, obviously, you're going to want to keep data for more than just one instance as we did above. In these cases, you need a way to keep track of data.

This functionality is offered to you through *variables*. You can keep track of data using variables and then change the data later by referring to it by some name that you define. You can define variables in JavaScript as the following:

var *variableName*;

You can also define it with an initial value. This is called initialization:

var myBananas = 3;

Alternatively, you can declare a variable and then define its value later:

var myBananas;
myBananas = 3;

232

So, why does all of this go together? First, the reason why we need to talk about data types was that JavaScript doesn't make you keep up with what kind of data a variable holds. This is good in some ways because it honestly makes it a much easier language to learn that it might be otherwise compared to something like C++ where you have to explicitly declare what type of data you're working with. Meanwhile, this can be difficult for a beginner who doesn't exactly understand how data works and how computers understand data. So, let's just assume that you're still starting to learn JavaScript. I decided that it's best to discuss how all of this works as opposed to just throwing you into the fire and expecting you to figure it out on your own. I may have just saved you a bit of time and future troubleshooting!

You can print out variables the same way you can print out individual data. This is because variables essentially just serve as boxes which can hold values. You can reach into these boxes and change the values, but the box will retain the same number of variable and refer to whatever is placed within it. When you create a variable, you're creating a box which may hold values. When you refer to that variable, you're saying "hey, whatever is in the box with that name, I want to work with that."

Let's try this with the last piece of data. Change your script as follows:

```
var number1 = 4;
var number2 = 4;
var number3 = number1 + number2;
document.write(number3);
```

Save it and reload the page; you'll end up with the following:

If that's the case, then perfect! You're well on your way to being adept at JavaScript. This is only the beginning, but much more can be done from here.

You can create a string variable by assigning a value with quotes around it; quotes indicate that a value is a string value. Note, too, that when you create these variables in JavaScript, they aren't created as the primitives but rather as the object wrappers – which, again, we'll talk about more in-depth later. When you try to connect strings, you do what's called a *concatenation*, which is where the characters from both of the strings are put together into one bigger string.

Anyhow, it's time that we move on to the next major part of this chapter, which uses all the knowledge we gained so far. We need to start discussing *math*.

## Math in JavaScript

Math in JavaScript isn't a terrible complicated thing. For the most part, it uses symbols that you're likely already familiar with. There won't be a whole lot for you to learn here, but rather this section is about taking the parts that you're most likely probably already familiar with and then using those in order to build a better base.

Math operations in JavaScript are written and carried out through the use of mathematical operators. These often will be very similar to their counterparts in other languages and, indeed, in math in general.

The operators in JavaScript are as follows:

a + b

This is the *addition* operator, as you've already seen. This will add two things together. It can also be used to concatenate strings or to connect them. If you add a number to a string, then the number will be added *to* the string; for example "hello " + 5 would equal "hello 5."

    a - b

This is the *subtraction* operator. The subtraction operator is used to subtract one value from another, as you might predict.

    a * b

This is the *multiplication* operator. This is used to multiply one thing by another.

    a / b

This is the *division* operator. This is used to divide one number by another.

    a % b

This is the modulo operator. This is used to find the remainder of a certain equation. For example, 5 % 2 would return 1 since 5 / 2 would give a remainder of 1.

    a**b

This is the exponentiation operator. The exponentiation operator will raise a "to the power" of b and return that number.

These are the basic mathematical operators of JavaScript. You can use these to easily perform complex mathematical operations in JavaScript. This may not seem like a big deal right now, but as we press on through the chapter, you'll see why math, more or less, is essential in anything you may do with JavaScript (or programming in general).

The other important operators to cover are the assignment operators. You can use the assignment operators in order to change a value in shorthand.

Assignment operators take a variable and then use any of the above operators with an equals sign. This will assign a new value to that variable. The most obvious assignment operator is the *equals sign*, which is used to assign a value to the left variable of the right side of the expression.

a += b

This is equal to a = a + b.

a -= b

This is equal to a = a - b.

a *= b

This is equal to a = a * b.

a /= b

This is equal to a = a / b.

a %= b

This is equal to a = a % b.

There are two more shorthand operators, the increment and decrement operators. These can be used to add or subtract one from a given variable, *a++* and *a--*, respectively, where *a* is the name of the variable that you're trying to increment or decrement.

We've covered most of the basic arithmetic and assignment operators that you're going to need for JavaScript. Now we're going to use this knowledge to build a foundation for understanding programmatic logic, which is a great and important foundation for being able to use all these.

## Foundations of Logic

So, why do we need to focus on logic specifically? What do we have to gain from it? The simple answer is that understanding logic allows you to let your computer understand logic. All of logic may be expressed in a mathematical way, and your computer, too, may come to understand logic in that sense. Computers, after all, are excellent at solving equations and able to make comparisons as a result of those equations.

This may not seem like a huge deal, but computers being able to think is a really good thing. Think about it; any time that your program is able to decide technically, it's using logic. You may not even have to think that hard. There are a lot of basic instances of logic. This will make more sense later on.

So what exactly is logic? Logic is, in one way or another, just a manner of systematically using statements. These statements can then be used to derive conclusions. Logic is used, often, in order to determine whether a given statement is true or false, both in computing and in real life.

Perhaps the most classic example of logic is in the old Socratic form: "All men are mortal; Socrates is a man; therefore, Socrates is mortal." This sort of transitive logic provides the foundation for much of what we know about *modern* logic and is perhaps one of the best examples of simple applications of logic used in different contexts.

Logic in computers is usually based on *expressions*. Expressions might be familiar to you from your old high school or college algebra courses, where you write out a certain statement written and determine if it's true or false. You can use algebra on these expressions to simplify them just by treating the expression operator as an equals sign.

This basic format stays the same. Expressions are essentially a method by which you can compare one value to another. You can set the standard of the comparison, for example, whether you're determining if two values are equivalent or not, if one is more or less than the other, so on. Expressions, therefore, are a great tool used in logic and play a part likewise in computer-based logic.

You form expressions through the use of logical operators. These logical operators are the very basis of expressions. The following are the logical operators that you can use in JavaScript:

$a == b$

This will compare value *a* to value *b* and return whether or not the two are equal to each other. If so, it will return true and false if otherwise.

$a === b$

This will compare the two values and return true if they are both equal to each other *and* if they are of the same type.

$a != b$

This will compare the two values and return true if they are *not* equal to each other *or* if they are not of the same type. This is logical *or*. So, they can be both *unequal* and *of the same type,* and it will still return true. I'll explain that later.

$a > b$

This will determine if a is greater than b.

$a < b$

This will determine if a is less than b.

$a >= b$

This will determine if a is greater than or equal to b.

$a <= b$

This will determine if a is less than or equal to b.

You can use these to form *individual expressions*. You can then use these expressions in logical statements, which will be discussed later. Note how these expressions return either true or false depending on whether they're true or not. This goes back to the boolean values that we discussed earlier. These return a boolean value, which may be either true or false depending on the statement.

Let's return to variables for a second. You can store a boolean value to a variable, like the following:

val myBool = true;

However, you can also store an *expression* to a variable, and it will store the true or false boolean value.

val myBool = 3 > 5;

The above would be false because 3 is obviously *not* greater than 5. Remember that the function of expressions is to compare values; therefore, you can compare any values. You can likewise compare variables instead of raw values. Make sure your variables are of the same type. If not, you might see some weird results in your comparison!

Anyway, you can chain these expressions into a longer expression to build more sophisticated logical systems. These systems will check *every* part of the greater expression to verify whether or not the logic behind them is true or not.

There are three more logical operators that we haven't covered yet which are tailored specifically toward the purpose of allowing you to build these larger expressions.

expressionA && expressionB

This is the logical *and* operator which checks if both expressions A and B are true. If so, the entire expression will return true and false if otherwise.

expressionA || expressionB

This is the logical *or* operator which checks if *either* expression A *or* B is true. If neither is true, then the entire expression will return false. If either expression is true, then the entire expression will return true. If, technically, one expression is true and the whole expression is true, then both expressions may be true since the technical limitation shows that either side is true and that it is satisfied even if both sides are true.

!(expression)

This is the logical, *not* operator. You can use this to test whether something is *not* true. If it's *not* true, then the entire expression will return true. If it *is* true, then the entire expression will return false.

Note that when you use these, you have to use the exact version that I've specified. For example, getting two equals signs but using one instead will significantly change the meaning of your expression. Likewise, using only one ampersand (&) or one pipe (|) sign will change the meaning of your expression at its very root by transforming it into a bitwise expression, that is, it will be evaluating things at the bit level or the smallest possible mathematical level that you're allowed access to by your computer. You cannot obtain the results that you wanted, *unless* you're specifically trying to do bitwise operations which, at this point, you almost certainly cannot. Just be cautious when working with these expressions.

With that said, hopefully, we've built a solid foundation of logical understanding. This is important because it's going to play a great role in the following sections of the chapter where we discuss the actual meat of control flow and all of the topics that make it up.

## Control Flow 101: Conditional Statements

That foray into control flow starts right as we speak. We're going to discuss how you can use the expressions that we covered in the last part of this chapter to build conditional statements. Conditional statements are the first essential part of control flow.

You may be wondering what control flow is. Control flow is the method by which you can direct your computer to obtain rudimentary forms of logic. By using the control flow, you can direct your computer (for instance, your web page) to make different decisions based on the current state of the given data.

Conditional statements exist in two forms, active and passive conditionals. Passive conditionals are the most basic form. So, we're going to be covering those first.

Passive conditionals are based on the idea of evaluating a single expression and then taking action if it's true. If it's true, then the code within will be run. If the condition is evaluated and turns out to not be true, then the code will be skipped over.

The basic form of a passive conditional in control flow is as follows:

```
if (expression) {
    // code within
}
```

Expression is any expression constructed as we discussed earlier. This is called a passive conditional because it allows you to create a statement that doesn't *require* anything on the end of the interpreter. For example, it doesn't require that your interpreter run a code if it comes out that the condition is false. This means that the condition, if necessary, can be skipped over altogether.

However, sometimes you're going to want something else of your statement. For example, if the code runs and it turns out that the statement isn't true, then you can have a backup code that will run in lieu of the conditional code. This ensures that no matter what, an action is always taken, which also gives you an opportunity to create a "backup" clause for your conditional statement by implementing another condition.

The syntax for the active conditional is as follows:

```
if (expression) {
    // code goes here
} else {
    // code
}
```

This will evaluate the expression. If the expression turns out not true, then it will proceed to the else statement, run the code within it, and then proceed to the next part of the program, instead of entirely skipping over the conditional statement as a whole.

However, sometimes you may want to have yet another condition that you can evaluate. This is pretty easy to set up. You can do so through the implementation of *else if* statements. *Else if* statements allow you to easily establish secondary expressions to evaluate. In *else if* statements, the first given expression will be evaluated. If it turns out not true, then the second expression will be evaluated. You can set up as many *else if* statements as you want, but take note that after a certain point, it will stop setting them up over and over.

You can set up an *else if* statement as follows:

```
if (expression) {
    // code goes here
} else if (expression) {
    // code goes here
} else {
    // code goes here
}
```

That is how you set up active conditionals in order to ensure that some codes will always run in a conditional statement. However, take note that this is not always what you wanted to happen. There are many cases, for example, where you may just want to evaluate to see if a single condition has taken place and then retain that code if that's not the case. In these cases, it is better to use a passive conditional.

## Arrays

Before we jump into the next part of the control flow, let us first discuss another extremely important concept: arrays. Arrays are a foundational part of programming, and they will inevitably find their way into your JavaScript programming. So, it's important that you understand arrays and how they function for you to be able to write better codes over the long term.

What exactly is an array? An array is a method of storing connected data together in an essential way. The use of an array may not be immediately obvious. Let us first take a look at arrays by imagining a scenario in which they *don't* exist. For example, let's say that we wanted to store all of the different guitar models that we had so that we can easily locate them later.

We could store the names of the guitars like the following:

```
val guitar1Name = "Gibson Les Paul";
val guitar2Name = "Fender Stratocaster";
val guitar3Name = "Ibanez s420WK";
```

As you can see above, this becomes very unwieldy very fast. It can be hard to access the data that you need. Additionally, if you are trying to increment through the data, for one reason or another, like listing all of the guitars that you own, you will have to do so in a sequential manner and slowly work through each variable, printing them out one by one.

This is not the best way to do this. The best way is to do it using an array. Arrays are implemented in many different ways across different programming languages, but the specific implementation of arrays in JavaScript is pretty simple, fortunately. Therefore, you will not encounter many issues in getting them to work, especially as opposed to a language like Java or C++ where they have far more rigid definitions to them which can be more complicated to set up.

Arrays are essentially a set of data, especially in the JavaScript implementation. Arrays allow you to store all of these in a single place and then refer to them by accessing them from that common location. In the original implementation of arrays, you can set up a memory in a contiguous manner such that it will be easy for the computer to refer to these locations and individual value storage locations. All of the data would literally be side by side, which allows you to easily work through this data piece by piece and access what you need instead of messing around with various different variable names and other confusing factors that might further complicate the development.

When you set up an array, you essentially set up individual side-by-side boxes of data, much like the variables that we discussed before. You can then access these boxes by referring to the location of the box. Imagine a bank's safety deposit room. There are several different boxes that you can reach for you to obtain a certain value, and you know which box to reach into by referring to its index.

How can we emulate this in our own code? What can we do there? We can set up our own safety deposit room, as a manner of speaking, and then refer to the box we want to reach into.

In order to do this, you must first declare an array (like any other value) and then feed it a set of data.

var guitars = ["Gibson Les Paul", "Fender Stratocaster", "Ibanez S420WK"];

See how simple that is? Now you can reach into this code and obtain your data any time you want. Let's test this out by creating this file for ourselves. Erase your current JavaScript and type the following:

var books = ["Moby Dick", "Pride and Prejudice", "Ulysses"];

Now, let's say that we want to print the first book from this set. How can we do that? First, we need refer to its safety deposit box. An individual piece of data from an array can be referred to as an *element*. Arrays are composed of many different elements which make up the entire array. These elements are located in different positions in the array, which are referred to as their *indices*, or an individual as an *index*. Array indices start at 0 due to practical computer science reasons that we aren't going to dig into right now.

So, if we want to print the first piece of data in this array, we can do that like the following:

```
var books = ["Moby Dick", "Pride and Prejudice", "Ulysses"];
document.write(books[0]);
```

If you save this and try to refresh your document, you will see the following:

Moby Dick

Easy, right? Know you can locate all the elements in the array. You can also reassign the value of a certain element by referring to its index and assigning it a new value, or you can use this as a means of printing or manipulating the data at these places. Now, let's say that we want to add an element to the array. How do we do it?

The easiest way is to use the *push* method. You simply call the push method and send it the argument of what data you want to add to your array. Let's test this out ourselves. Write the following code:

```
books.push("On the Road");
```

```
document.write("<br/>" + books[3]);
```

Save your page and then refresh it. You should see the following:

Moby Dick
On the Road

With that, we've worked through the basics of arrays. You're going to see why this is particularly useful in the next part of this chapter.

## Control Flow 102: Loops

What exactly are loops and how can you use them? Loops are an integral part of logic and control flow. You may not realize it, but you use loop logic all the time.

Imagine this: you're sitting there trying to type a text message for your best friend or significant other or somebody. What do you do? It's really simple; you just type each character and then press send, right? But this is an application of loop logic in and of itself.

Think about it. First, you want to type a message, so you open your messaging app. Then, you start typing the message. You seek the character on your keyboard and then you press it and you verify that you pressed the right character. You do this for every character. You also check to see if you typed the final character of the message. Then, you press send and close the messaging app and the loop has been terminated. This is how you can think of many simple activities in terms of loop logic. We tend to not think about this too much because, let's be honest, it's not that fun of a topic to mull over. Regardless of that, it's an extremely important part of loop logic. Therefore, we're going to talk about it nonetheless.

In JavaScript, there are two main kinds of loops, *for loops* and *while loops*. These loops are both similar in terms of their essential logic (do something under these terms), but they have immensely different cases which entails us to use either of them. We're going to spend a bit of time examining these two loops and their optimal use cases in the next section.

Let's start with the easier one – the *while* loop. The while loop is pretty simple because, in a lot of ways, it just mirrors many of the topics that we've already discussed throughout the course of the chapter, specifically the *if* statement. The *while* loop works by repeatedly running through the code contained within it. On every iteration of the while loop, the loop will evaluate the stated condition and determine whether or not it is still true. If it does happen to be true, the loop will run again. The loop will continue to ad nauseum until it determines that the condition for the loop is not true after all. At this point, the loop will terminate and the code will move on to the next point. Hopefully, this is an adequate explanation, but just in case it isn't, don't worry, we're going to be looking at the structure of these now.

So, the structure of a while loop looks like the following:

```
while (expression) {
    // code here
}
```

Let's say, for example, that we want to count from 1 to 10 using this. First, we must define our variable just as the following:

```
var i = 0;
```

Now, we need to set up our while loop. This is going to run for as long as it is less than 10:

```
while (i < 10) {
}
```

On every iteration of this loop, we want to have an *i* increment by one (we'll use a pre-fix so that it prints *i* after it's been incremented rather than a post-fix), and we want to print that increment as well as an HTML line break. The code will end up looking like the following:

```
var i = 0;
```

247

```
    while (i < 10) {
        document.write(++i + "<br / >");
    }
```

The outcome of this code will look like the following:

```
1
2
3
4
5
6
7
8
9
10
```

However, as you can see above, this isn't exactly the best way to do this. It's a little unwieldy and hard to understand, and you have to go out of your way to do some things that ideally you really wouldn't have to, such as defining a variable that you will use for the loop before you do so.

Loops are useful in checking singular conditions that will become false upon an event. In other words, loops are more preferred if you don't know *how long* a loop is going to run. For a loop like this, where you know exactly how many times it's going to run, it's better to use an incremental loop such as a *for* loop. We'll get to that momentarily.

Based on this, loops are commonly used in the form of a *game loop*. Game loops aren't only for games, of course. Game loops are called so because they follow the basic idea that games do.

A game loop has a certain boolean variable that is evaluated with every run of the loop. For example, you may have a boolean called *running* which is set to be true.

In games, you have a certain win or loss condition that must be met. Until this is met, the same thing will happen repeatedly. For instance, if a player hasn't fallen in lava or been hit three times, then that player is still alive! You don't know how long they'll stay alive, and therefore you don't know how many times you'll need to run your basic logical loop. So, you can't use an incremental loop. It is better to use the *while* loop instead for cases like this.

If you step in lava or your hit counter does hit 3, then you can set the variable running to false. This will indicate to the *while* loop that playtime is over, that the player has lost. Them you can quit running this internal logic and then proceed to the next part of the code, which is a game over screen presumably.

This is a vast simplification but hopefully it does a good job in explaining *what* a game loop is and why *while* loops are so well fit for them. *While* loops are very useful in terms of constantly evaluating a function and repeatedly running the logic in situations where the actual context surrounding it all vary tremendously. If you don't know exactly how much you're going to need to run the code, then *while* loops allow you to check that code for you to be able to obtain a more dynamic interpretation.

*While* loops are the opposite of *for loops*. *For* loops are used to *iterate* through the code. Instead of just repeatedly running the same chunk until a given condition isn't true, you can define the running terms of the function. This may not immediately make sense, but it will, don't worry.

Earlier, we talked about arrays and mentioned that one of the problems you may run into would be iterating through the guitar variables if you need to. The explanation of the arrays themselves didn't make much sense either in that context. Now, let's dive more into that.

Erase your code for the *while* loop and then bring back the book list code. It should look like the following:

    books = ["Moby Dick", "Pride and Prejudice", "Ulysses"];

```
document.write(books[0]);
books.push("On the Road");
document.write("<br/>" + books[3]);
```

Now, let's say that we want to iterate through all these. Remove our write lines so that what remains is our declaration and push method. Then, create a *for* loop. How do for loops work?

For loops work on the basis of iterating through data, as we mentioned earlier. *For* loops have three parts. The first part is the initialization of an iterator variable. This iterator variable serves as the starting point of your loop's "counting". The second part is the condition. This is the condition under which your loop continues to run. This will often be similar to what it would be in a *while* loop of the same function, but sometimes there will be a small change made between them. The third part is the incrementation step. This is the step by which your initialized loop variable moves with every loop of the equation. If, for example, you were to set this to an increment by one (variable++), then on every run of the loop, this variable will change by a degree of one.

The structure of a *for* loop looks like the following:

```
for (initializer variable; condition of running; increment) {
    // code within
}
```

If we want to print every book on our list, what do we do first? Remember that array indices are accessed through referring to their element. These elements start at zero. By starting our initialization variable at 0 and then referring to the index by the initialization variable, we can move through our whole list of books!

Now, how do we define the running length of our loop? In order to define the running length of this loop, you must obtain the length of the array by accessing the array's *length* property.

Then, you must increment by 1 each time.

With all of that in mind, our loop will probably start to look like the following:

```
for (var i = 0; i < books.length; i++) {
    document.write(books[i] + "<br/>");
}
```

Our end code will also look like the following:

```
var books = ["Moby Dick", "Pride and Prejudice", "Ulysses"];
books.push("On the Road");
for (var i=0; i<books.length;i++) {
    document.write(books[i] + "br/>");
}
```

Now, save and run this code and see how it comes out. It should look a little bit like the following:

Moby Dick
Pride and Prejudice
Ulysses
On the Road

With that, perfect! You've made a working for loop in JavaScript. Now, let's talk about functions. Functions are an important catalyst for developing a great working knowledge of JavaScript.

## Functions

What exactly *is* a function? A function, to some, may send a person back to memories of their old high school or college math courses where worked with things such as $f(x) = y$. In this function, the function $f()$ takes an argument of $x$. The argument $x$ can be manipulated by the function $f(x)$ to produce the output of $y$.

However, there are, in fact, some differences between this definition of a function and the one that we're forced to work with in computer science. Computer science was, in many ways, developed as an extension of mathematics after all. It makes sense that computer science carries over many concepts from mathematics.

How do computer science functions differ? Computer science functions don't just have to take one argument. They also don't have to take *any* arguments. We'll talk about that in just a second. (There are some multivariable functions in higher-level mathematics, but this book isn't going to assume that you have that background.)

Computer science functions can take zero, one, or multiple arguments. These arguments can then be manipulated in the target data to give you a dynamic function to work with.

This is a parallel. For example, let $f(x) = 3x + 5 = y$. Let's say that we sent in the argument of $3$ for this function. We substitute x for 3 since x is the argument and then obtain our final value $y$. $3(3) + 5 = 9 + 5 = 14 = y$. Therefore, y = 14, and our function *returns* the value of 14.

Just as a function can *return* a value, our own functions can return values too. These functions can be the end result of all of the mathematics and operations that you did in the function. However, a function doesn't necessarily have to *return* anything either.

What is the purpose of functions then? Functions allow you to abstract certain chunks of code in your program that you're repeatedly reusing. This has many uses from a programmer's point of view, but perhaps the biggest deal is the fact that it makes your code more modular. It simplifies and makes things so that you can start using them in multiple different ways even if you use the same chunk of code, without the need for you to repeatedly reuse the code.

Let's work with this idea for a moment. Let's say that we need a function to return the volume of a given rectangular prism. The following is how you define a function in JavaScript:

```
function functionName(arguments) {
    // code
    return value; // (if necessary)
}
```

Let's say that we want to develop a function that can return the volume of a prism. The volume of a prism is just length by width by height as follows:

```
function volumeOfPrism(length, width, height) {
    return length * width * height;
}
```

This will give back the value of the volume. This is one of the coolest parts of JavaScript and scripting in general. Just like any other values in JavaScript, you can save this to a variable and use it later. This gives you a lot of utility and flexibility as a programmer. You can also save it outside of a variable and just print the raw value of the function like the following:

```
document.write(volumeOfPrism(3,4,5));
```

This will print the value 60. You can save it like the following also:

```
volume = volumeOfPrism(3,4,5);
```

This will store the value of volume as 60, which you can then verify by printing it out:

```
document.write(volume);
```

Now, with all of that said, let's cover the last topic. We will not cover it entirely in-depth, but it's important that we do so that you will be aware of what you're dealing with.

## Object-Oriented Programming: An Introduction

We're not going to tackle all the complex coding of object-oriented programming right now. We're just going to be dealing with the raw concepts at heart: classes and objects. In order to understand these, we must first discuss classes. This will make some of the things that we said earlier – like object wrappers – make more sense.

What is a class? The utility of classes comes from the fact that sometimes you need more complex structures than what the code automatically gives you. This occurs rarely in languages like JavaScript. Object-oriented programming is about this abstraction at its core: the ability to take smaller concepts and then integrate them into bigger structures that utilize these concepts.

A better way to think about it is to try to imagine a dog. All dogs have features in common; for example, they have 2 eyes, 4 legs, and a wagging tail. They can also bark. However, there can be a lot of variance, too. For example, dogs can have separate breeds and other things which set them apart, like their size or weight.

However, there are still unifying concepts and properties that apply to all dogs, regardless their breed, size, and weight, which are *properties* they all have in common. These can be portrayed as individual data members of a larger structure. This structure can be referred to as a *dog*. These individual data members are called the properties of the dog class. Each class can also have standard functions, like *bark* or *wagTail*, which are common among all instances of the class.

A singular instance of a class is referred to as an object. Each object has its own name and can be treated as its own variable. So, if you define a class *dog*, you can create a dog variable known as *myDog* or any other standard variable name. Then, access the properties and alter them however you wish. This standardization and abstraction are the major appeals of object-oriented programming.

Therefore, whenever something is referred to as an *object*, it means that a class was constructed which consists of smaller data types and pieces of data that all make up the bigger concept that is represented both through the object and through its constituent class.

With that, we've worked through the bulk of the stuff that you need to know as an new JavaScript programmer. These are the foundations of all the knowledge you gained from this book, and it's important that you understand all these before continuing.

# Chapter 4

# The Future of JavaScript

At this point, you might be wondering, what exactly is the future of JavaScript? What can I expect to gain from learning all these?

Since the whitepaper that brought Ajax to the forefront, JavaScript has only been gaining steam constantly. There are a huge number of new JavaScript frameworks that are being introduced every year that are fantastic for their various different purposes, and more frameworks will be expected.

The future of JavaScript is more about the future of you. JavaScript is only going to become more popular if further features are added into the future ECMA standardizations, if the web in general is used by more people, and if web platforms mature. Likewise, JavaScript matures alongside PHP and CSS. It is expected that JavaScript will continue to develop in the future.

If you want to be a web developer, you must learn JavaScript and be aware of its frameworks, because those will allow you to keep up with the trends.

As technology grows more and more advanced, JavaScript programmers will also be more in demand. There are a number of things right now that are currently relegated to other common scripting languages, like Python, that can be ported to JavaScript. Natural language processing and machine translation are just two examples that will inevitably be ported to JavaScript which therefore increases demand.

256

JavaScript isn't just for creating pretty web pages; the actual utility of web pages is expanding. With this in mind, JavaScript will advance to this because web pages are now able to perform very complicated actions. The advent of browser-based HTML/CSS/JavaScript games only goes to support this.

As a JavaScript programmer, expect that more programmers will be needed in the industry. Therefore, one of the best things that you can do for yourself is to learn JavaScript and advance your learning.

# Conclusion

Thank you for making it through the end of *JavaScript*. Let's hope that it was informative and able to provide you with all of the tools you need to achieve your goals whatever they may be.

The next step is to use this knowledge. Get out there and start working with some JavaScript frameworks. The way to reinforce all that you've learned is by doing it. You won't be familiar with all of them, and sometimes you're even going to be left really confused, but if you keep pushing through, then I guarantee that it will be worth it and you'll come out the other end as a fantastic web developer.

Lastly, if you found this book useful in anyway, a review on Amazon is always appreciated!

# HTML

*Basic Fundamental Guide for Beginners*

# Introduction

Congratulations and thank you for purchasing *HTML: Basic Fundamental Guide For Beginners*! Whether you're interested in learning HTML to build your own basic website or you'd just like to expand your understanding of markup languages, this book is a great starting point and will provide you with easy-to-understand explanations and examples. In no time you'll be able to use your newly learned HTML skills to create a simple yet functional website.

Never used a programming or markup language before? Don't panic! You don't need much to begin—in fact, all you need to get started with learning HTML is a simple program for editing text (like Notepad or TextEdit) and a web browser to view your creations. In the following chapters, you'll learn not only what HTML is and what it can be used for but also gain an understanding of basic HTML through descriptions and samples that you can easily reproduce yourself. Excited about designing your very own website? By the time you complete this book, you will be able to apply what you've learned to create a simple page with different fonts, eye-catching colors, a unique layout, tables, lists, and even a form that will accept input from a user!

There are many books available on this subject, so thanks again for choosing this one. Good luck and have fun getting started with HTML!

# Chapter 1

## Getting Started With Basic HTML Tags

B efore getting started with writing your first small chunk of HTML, it's necessary that you understand what HTML is. Literally, HTML is an initialism for HyperText Markup Language, which is a set of codes and symbols used to mark up a file so that a web browser knows how to display the content of the file. *Without* HTML, a browser would just display your web page as plain text without any sorts of fonts, colors, or layout; *with* HTML, a browser knows how to display your web page in exactly the style and format that you want. Generally speaking, HTML defines the way that a web page—and the internet as a whole—will appear to users.

In order to give a browser instructions about how to display a file, HTML uses something called tags to signify the beginnings and ends of elements. These tags contain information called attributes which allow a browser to know how the element should appear. The next few sections discuss how elements, tags, and attributes work to define how your web page content will look.

### What are elements, tags, and attributes?

In HTML, an element is a single component of your web page. Generally, each element on your page will have both a start and end tag as well as some sort of content, though certain "empty elements" only require a start tag. Both kinds of tags are labels enclosed in the <> symbols that a browser uses to know how to display a page, but the tags themselves are not displayed. Tags are commonly written in lowercase despite the fact that HTML is not case sensitive. Take a look at the format of an HTML element:

A little bit of content

You can see that the element begins with a tag called "sometagname" which is enclosed in the <> symbols. At the end of the content, you can see the end tag. You'll notice that the end tag is almost identical to the start tag with the addition of the / symbol before the tag name inside the <> symbols. Some elements will display accurately even if the end tag is missing, but sometimes a missing end tag will create an error, so it's best to ensure that your end tags are always in place.

The start tag for an element can define attributes for the element which can give the browser a little bit more information about how the element should be displayed. For instance, an attribute of a link element could be the URL destination for the link. Attributes of an image might include its display height and width. For text, attributes could be styling information like what color, size, or font it should be displayed as. An element can have multiple attributes, so you can fully customize the components of your web pages.

Attributes are contained within the start tag after the tag name and consist of the attribute name followed by the = symbol and then the attribute information in quotation marks. The basic format should look like this:

<sometagname someattributename="attribute value">

A little bit of content

</sometagname>

Similar to the tag name, the attribute name should be written in lowercase. The attribute value should be contained in either single or double quotations. It is worth noting here that if your attribute value itself contains single or double quotation marks, you will need to use the opposite to enclose the attribute value. For instance, if your attribute value is the phrase "You're awesome!" you'll need to enclose it with double quotes, like so:

someattributename="You're awesome!"

Alternatively, if your attribute value is something like "Amanda "Mandy" Jones," then you should enclose it with single quotes:

someattributename='Amanda "Mandy" Jones'

If this seems a little overwhelming, don't worry! Over the course of the next couple of sections, you'll have the opportunity to view some actual examples of working HTML and you'll have the opportunity to gain some hands-on experience.

## How do I get started with my first web page?

Now that you have a basic idea of how HTML uses tags to tell a browser how to display content, it's time to put that knowledge to use! Throughout this next section, you'll learn some ways that you can use HTML to put together a very basic web page. Open up Notepad, TextEdit, or your favorite text editor and follow along.

*Note: if you're a Mac user using TextEdit, you may need to adjust some settings in order to view and save things properly. Under Preferences and then Format, you'll want to select "Plain Text," and under Open and Save, you'll need to check a box that says "Display HTML files as HTML code instead of formatted text."*

The very first thing you'll need to include whenever you start writing an HTML document is the following line:

<!DOCTYPE html>

This line is not an element even though it uses the <> symbols just like element tags do. This line is a declaration, and it lets the browser know that the document is written using HTML. If this line is not present, the browser may attempt to display the web page using some default styles, but certain elements may not show up correctly. It's important to always include this line.

The next component of your HTML file will be the root element of your page, and it will surround the remainder of the HTML in your file. This root element will have <html> start and end tags, so your HTML document so far will look like this:

```
<!DOCTYPE html>
<html>

</html>
```

You'll notice that there's some space between the <html> start and end tags—that's where the rest of your elements will be written. HTML allows elements to be nested, which means an element can actually contain another element or even multiple elements. The first element that will be contained inside of the <html> root element will be the <head> element, which contains metadata or data about the HTML document. This metadata can define information like the title of a document, scripts, links to CSS stylesheets, descriptions of your web page, and styles. For this first example, we'll just be putting the title of the document you're wanting to create into the <head> element, so the HTML document will look similar to this:

```
<!DOCTYPE html>
<html>
<head>
<title> Just an Example Web Page </title>
</head>
</html>
```

The text that is contained inside of the <title> element—in this example, Just an Example Web Page—is what will show up in a browser tab as the name of the page. It's also what the page will be called if you add it to your favorites or find it somewhere online, such as in results from a search engine.

265

You may notice that in our sample, the <head> element start and end tags are indented under the root <html> element, and after that the <title> element is indented within the <head> element. This is not necessary, but it can help when writing your HTML document to see how elements are laid out. The page will display the same whether or not the element tags are indented, however, so it's up to you to write your HTML documents in whichever way you feel the most comfortable.

Of course, you won't just want your web page to be a blank page with a title, so you'll need to have a space to put all of the content you want to be displayed on your page. You'll do this within another element within the <html> element called the <body> element. It will come after the <head> element like so:

```
<!DOCTYPE html>
<html>
<head>
<title> Just an Example Webpage </title>
</head>
<body>

</body>
</html>
```

The <body> element of your HTML document will contain everything that is visible on your web page like text, pictures, links, and media. For this simple example, we'll just be adding a couple lines of text to your page: one large heading and one smaller paragraph. Now, your HTML document will look like this:

```
<!DOCTYPE html>
<html>
<head>
<title> Just an Example Webpage </title>
</head>
<body>
```

```
        <h1> Example of headings in HTML. </h1>
        <p> Example of paragraphs in HTML. </p>
        <p> Second example of paragraphs in HTML </p>
    </body>
    </html>
```

The heading element starts with the <h1> tag and ends with the </h1> tag, and the paragraph elements start and end with the <p> and </p> tags. You can see that the heading and the paragraph elements are separate from each other but are all contained within the <body> element. Make sure to use end tags, and be sure to put them in the appropriate places.

That's it! You now have a simple HTML document that will display a simple web page in a browser. In order to test it out, you'll first need to save your HTML document with the correct file extension. Click "Save as" in the menu, and then put the file name **myexamplewebpage.html** in the "File name" box. Don't forget the .html extension! Next, change the "Save as type" to "All Files (*.*)" and click Save. Now you can open your HTML file in your browser window either by double-clicking on it from where you saved it or by clicking the file with your right mouse button and picking "Open with." When your page opens, it should look something like this:

# This line is a heading.

This line is a paragraph.

This line is also a paragraph.

In the URL bar, you should be able to see the file path to the HTML document you created; it will probably look similar to this, but not exactly the same. You can see from this example how the page title, heading, and paragraphs are displayed. The browser utilizes the HTML tags to decide how to show the text content, but the tags themselves are not shown.

## How can I change the appearance of the elements on my web page?

Now that you have a basic framework for your HTML pages, you'll undoubtedly want to start adding custom elements to create a page that fits your personal needs. Check out some of the different tags below that you can use to completely customize your sites:

### <title> </title>

The <title> element contains the name of your web page, which is displayed in a browser tab or within search engine results. Be sure to title your page something informative!

### <style> </style>

These tags contain information about the default styles your document will use and are located inside the <head> element of your HTML document. Alternatively, one can set the style for an individual element within its start tag.

### <meta>

This tag and its attributes define information about your web page, like a page description, page author, or keywords relevant to your page. This tag is contained in the <head> element and does not show anything on your page itself.

## \<script> \</script>

These tags contain JavaScript code that can be used elsewhere on your page to perform actions like manipulating images or validating forms.

## \<p> \</p>

These tags signify the beginning and end of a paragraph. You used these in the example in the previous section. A paragraph is simply text that is spaced apart from surrounding elements.

## \<b> \</b>

These tags signify that the contained text should be bold.

## \<u> \</u>

These tags signify that the contained text should be underlined.

## \<i> \</i>

These tags signify that the contained text should be italicized.

## \<del> \</del>

These tags signify that the contained text was deleted and the text is displayed with a line through it.

## \<mark> \</mark>

These tags signify that the contained text should be highlighted.

## \<h1> \</h1>

These tags are used to display a large or very important heading.

## \<h2> \</h2>

These tags are used to display a heading that is large and important, but less so than h1.

### \<h3> \</h3>

These tags are used to display smaller or less important heading than h2.

### \<h4> \</h4>

These tags are used to display smaller or less important heading than h3.

### \<h5> \</h5>

These tags are used to display smaller or less important heading than h4.

### \<h6> \</h6>

These tags are used to display the smallest-sized or least important heading.

### \<a> \</a>

These tags are used to define a link. You'll use the href attribute to specify the destination for the link and the link will be displayed as the text that is placed between the two given tags.

### \<img>

This tag is used to define an image and does not use an end tag. You can use attributes to control the source file for the image, the image size, and any alternative text for the image.

### \<button> \</button>

These tags signify a button that can be clicked. You can use buttons along with JavaScript to perform certain actions when the buttons are clicked.

### \<br>

This tag signifies a line break and doesn't require an end tag. A line break is simply an empty line. You can use one or multiple line breaks between the elements on your page to space them out and prevent your layout from appearing jumbled.

HTML also uses certain element tags to help define the layout of your web page, such as the following:

## <header> </header>

This element defines a section or document header.

## <nav> </nav>

This element contains the navigation links for a web page.

## <section> </section>

This element determines a section within a document.

## <aside> </aside>

This element contains additional sidebar content on a web page.

## <footer> </footer>

This element defines a section or document footer.

## <details> </details>

This element contains additional details about the page.

You'll also want to familiarize yourself with the attributes that can be used with each of these tags. Some of the most common and important ones are as follows:

## href

This attribute defines the URL for a link element. You'll want to use the full URL, including the http:// at the beginning.

### src

This attribute signifies where the source file for an image can be found. This can be a file path or a URL. If the file in question and the HTML document are both saved in the same folder, you can simply use the filename and extension here; otherwise, you should use an absolute file path.

### title

This attribute gives additional information about an element which is displayed when a cursor hovers over it. This can help users understand how to use certain aspects of your web page.

### alt

This attribute provides alt text for an image which is displayed when the image itself can't be shown.

### id

This attribute assigns a unique id to an element. Each id should only be used once per web page; an id is often used as a unique identifier for a particular element.

### disabled

This attribute signifies that an element should be displayed as disabled on your web page. Disabled elements are usually greyed out, which prevents users from interacting with them.

### height

This attribute defines how tall an element should be on your web page. It can be a set amount of pixels or even a percentage value.

## width

This attribute defines how wide an element should be on your web page. It can be a set amount of pixels or even a percentage value.

## style

This attribute can be used to define how an element is styled in terms of size, color, or font.

There are many other tags and attributes available for you to use, but they won't all be necessary for every web page you build, and certain elements can tend to be complex to use. For this beginner's tutorial, we'll be sticking to some of the simpler elements to create your page. Open up your text editor again and follow along!

For this example, we'll start off in the same way that we did with the first example, by beginning the document with the HTML declaration and the <html> start tag:

```
<!DOCTYPE html>
<html>
```

Then, we'll add some information into the <head> element, so put the <head> start tag on the next line:

```
<!DOCTYPE html>
<html>
    <head>
```

On the next line, we'll define the title of our web page, just like we did in our first sample:

```
<!DOCTYPE html>
<html>
    <head>
    <title> Another web page! </title>
```

Now we can add in something different. By using the <style> element, we can set default style information for our web page. Let's make it so that our web page has a blue background, white headings, and red paragraphs with a white background:

```
<!DOCTYPE html>
<html>
  <head>
  <title> Another web page! </title>

  <style>
      body {background-color: blue;}
      h1 {color: white;}
      p {color: red; background-color: white;}
  </style>
```

Next, let's use the <meta> element to add some information about our web page to our document, like an author, a description, and some keywords for search engines to use:

```
<!DOCTYPE html>
<html>
  <head>
      <title> Another web page! </title>
      <style>
          body {background-color: blue;}
          h1 {color: white;}
          p {color: red; background-color: white;}
      </style>
      <meta name="author" content="Your Name">
      <meta name="description" content ="A basic web page sample">
      <meta name="keywords" content="HTML, sample, beginner">
```

Great! If you want to define any JavaScript functions or link to a CSS stylesheet you would also do that here in the <head> element, but for now, let's end the <head> element and put some customized elements into the <body> element:

```
<!DOCTYPE html>
<html>
  <head>
    <title> Another web page! </title>
    <style>
        body {background-color: blue;}
        h1 {color: white;}
        p {color: red; background-color: white;}
    </style>
    <meta name="author" content="Your Name">
    <meta name="description" content ="A basic web page sample">
    <meta name="keywords" content="HTML, sample, beginner">
  </head>
  <body>
```

First, let's add in a few different headings. Remember in the <head> element that you set the default color for <h1> elements to white. Let's add an <h1> element without any attributes, an <h1> element with a specified color attribute, and some other heading elements with various attributes to see how their sizes and styles compare:

275

```
<!DOCTYPE html>
<html>
  <head>
    <title> Another web page! </title>
    <style>
      body {background-color: blue;}
      h1 {color: white;}
      p {color: red; background-color: white;}
    </style>
    <meta name="author" content="Your Name">
    <meta name="description" content ="A basic web page
    sample">
    <meta name="keywords" content="HTML, sample,
    beginner">
  </head>
  <body>
    <h1> This is a heading using the defined default style. </h1>
    <h1 style="color:aqua;"> Example of headings being given
    defined color attributes. </h1>
    <h2 style="text-align:center;"> Example of centering
    subheadings using CSS properties. </h2>
    <h3 > This is a smaller subheading with the default style.
    </h3>
    <h4 style="background-color:black; color:white;"> This is
    an even smaller subheading with a defined color and
    background color. </h4>
    <h5 style="text-align:right;"> This is an even smaller
    subheading, and it's right justified! </h5>
    <h6 style="background-color:green;"> This is the smallest
    heading with a defined background color. </h6>
```

Now, let's add some text and some line breaks below your headings.
Remember, one is able to nest elements within other ones!

```
<!DOCTYPE html>
```

```html
<html>
    <head>
        <title> Another web page! </title>
        <style>
            body {background-color: blue;}
            h1 {color: white;}
            p {color: red; background-color: white;}
        </style>
        <meta name="author" content="Your Name">
        <meta name="description" content ="A basic web page
        sample">
        <meta name="keywords" content="HTML, sample,
        beginner">
    </head>
    <body>
        <h1> This is a heading using the defined default style. </h1>
        <h1 style="color:aqua;"> Example of headings being given
        defined color attributes </h1>
        <h2 style="text-align:center;"> Example of centering
        subheadings using CSS properties. </h2>
        <h3 > This is a smaller subheading with the default style.
        </h3>
        <h4 style="background-color:black; color:white;"> This is
        an even smaller subheading with a defined color and
        background color. </h4>
        <h5 style="text-align:right;"> This is an even smaller
        subheading, and it's right justified! </h5>
        <h6 style="background-color:green;"> This is the smallest
        heading with a defined background color. </h6>
```

```
<p> Example of paragraphs using default style definition.
</p>
<p style="background-color:blue; color:black;"> Example
of the background color removed and a text color defined.
</p>
<p style="font-size:200%;"> Example of doubling font size
in paragraph. </p>
<p style="color:black;"> Example of <b> bold </b> , <i>
italicized </i> , <u> underlined </u> , and <mark>
highlighted </mark> words. </p>
<p> This is an example of <br> breaking up lines in HTML.
</p>
<p style="font-family:courier; background-color:black;
color:white;"> Example of a different font and a defined
background color and text color. </p>
<p title="Hello!"> This paragraph shows some text when
you hover over it. </p>
```

Next, let's put a link on our page that sends the user to the Google homepage when they click it:

```html
<!DOCTYPE html>
 <html>
    <head>
        <title> Another web page! </title>
        <style>
            body {background-color: blue;}
            h1 {color: white;}
            p {color: red; background-color: white;}
        </style>
        <meta name="author" content="Your Name">
        <meta name="description" content ="A basic web page
        sample">
        <meta name="keywords" content="HTML, sample,
        beginner">
    </head>
    <body>
        <h1> This is a heading using the defined default style. </h1>
        <h1 style="color:aqua;"> Example of headings being given
        defined color attributes </h1>
        <h2 style="text-align:center;"> Example of centering
        subheadings using CSS properties. </h2>
        <h3 > This is a smaller subheading with the default style.
        </h3>
        <h4 style="background-color:black; color:white;"> This is
        an even smaller subheading with a defined color and
        background color. </h4>
        <h5 style="text-align:right;"> This is an even smaller
        subheading, and it's right justified! </h5>
        <h6 style="background-color:green;"> This is the smallest
        heading with a defined background color. </h6>

        <p> Example of paragraphs using default style definition.
        </p>
```

```
<p style="background-color:blue; color:black;"> Example
of the background color removed and a text color defined.
</p>
<p style="font-size:200%;"> Example of doubling font size
in paragraph. </p>
<p style="color:black;"> Example of <b> bold </b> , <i>
italicized </i> , <u> underlined </u> , and <mark>
highlighted </mark> words. </p>
<p> This is an example of <br> breaking up lines in HTML.
</p>
<p  style="font-family:courier;  background-color:black;
color:white;"> Example of a different font and a defined
background color and text color. </p>
<p title="Hello!"> This paragraph shows some text when
you hover over it. </p>

<a  style="color:white;"  href="http://www.google.com">
Outgoing anchor to Google </a>
```

Finally, let's put a picture onto your web page. You can use an image that you have saved on your computer or you can use one online. To use an image from your own computer, you'll need to save the image in the same location as your HTML document. For instance, if your HTML document is saved on your desktop, your image should also be saved on your desktop; if your HTML document is saved in a folder, your image should be saved in the same folder. Let's add an image that's saved as shapes.png:

```
<!DOCTYPE html>
<html>
    <head>
        <title> Another web page! </title>
        <style>
            body {background-color: blue;}
            h1 {color: white;}
            p {color: red; background-color: white;}
        </style>
        <meta name="author" content="Your Name">
        <meta name="description" content ="A basic web page sample">
        <meta name="keywords" content="HTML, sample, beginner">
    </head>
    <body>
        <h1> This is a heading using the defined default style. </h1>
        <h1 style="color:aqua;"> Example of headings being given defined color attributes </h1>
        <h2 style="text-align:center;"> Example of centering subheadings using CSS properties. </h2>
        <h3 > This is a smaller subheading with the default style. </h3>
        <h4 style="background-color:black; color:white;"> This is an even smaller subheading with a defined color and background color. </h4>
        <h5 style="text-align:right;"> This is an even smaller subheading, and it's right justified! </h5>
        <h6 style="background-color:green;"> This is the smallest heading with a defined background color. </h6>
        <p> Example of paragraphs using default style definition. </p>
        <p style="background-color:blue; color:black;"> Example of the background color removed and a text color defined. </p>
```

```
<p style="font-size:200%;"> Example of doubling font size
in paragraph. </p>
<p style="color:black;"> Example of <b> bold </b> , <i>
italicized </i> , <u> underlined </u> , and <mark>
highlighted </mark> words. </p>
<p> This is an example of <br> breaking up lines in HTML.
</p>
<p  style="font-family:courier;  background-color:black;
color:white;"> Example of a different font and a defined
background color and text color. </p>
<p title="Hello!"> This paragraph shows some text when
you hover over it. </p>

<a  style="color:white;"  href="http://www.google.com">
Outgoing anchor to Google </a>

<img src="shapes.png">
```

If you'd like to change the size of the image, you can do so using the
width and height attributes. You can also add some alternative text to
the image using the alt attribute:

```
<!DOCTYPE html>
<html>
    <head>
        <title> Another web page! </title>
        <style>
            body {background-color: blue;}
            h1 {color: white;}
            p {color: red; background-color: white;}
        </style>
        <meta name="author" content="Your Name">
        <meta name="description" content ="A basic web page
        sample">
        <meta  name="keywords"  content="HTML,  sample,
        beginner">
```

```html
</head>
<body>
    <h1> This is a heading using the defined default style. </h1>
    <h1 style="color:aqua;"> Example of headings being given defined color attributes </h1>
    <h2 style="text-align:center;"> Example of centering subheadings using CSS properties. </h2>
    <h3 > This is a smaller subheading with the default style. </h3>
    <h4 style="background-color:black; color:white;"> This is an even smaller subheading with a defined color and background color. </h4>
    <h5 style="text-align:right;"> This is an even smaller subheading, and it's right justified! </h5>
    <h6 style="background-color:green;"> This is the smallest heading with a defined background color. </h6>
    <p> Example of paragraphs using default style definition. </p>
    <p style="background-color:blue; color:black;"> Example of the background color removed and a text color defined. </p>
    <p style="font-size:200%;"> Example of doubling font size in paragraph. </p>
    <p style="color:black;"> Example of <b> bold </b> , <i> italicized </i> , <u> underlined </u> , and <mark> highlighted </mark> words. </p>
    <p> This is an example of <br> breaking up lines in HTML. </p>
    <p style="font-family:courier; background-color:black; color:white;"> Example of a different font and a defined background color and text color. </p>
    <p title="Hello!"> This paragraph shows some text when you hover over it. </p>
```

```
<a    style="color:white;"    href="http://www.google.com">
Outgoing anchor to Google </a>

<img src="shapes.png">

<img src="shapes.png" width="750" height="500" alt="A
square, a circle, and a triangle.">
```

Great! Now, close the <body> and <html> elements, and you should have an HTML document that looks like this:

```
<!DOCTYPE html>
<html>
  <head>
    <title> Another web page! </title>
    <style>
        body {background-color: blue;}
        h1 {color: white;}
        p {color: red; background-color: white;}
    </style>
    <meta name="author" content="Your Name">
    <meta name="description" content ="A basic web page
    sample">
    <meta    name="keywords"    content="HTML,    sample,
    beginner">
  </head>
  <body>
    <h1> This is a heading using the defined default style. </h1>
    <h1 style="color:aqua;"> Example of headings being given
    defined color attributes </h1>
    <h2    style="text-align:center;">    Example    of    centering
    subheadings using CSS properties. </h2>
    <h3 > This is a smaller subheading with the default style.
    </h3>
```

```html
<h4 style="background-color:black; color:white;"> This is
an even smaller subheading with a defined color and
background color. </h4>
<h5 style="text-align:right;"> This is an even smaller
subheading, and it's right justified! </h5>
<h6 style="background-color:green;"> This is the smallest
heading with a defined background color. </h6>
<p> Example of paragraphs using default style definition.
</p>
<p style="background-color:blue; color:black;"> Example
of the background color removed and a text color defined.
</p>
<p style="font-size:200%;"> Example of doubling font size
in paragraph. </p>
<p style="color:black;"> Example of <b> bold </b> , <i>
italicized </i> , <u> underlined </u> , and <mark>
highlighted </mark> words. </p>
<p> This is an example of <br> breaking up lines in HTML.
</p>
<p style="font-family:courier; background-color:black;
color:white;"> Example of a different font and a defined
background color and text color. </p>
<p title="Hello!"> This paragraph shows some text when
you hover over it. </p>
<a style="color:white;" href="http://www.google.com">
Outgoing anchor to Google </a>
<br>
<br>
<img src="shapes.png">
<br>
<br>
<img src="shapes.png" width="750" height="500" alt="A
square, a circle, and a triangle.">
</body>
</html>
```

When you save this document with a .html extension and open it using a browser, it will look something like this:

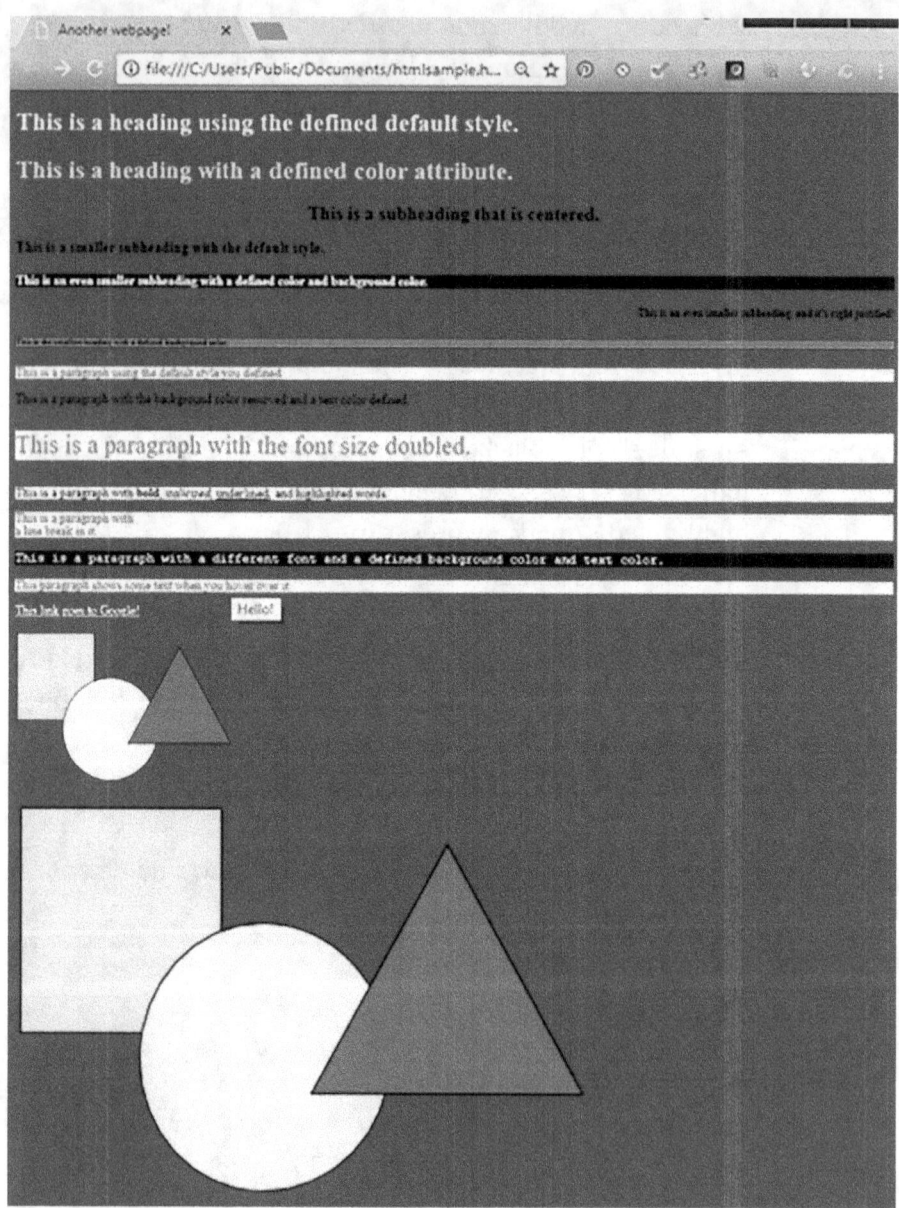

Congratulations! You've made an HTML page with customized elements. Feel free to play around with the tags and attributes for these sample elements to make a simple web page that suits your personal needs. Try to practice creating different custom elements, like an image that links to another website, or a heading that shows a message when you hover over it with a cursor.

# Chapter 2

# Creating HTML Lists And Tables

In addition to headings and paragraphs, you may want to display your text in other formats, such as a list or a table. Fortunately, HTML makes this simple to do using tags just like the ones you practiced using in the previous chapter. Follow along through the next sections to see additional ways you can format the content of your web page.

## How can I display my content as a list?

If you'd like to display a portion of the content on your web page as a list, you actually have a couple of different options to do so. For lists in which you would like the items to have a defined order, you can create what is called an ordered list, which uses numbers, letters, or numerals next to the list items. Ordered lists are defined using the <ol> tag, and each item in the list uses a <li> tag. For instance, if you'd like to create a list of race participants by the order in which they finished, you might have something like this:

```
<ol>
    <li> Susan </li>
    <li> Mark </li>
    <li> Amanda </li>
    <li> Jon </li>
</ol>
```

which will number the participants from 1 to 4. You can use the **type** attribute to change the numbering system to upper or lowercase letters or upper or lowercase Roman numerals like so:

```
<ol type="1">
   <li> Susan </li>
   <li> Mark </li>
   <li> Amanda </li>
   <li> Jon </li>
</ol>

<ol type="A">
   <li> Susan </li>
   <li> Mark </li>
   <li> Amanda </li>
   <li> Jon </li>
</ol>

<ol type="a">
   <li> Susan </li>
   <li> Mark </li>
   <li> Amanda </li>
   <li> Jon </li>
</ol>

<ol type="I">
   <li> Susan </li>
   <li> Mark </li>
   <li> Amanda </li>
   <li> Jon </li>
</ol>

<ol type="i">
   <li> Susan </li>
   <li> Mark </li>
   <li> Amanda </li>
   <li> Jon </li>
</ol>
```

If you'd like, you also have the option to start numbering your ordered list from a specified point using the **start** attribute:

```
<ol start="10">
    <li> Brian </li>
    <li> David </li>
    <li> Lynn </li>
    <li> Sabrina </li>
</ol>

<ol start="50">
    <li> Louise </li>
    <li> Morgan </li>
    <li> Jana </li>
    <li> Peter </li>
</ol>
```

Alternatively, if the order of your list items doesn't matter, you can create an unordered list. Unordered lists use markers or bullets to mark individual list items, and are defined using the <ul> tag. Similarly to ordered lists, each individual list item is defined with the <li> tag, as follows:

```
<ul>
    <li> square </li>
    <li> triange </li>
    <li> rectangle </li>
    <li> circle </li>
</ul>
```

Unordered lists can also be customized using the **style** attribute. The default style is to use bullets, but you can also use squares, circles, or no markers at all to mark each item in your list, like so:

```
<ul style="list-style-type:square">
    <li> square </li>
    <li> triange </li>
    <li> rectangle </li>
    <li> circle </li>
</ul>
```

```
<ul style="list-style-type:circle">
    <li> square </li>
    <li> triange </li>
    <li> rectangle </li>
    <li> circle </li>
</ul>

<ul style="list-style-type:none">
    <li> square </li>
    <li> triange </li>
    <li> rectangle </li>
    <li> circle </li>
</ul>
```

You can further customize your lists by using the <b> , <i> , <u> , <a>, or <mark> tags around your text, just like you did with your paragraph text in the previous chapter. You can also nest lists within lists, like so:

```
<ul>
    <li> words </li>
        <ul>
                <li> normal </li>
                <li> <b> bold </b> </li>
                <li> <i> italicized </i> </li>
                <li> <mark> highlighted </mark> </li>
                 <li>  <a  href="http://www.google.com">  link
                </a> </li>
        </ul>

    <li> numbers </li>
        <ol>
                <li> one </li>
                <li> two </li>
                <li> three </li>
        </ol>
</ul>
```

Let's create another simple web page using headings and lists to see how different list types and styles appear in a browser. Type or copy and paste this next bit of HTML into your text editor:

```html
<!DOCTYPE html>
<html>
  <head>
        <title> Lists! </title>
  </head>
  <body>
        <h3> An ordered list: </h3>
        <ol>
                <li> Susan </li>
                <li> Mark </li>
                <li> Amanda </li>
                <li> Jon </li>
        </ol>

        <h3> An ordered list using uppercase letters: </h3>
        <ol type="A">
                <li> Susan </li>
                <li> Mark </li>
                <li> Amanda </li>
                <li> Jon </li>
        </ol>


        <h3> An ordered list using lowercase letters: </h3>
        <ol type="a">
                <li> Susan </li>
                <li> Mark </li>
                <li> Amanda </li>
                <li> Jon </li>
        </ol>
```

```
<h3> An ordered list using uppercase roman numerals:
</h3>
<ol type="I">
        <li> Susan </li>
        <li> Mark </li>
        <li> Amanda </li>
        <li> Jon </li>
</ol>


 <h3> An ordered list using lowercase roman numerals:
 </h3>
<ol type="i">
        <li> Susan </li>
        <li> Mark </li>
        <li> Amanda </li>
        <li> Jon </li>
</ol>

<h3> An ordered list starting at 10: </h3>
<ol start="10">
        <li> Brian </li>
        <li> David </li>
        <li> Lynn </li>
        <li> Sabrina </li>
</ol>


<h3> An unordered list: </h3>
<ul>
        <li> square </li>
        <li> triange </li>
        <li> rectangle </li>
        <li> circle </li>
</ul>
```

```html
<h3> An unordered list using square markers: </h3>
<ul style="list-style-type:square">
        <li> square </li>
        <li> triange </li>
        <li> rectangle </li>
        <li> circle </li>
</ul>

<h3> An unordered list using circle markers: </h3>
<ul style="list-style-type:circle">
        <li> square </li>
        <li> triange </li>
        <li> rectangle </li>
        <li> circle </li>
</ul>

<h3> An unordered list using no markers: </h3>
<ul style="list-style-type:none">
        <li> square </li>
        <li> triange </li>
        <li> rectangle </li>
        <li> circle </li>
</ul>


<h3> Nested lists: </h3>
<ul>
        <li> words </li>
                <ul>
                        <li> normal </li>
                        <li> <b> bold </b> </li>
                        <li> <i> italicized </i> </li>
                        <li> <mark> highlighted
                        </mark> </li>
```

```
                              <li>    <a    href="http://www.
                              google.com"> link </a> </li>
                    </ul>
               <li> numbers </li>
                    <ol>
                              <li> one </li>
                              <li> two </li>
                              <li> three </li>
                    </ol>
          </ul>
     </body>
</html>
```

Now save the document with a .html extension and then open it up using a browser. Your web page should look something like this:

**An ordered list:**

1. Susan
2. Mark
3. Amanda
4. Jon

**An ordered list using uppercase letters:**

A. Susan
B. Mark
C. Amanda
D. Jon

**An ordered list using lowercase letters:**

a. Susan
b. Mark
c. Amanda
d. Jon

**An ordered list using uppercase roman numerals:**

I. Susan
II. Mark
III. Amanda
IV. Jon

**An ordered list using lowercase roman numerals:**

i. Susan
ii. Mark
iii. Amanda
iv. Jon

**An ordered list starting at 10:**

10. Brian
11. David
12. Lynn
13. Sabrina

An unordered list:

- square
- triange
- rectangle
- circle

An unordered list using square markers:

- square
- triange
- rectangle
- circle

An unordered list using circle markers:

o square
o triange
o rectangle
o circle

An unordered list using no markers:

square
triange
rectangle
circle

Nested lists:

- words
    o normal
    o **bold**
    o *italicized*
    o highlighted
    o link
- numbers
    1. one
    2. two
    3. three

## How can I display my content as a table?

You may also occasionally want to display content as a table on your web page. You can accomplish this by using the <table> , <tr> , <th> and <td> tags. The <tr> tag signifies a row of the table, while the <th> and <td> tags specify table headers and table date respectively. Consider

297

a table with three columns that contain the first name, last name, and birthday for a set of individuals. Your HTML might look something like this:

```
<table>
    <tr>
            <th> First Name </th>
            <th> Last Name </th>
            <th> Birthday </th>
    </tr>
    <tr>
            <td> Rebecca </td>
            <td> Jones </td>
            <td> May 2 </td>
    </tr>
    <tr>
            <td> Tony </td>
            <td> White </td>
            <td> April 14 </td>
    </tr>
    <tr>
            <td> Jamie </td>
            <td> Parker </td>
            <td> August 27 </td>
    </tr>
</table>
```

You can use attributes to customize the size and text alignment of the elements in your table. For instance, you can alter the <table> element's **style** attribute to set your table to cover a set width or the whole width of your web page, and you can use the **text-align** attributes for the headers and cells to left align, center align, or right align your text. *Note: you can put the text-align attribute into the start tags of each of your cells, but if you're using the same formatting for an entire table, it will* *probably be easier to include this styling information within the document's **\<head\>** element, like you did in Chapter 1.*

Give it a try! Type the following HTML into your text editor:

```
<!DOCTYPE html>

    <html>
      <head>
              <title> Tables! </title>
              <style>
                     th {text-align:left;}
                     td {text-align:center;}
              </style>
      </head>
      <body>
              <h3> A table with 3 columns that spans 75% of the
              window width: </h3>
              <table style="width:75%">
                     <tr style="background-color:grey;">
                             <th> First Name </th>
                             <th> Last Name </th>
                             <th> Birthday </th>
                     </tr>
                     <tr style="color:green;">
                             <td> Rebecca </td>
                             <td> Jones </td>
                             <td> May 2 </td>
                     </tr>
                     <tr style="color:blue;">
                             <td> Tony </td>
                             <td> White </td>
                             <td> April 14 </td>
                     </tr>
                     <tr style="color:purple;">
                             <td> Jamie </td>
```

```
            <td> Parker </td>
            <td> August 27 </td>
        </tr>
    </table>
  </body>
</html>
```

When you save it with the .html file extension and open it with your browser, it should look like this:

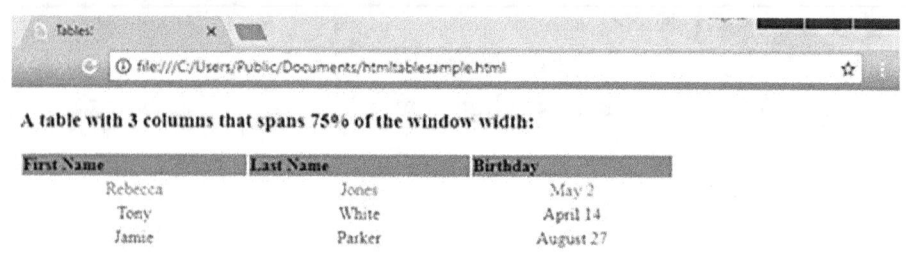

A table with 3 columns that spans 75% of the window width:

| First Name | Last Name | Birthday |
|---|---|---|
| Rebecca | Jones | May 2 |
| Tony | White | April 14 |
| Jamie | Parker | August 27 |

If you'd like, you can add borders to your table elements using the **border** attribute. You can instruct these separate borders to mesh into one border with the **border-collapse** attribute:

```
<style>
    table, th, td {border: 1px solid black; border-collapse:collapse;}
</style>
```

You can also use the colspan and rowspan attributes to create cells that cover multiple columns or rows. For instance, if two individuals had the same birthday in the above example, you might want to display it like so:

```
<tr>
    <th> First Name </th>
    <th> Last Name </th>
    <th> Birthday </th>
</tr>
<tr>
```

```
   <td> Rebecca </td>
   <td> Jones </td>
   <td rowspan="2"> May 2 </td>
</tr>
<tr>
   <td> Tony </td>
   <td> White </td>
</tr>
<tr>
   <td> Jamie </td>
   <td> Parker </td>
   <td> August 27 </td>
</tr>
```

Try it yourself! Copy and paste or manually type the following bit of HTML into your own text editor:

```
<!DOCTYPE html>
<html>
   <head>
         <title> Tables! </title>
         <style>
               table, th, td {border: 1px solid black; border-
               collapse:collapse;}
               th {text-align:left;}
               td {text-align:center;}
         </style>
   </head>
   <body>
               <h3> A table with 3 columns that uses the default
               width and colors: </h3>
         <table>
               <tr>
                     <th> First Name </th>
```

```
                <th> Last Name </th>
                <th> Birthday </th>
        </tr>
        <tr>

                <td> Rebecca </td>
                <td> Jones </td>
                <td> May 2 </td>
        </tr>
        <tr>

                <td> Tony </td>
                <td> White </td>
                <td> April 14 </td>
        </tr>
        <tr>

                <td> Jamie </td>
                <td> Parker </td>
                <td> August 27 </td>
        </tr>
</table>


<h3> A table with 3 columns that spans 75% of the
window width and uses defined colors: </h3>
<table style="width:75%">
        <tr style="background-color:grey;">
                <th> First Name </th>
                <th> Last Name </th>
                <th> Birthday </th>
        </tr>
        <tr style="color:green;">
                <td> Rebecca </td>
                <td> Jones </td>
                <td> May 2 </td>
        </tr>
        <tr style="color:blue;">
                <td> Tony </td>
```

```html
                    <td> White </td>
                    <td> April 14 </td>
            </tr>
            <tr style="color:purple;">
                    <td> Jamie </td>
                    <td> Parker </td>
                    <td> August 27 </td>
            </tr>
    </table>

    <h3> A table with 3 columns that spans 75% of the
    window width and uses merged rows: </h3>
    <table style="width:75%">
            <tr>
                    <th> First Name </th>
                    <th> Last Name </th>
                    <th> Birthday </th>
            </tr>
            <tr>
                    <td> Rebecca </td>
                    <td> Jones </td>
                    <td rowspan="2"> May 2 </td>
            </tr>
            <tr>
                    <td> Tony </td>
                    <td> White </td>
            </tr>
            <tr>
                    <td> Jamie </td>
                    <td> Parker </td>
                    <td> August 27 </td>
            </tr>
    </table>
    </body>
</html>
```

Once you save this HTML with the .html extension and open it with a browser, your web page should look something like this:

A table with 3 columns that uses the default width and colors:

| First Name | Last Name | Birthday |
|---|---|---|
| Rebecca | Jones | May 2 |
| Tony | White | April 14 |
| Jamie | Parker | August 27 |

A table with 3 columns that spans 75% of the window width and uses defined colors:

| First Name | Last Name | Birthday |
|---|---|---|
| Rebecca | Jones | May 2 |
| Tony | White | April 14 |
| Jamie | Parker | August 27 |

A table with 3 columns that spans 75% of the window width and uses merged rows:

| First Name | Last Name | Birthday |
|---|---|---|
| Rebecca | Jones | May 2 |
| Tony | White | |
| Jamie | Parker | August 27 |

### What other ways can I display my content?

In addition to lists and tables, you can also use HTML to format your text into block quotations, subscripts, superscripts, computer code, and even reversed text. Check out the following HTML to see how to use tags to format your page using these different techniques:

```
<!DOCTYPE html>
<html>
    <head>
            <title> Other Formats! </title>
    </head>
    <body>
            <h3> The following is a block quotation: </h3>
            <blockquote> This is a block quotation. Usually,
            browsers indent block quotations. You can use this tag
            when you want to quote long pieces of text from other
            sources. </blockquote>
            <h3> The following text contains subscript and
            superscript: </h3>
            <p> This paragraph uses <sub> subscript </sub> and
            <sup> superscript </sup> elements, which can be useful
            when working with math. </p>
            <h3> The following text is formatted to look like
            computer code: </h3>
            <code> If your page is relevant to programming, you
            might want to use this tag. </code>
            <h3> The following text is displayed right to left: </h3>
            <bdo dir="rtl"> Right to left! </bdo>
    </body>
</html>
```

Save the code prior in an HTML file and then open the file in your browser, and it should display like so:

**The following is a block quotation:**

> This is a block quotation. Usually, browsers indent block quotations. You can use this tag when you want to quote long pieces of text from other sources.

**The following text contains subscript and superscript:**

This paragraph uses $_{subscript}$ and $^{superscript}$ elements, which can be useful when working with math.

**The following text is formatted to look like computer code:**

`If your page is relevant to programming, you might want to use this tag.`

**The following text is displayed right to left:**

!tfel ot thgiR

Now that you've seen many of the different ways you can format and style the elements on your web page, try your hand at combining the techniques you've learned to further customize your page. Will you make a table with links? A page full of quotes? Interesting color coded informational tables? It's up to you!

# Chapter 3

# Creating HTML Forms And Handling Input

Oftentimes, when you are creating web pages, you are doing so with the intention of interacting with people who visit your page. One simple way to accomplish this is by incorporating an HTML form into your page to request input from your users.

## What kinds of input can I accept from users?

Depending on the type of information you'd like to request from your users, you can incorporate a number of different input options into your forms. For instance, if you'd like a way for users to input their names, you could use a text input field. If you want users to choose from different available options, you could use radio buttons or a dropdown list of choices. Check out the options below for ways that you can use forms to request information from your users:

**Text Fields:** You can create a text field that is one line high through setting the input tag as **"text"** like so:

> Type your first name here:
> <br>
> <input type="text"> </input>

Or, if you want to accept a larger quantity of text, like a message, you can create a text area using the <textarea> and </textarea> start and end tags.

**Number Fields:** You can create a field where users can input numerical values through setting the input tag as **"number"** like this:

> Please enter a number:
> <br>
> <input type="number"> </input>

A number field will not allow the user to enter in any characters besides numbers.

**Password Fields:** You can create a field where users can enter their password by setting the input tag as **"password"** like so:

> Type your password here:
> <br>
> <input type="password"> </input>

When a user types text into a password field, the characters are hidden for privacy.

**Email Fields:** You can create a field that accepts email addresses by setting the input tag as **"email"**, like this:

> Type your email address here:
> <br>
> <input type="email"> </input>

This field will require a user to enter a text value containing the @ symbol.

**Radio Buttons:** You can set the input tag to **"radio"** to create radio buttons like so:

> <input type="radio" name="radiobuttons"> Option 1 </input>
> <input type="radio" name="radiobuttons"> Option 2 </input>
> <input type="radio" name="radiobuttons"> Option 3 </input>

Your user will only be able to select one of the available radio buttons at a time for radio buttons with the same **name** attribute value.

**Checkboxes:** You can create checkboxes for your forms by setting the input tag as **"checkbox"** as follows:

```
<input type="checkbox"> I like coffee </input>
<input type="checkbox"> I like tea </input>
```

Using checkboxes will let you users select none, some, or all of the options provided.

**Drop-Down Lists:** If you'd like to create a drop-down list with options for a user to choose from, you can do so by using the <select> and <option> tags like this:

```
<select>
   <option> Square </option>
   <option> Circle </option>
   <option> Triangle </option>
   <option> Hexagon </option>
</select>
```

Depending on the attributes you use, your user will be able to select either a single or multiple options from the drop-down list at a time.

**Buttons:** You can create a button that users can click on by setting the input tag to **"button"**. You can assign text to the button using the **value** attribute like so:

```
<input type="button" value="I'm a button!"> </input>
```

Note: nothing will happen when you click this button as is; you will need to assign it an action when it is clicked using the **onclick** attribute, which you'll see in the next section.

**Color Choosers:** You can allow your users to select a color using a color picker by setting the input tag to **"color"** like this:

```
Please choose your favorite color:
<br>
<input type="color"> </input>
```

**Date Selectors:** You can allow your users to select a date from a calendar by setting the input tag to **"date"** like this:

Please select your birthdate:
<br>
<input type="date"> </input>

**Range Sliders:** Your users can select a relative value on a sliding scale with a range slider which you can create by setting the input tag to **"range"** like so:

Cold
 <input type="range"> </input>
Hot

**Submit Buttons:** The submit button sends the data from your form to a handler, which processes the data from the form. You can create a submit button by setting the input tag to **"submit"** like this:

<input type="submit"> </input>

The submit button refers to the **action** attribute in the <form> start tag to know where to send the data, which is generally a page with a data processing script.

**Reset Buttons:** If you would like your users to be able to set all of the options in your form back to their original default values, you can incorporate a reset button by setting the input tag to **"reset"** like so:

<input type="reset"> </input>

Each form you create will use the <form> and </form> start and end tags to specify where the form begins and ends. This allows certain elements to know what to send when the form is submitted and enables you to have multiple forms on one page which can be submitted individually. Copy and paste or manually type in the following HTML into your text editor to see how different basic form elements appear in by default:

```
<!DOCTYPE html>
<html>
   <head>
           <title> Forms! </title>
   </head>
   <body>
           <h2> A form with multiple input types: </h2>
           <form>
                   <h3> A text field: </h3>
                   Type your name below:
                   <br>
                   <input type="text"> </input>

                   <h3> A number field: </h3>
                   Please enter your favorite number:
                   <br>
                   <input type="number"> </input>

                   <h3> A password field: </h3>
                   Type your password below:
                   <br>
                   <input type="password"> </input>

                   <h3> An email field: </h3>
                   Type your email below:
                   <br>
                   <input type="email"> </input>

                   <h3> Radio buttons: </h3>
                   <input    type="radio"    name="radiobuttons">
                   Option 1 </input>
                   <input    type="radio"    name="radiobuttons">
                   Option 2 </input>
                   <input    type="radio"    name="radiobuttons">
                   Option 3 </input>
```
311

```html
<h3> Checkboxes: </h3>
<input type="checkbox"> I like coffee </input>
<input type="checkbox"> I like tea </input>

<h3> A drop-down list: </h3>
<select>
        <option> Square </option>
        <option> Circle </option>
        <option> Triangle </option>
        <option> Hexagon </option>
</select>

<h3> A color picker: </h3>
Please choose your favorite color:
<br>
<input type="color"> </input>

<h3> A date picker: </h3>
Please select your birthdate:
<br>
<input type="date"> </input>

<h3> A slider: </h3>
Cold
<input type="range"> </input>
Hot

<h3> Standard, submit, and reset buttons: </h3>
<input type="button" value="I'm a button!">
</input>
<input type="submit"> </input>
<input type="reset"> </input>
        </form>
    </body>
</html>
```

When you save this HTML in a file using the .html extension and then open it with a browser, your page should look something like this:

## A form with multiple input types:

### A text field:

Please enter your name:

### A number field:

Please enter your favorite number:

### A password field:

Please enter your password:

### An email field:

Please enter your email address:

### Radio buttons:

○ Option 1   ○ Option 2   ○ Option 3

### Checkboxes:

☐ I like coffee   ☐ I like tea

### A drop-down list:

Square ▼

### A color picker:

Please choose your favorite color:

### A date picker:

Please select your birthdate:
mm/dd/yyyy

### A slider:

Cold   🔘   Hot

### Standard, submit, and reset buttons:

I'm a button!   Submit   Reset

## How can I customize the forms on my web page?

Just like you can use attributes to change certain aspects of the text and images on your page, you can use attributes to enhance the elements in your forms. Some of the most common attributes you might use when creating forms are the following:

**name:** You should use the **name** attribute to assign a reference name to elements or groups of elements. This will enable other elements to interact with the element and form handlers to know what each piece of input data should refer to. Certain elements need to have a **name** attribute value assigned in order to work correctly like the radio buttons in the last section. You should use descriptive values to define this attribute.

**value:** The **value** attribute allows you to assign default values to the elements in your forms. For instance, you could have a word or phrase populate in a text field when your form is generated, or you could have a radio button pre-selected.

**required:** This attribute signifies that the field is required and that the form cannot be submitted without a value entered.

**disabled:** This attribute signifies that the current field should be disabled and unable to accept any input from a user.

**max:** The value for this attribute will define the maximum value that the input field is able to accept.

**maxlength:** Similarly to the **max** attribute, the value of the **maxlength** attribute defines how many characters an input field is able to accept from the user.

**min:** The value for this attribute will define the minimum value that the input field is able to accept.

**size:** The value assigned to the **size** attribute defines how many characters wide an input field should be.

314

Other attributes only pertain to specific input types. Read through the HTML below to view some examples of attributes used for form elements:

```
<!DOCTYPE html>
<html>
   <head>
           <title> Forms! </title>
   </head>
   <body>
           <h2> A form with multiple input types: </h2>
           <form>
                   <h3> A text field with a specified size, a default
value, and a maximum input length: </h3>
                   Please enter your first name:
                   <br>
                   <input        type="text"        value="Mario"
maxlength="10" size="12" name="firstname"> </input>


                   <h3> A disabled text field: </h3>
                   Please enter your last name:
                   <br>
                   <input type="text" name="lastname" disabled>
</input>


                   <h3> A large text area: </h3>
                   Please write a message:
                   <br>
                   <textarea        rows="5"        cols="35"
name="msgbox"> Some default text! </textarea>


                   <h3> A number field with a maximum accepted
value of 10: </h3>
                   Please enter your favorite number less than or
equal to 10:
```

\<br\>

\<input type="number" max="10" name="favnum"\> \</input\>

### \<h3\> A number field with a specified step value: \</h3\>

Please enter a multiple of 5:

\<br\>

\<input type="number" step="5" name="favnum"\> \</input\>

### \<h3\> A long password field: \</h3\>

Please enter your password:

\<br\>

\<input type="password" name="password" size="60"\> \</input\>

### \<h3\> An email field that requires input: \</h3\>

Please enter your email address:

\<br\>

\<input type="email" name="email" required\> \</input\>

### \<h3\> Radio buttons with one checked by default: \</h3\>

\<input type="radio" name="textstyle"\> \<b\> bold \</b\> \</input\>

\<input type="radio" name="textstyle" checked\> \<i\> italics \</i\> \</input\>

\<input type="radio" name="textstyle"\> \<mark\> highlighted \</mark\> \</input\>

### \<h3\> Checkboxes that are checked by default: \</h3\>

<input type="checkbox" name="beverages" checked> I like coffee </input>
<input type="checkbox" name="beverages" checked> I like tea </input>

<h3> A drop-down list that allows users to pick one option, with one selected by default: </h3>
<select name="ashape">
    <option> Square </option>
    <option> Circle </option>
    <option selected> Triangle </option>
    <option> Hexagon </option>
</select>

<h3> A drop-down list that shows 2 options at a time and allows users to pick multiple options using the ctrl key: </h3>
<select name="shapes" size="2" multiple>
    <option> Square </option>
    <option> Circle </option>
    <option> Triangle </option>
    <option> Hexagon </option>
</select>

<h3> A color picker: </h3>
Please choose your favorite color:
<br>
<input type="color" name="favcolor"> </input>

<h3> A date picker with date restrictions: </h3>
Please select a date in 2000:
<br>
<input type="date" name="somedate" min="2000-01-01" max="2000-12-31"> </input>

```html
<h3> A slider set to the minimum value by
default: </h3>
Cold
<input type="range" value="0"> </input>
Hot

<h3> Standard, submit, and reset buttons: </h3>
<input    type="button"    onclick="alert('You
clicked me!')" value="I'm a button!"> </input>
<input type="submit" value="Submit form!">
</input>
 <input  type="reset"  value="Reset  form!">
</input>
</form>
</body>
</html>
```

Save this HTML with a .html extension and open it with your browser.
It should look like this:

## A form with multiple input types:

### A text field with a specified size, a default value, and a maximum input length:

Please enter your first name
Mario

### A disabled text field:

Please enter your last name

### A large text area:

Please write a message
Some default text!

### A number field with a maximum accepted value of 10:

Please enter your favorite number less than or equal to 10

### A number field with a specified step value:

Please enter a multiple of 5

### A long password field:

Please enter your password

### An email field that requires input:

Please enter your email address

### Radio buttons with one checked by default:

○ **bold** ● *italics* ○ highlighted

### Checkboxes that are checked by default:

☑ I like coffee ☑ I like tea

### A drop-down list that allows users to pick one option, with one selected by default:

Triangle ▾

### A drop-down list that shows 2 options at a time and allows users to pick multiple options using the ctrl key:

Square
Circle

### A color picker:

Please choose your favorite color

### A date picker with date restrictions:

Please select a date in 2000
mm / dd / 2000

### A slider set to the minimum value by default:

Cold ▫————————— Hot

### Standard, submit, and reset buttons:

I'm a button! | Submit form! | Reset form!

319

Great job! Now, play around with the elements of your form. What happens if you try to enter a value of 11 into the number field with a maximum value of 10? What about if you try to type more than 10 characters into the first text field? See how you can manipulate the different elements of your HTML form in ways that can be useful for your web page!

# Chapter 4

# HTML And CSS

In previous examples, you learned how to define the style for your elements in 2 different ways: in the start tag for the element itself, or within the <style> element within the <head> element of your HTML file. In doing so, you were actually using CSS already using inline and internal techniques. Next, let's look at how to define styles for your page and its elements externally using a separate CSS file.

**What is CSS?**

The initials CSS literally stand for the words Cascading Style Sheets. With CSS, you can define the style for a specific element, a type of element, or for your entire webpage easily and efficiently. Although you can use CSS within your HTML document or even within an individual element, perhaps the most efficient way to use CSS is by defining the styles for your website within an external document saved with a .css extension. By doing so, you enable yourself to alter the appearance of your entire website by changing a single file instead of individual pages or elements.

An external style sheet cannot contain any HTML code. The contents of your external CSS file will resemble the contents of the <style> element within the <head> element of an HTML document. If you've been following along with the examples in the previous chapters, this should look familiar to you! A simple .css file might look like this:

```css
body {
    background-color: black;
}
h2 {
    color: white;
}
p {
    background-color: white;
    color: blue;
    font-family: courier;
}
```

Type the CSS from above into your text editor and save it with a .css extension as something like styles.css. To use the .css file with an HTML document, you will first need to define a link to the .css file within the <head> element of your HTML. Let's use a simple HTML example:

```html
<!DOCTYPE html>
<html>
    <head>
            <title> CSS! </title>
            <link rel="stylesheet" href="styles.css"> </link>
    </head>
    <body>
            <h2> This heading uses the styles defined in your
            external CSS file! </h2>
            <p> This paragraph uses the styles defined in your
            external CSS file! </p>
    </body>
</html>
```

Save this HTML with a .html file extension in the same folder as your styles.css file. When you open the .html file using your browser, you should be able to see a heading and paragraph displayed using the styles you defined in your CSS file:

## How can CSS enhance my web page?

You've already used CSS throughout this tutorial to style the elements of your webpage. By using an external .css style sheet, you can make the process of styling your webpage even simpler by containing all of your style rules in one place. You can use your style sheet to define how different types of elements should each be displayed in terms of sizes, fonts, colors, outlines, margins, and alignment, and then link to the same .css file from multiple HTML documents. Even if your website has 100 pages, you'll only have to write your CSS once!

In addition to assigning styles to specific element types like headings and paragraphs, you can also assign unique styles to individual elements using CSS. Let's take a look at a couple of different ways we can do this. The first way uses the id attribute within the start tag of an element.

For instance, let's slightly alter the HTML and CSS examples from the last section:

```
<!DOCTYPE html>
<html>
   <head>
         <title> CSS! </title>
         <link rel="stylesheet" href="styles.css"> </link>
   </head>
   <body>
         <h2> This is a normal h2 heading </h2>
         <p> This is a normal paragraph </p>
         <p id="special"> Example of a special id </p>
   </body>
</html>
```

Now, update your styles.css file to the following:

```
body {
    background-color: black;
}
h2 {
    color: white;
}
p {
    background-color: white;
    color: blue;
    font-family: courier;
}
#special {
    color: green;
}
```

Upon opening your file with your web browser, you should be able to see that the element with the **"special"** id uses the style defined by **#special** in the .css file:

```
This is a normal h2 heading
This is a normal paragraph
This is a paragraph with a special id
```

Note: no 2 elements should be given the same id within a single page, so this method should only be used to alter individual elements.

Alternatively, you can use classes to style subsets of element types with CSS. For example, you could divide your paragraphs into normal and special classes and then use CSS to assign a different color to the special paragraph class. Copy and paste or manually type the following CSS code within your editor of choice and save it as styles.css:

```
body {
    background-color: black;
}
h2 {
    color: white;
}
p {
    background-color: white;
    color: blue;
    font-family: courier;
}
p.special {
    background-color: grey;
    color: aqua;
}
```

Now copy and paste or manually type the following HTML into your text editor:

```
<!DOCTYPE html>
<html>
  <head>
          <title> CSS! </title>
          <link rel="stylesheet" href="styles.css"> </link>
  </head>
  <body>
          <h2> This is a heading </h2>
          <p> This is a normal paragraph </p>
          <p class="special"> Example of a special class </p>
  </body>
</html>
```

Once you save the HTML document and then open it with a browser, your page should resemble the following:

**This is a heading**

This is a normal paragraph

This is a paragraph with a special id

Since multiple elements can have the same class value, you can use this method to assign specific styles to large subsets of element types. Even better, you can update the style of all of the elements with the same class name by simply updating your .css file—there's no need to update each individual element inline!

To get an idea of how to further use an external style sheet to define how your HTML page is displayed, copy and paste or manually type the following CSS code within your editor of choice and save it as styles.css:

```
body {
    background-color: aqua;
    font-family: courier;
}
h1 {
}
h2 {
    color: purple;
    text-align: center;
}
h3 {
    color: green;
    font-family: verdana;
}
h4 {
    color: grey;
    font-family: times;
    text-align: right;
}
h5 {
    background-color: black;
    color: white;
```

```css
}
h6 {
    text-align: center;
}
h6.error {
    color: red;
    font-weight: bold;
}
p {
    background-color: white;
    color: blue;
    font-family: verdana;
}
p.fancy {
    background-color: grey;
    color: aqua;
    font-family: cursive;
}
p.important {
    font-weight: bold;
    font-size: 200%;
    text-transform: capitalize;
    text-align: center;
}
p.right {
    text-align: right;
}
#special {
    font-size: 300%;
    background-color: aqua;
    color: green;
}
img {
    background-color: black;
}
```

```css
img.big {
    width: 100%;
    height: 100%;
}
img.bordered {
    border-color: white;
    border-width: medium;
    border-style: solid;
}
img.dashborder {
    border-width: medium;
    border-color: white;
    border-style: dashed;
}
```

Then, copy and paste or manually type the following HTML into your text editor:

```html
<!DOCTYPE html>
<html>
  <head>
        <title> CSS! </title>
        <link rel="stylesheet" href="styles.css"> </link>
  </head>
  <body>
        <h1> This is an h1 heading </h1>
        <h2> This is an h2 heading </h2>
        <h3> This is an h3 heading </h3>
        <h4> This is an h4 heading </h4>
        <h5> This is an h5 heading </h5>
        <h6> This is an h6 heading </h6>
        <h6 class="error"> This is an h6 error heading </h6>
        <p> This is a paragraph </p>
        <p class="fancy"> This is a fancy paragraph </p>
```

```
            <p class="important"> This is an important paragraph
</p>
            <p class="right"> This is a right aligned paragraph </p>
            <p id="special"> Example of a special id </p>
            <p class="fancy"> Another fancy paragraph! </p>
            <img src="shapes.png">
            <br>
            <img src="shapes.png" class="big">
            <br>
            <img src="shapes.png" class="bordered">
            <br>
            <img src="shapes.png" class="dashborder">
        </body>
    </html>
```

Save both files in the same folder along with an image called shapes.png and then open the HTML document with your web browser. The elements of your page will be aligned, sized, colored, and bordered in the ways that you specified in your .css file!

Now that you've got a basic idea of how you are able to use external CSS files to specify different styles for the elements in your HTML documents, take some time to practice. The previous example used a .css file to define styles for headings, paragraphs, and images. See if you can apply the same techniques to style other elements like links, tables, lists, or form elements. You'll be efficiently making unique web pages with custom styles in no time!

# Chapter 5

## Using Div Elements

In HTML, and especially with the advent of HTML5, there are many different dividing elements one can use in order to break your document up into several different sections, all of which have their own specialty but function in similar ways.

Remember, HTML is ultimately a *markup* language. It's intended to take text and present it in a certain way using codified standards. This means that, to one extent or another, the language itself should ideally be easy to understand. In order to aid in making HTML easier to understand, certain conventions have been created that allow people to write better markup. Among these are these new divider elements.

The oldest divider element, and in fact one which has been around for quite a while, is the *div* element. The div element normally will take either an *ID* or a *class* (or both). These are defined in the markup for the div element.

We've already talked about both of these in passing but since IDs and classes are actually a concept that you're going to run into fairly often when you're working with HTML and CSS, it's worth taking a second to really start to understand what they are and what the difference is between them. They are different and you can absolutely use both in order to mark a single element.

IDs and classes are similar but functionally different in a fundamental way. IDs serve as a means for designating a single element. In this way, an ID is an identifier, hence the name "ID." You cannot have two elements with the same identifier. All identifiers must be unique.

Classes are parallel to identifiers. They allow you to designate a single *type* of element. So, if you wanted every element of your site that was designated as a *content-box* to have a drop shadow, you could do so by setting these to be of the class *content-box*.

Something may be designated through both an ID and a class. If you were to do this, then it would take the style properties from both (something we'll talk about more in-depth in the book specifically geared at CSS). If they both have a similar property, like border-color for instance, then the class definition will be superseded by the ID definition.

IDs and classes can be written in your markup like so:

```
<div id="idName" class="className">
    <!-- content -->
</div>
```

Note that you don't necessarily have to have both of these. You can have only one and that would be perfectly fine. You also don't have to have either of these. However, if you decide to use these, then that will give you a way to define further things for these markup elements both within your CSS and within any JavaScript or PHP code that you write. As a result, getting into the habit of using these is extremely important. You can use them with pretty much any element that you want to style, but there is a way to use them excessively and in places where they don't really belong, so only use them when they have a specific purpose within the context of your code.

Another divider element that you should know is the *nav* element. The nav element is intended to give you an easy way to mark out where the navigation bar in your code is. Like so:

```
<nav>
    <a href=""> Link 1 </a>
    <a href=""> Link 2 </a>
    <a href=""> Link 3 </a>
</nav>
```

One can also try the section element, which will allow one to break their code into sections. This is functionally similar to the *div* element, but the language is a bit clearer. Where div can be used for generally any division, the *section* element is particularly useful within the context of modern web design where one-page designs that are broken into singular sections in the code are the modus operandi.

While we're discussing dividing elements, it's also important that you understand how they work in the context of linking back to your site. You can actually use identifiers in order to link to a certain place on your page. For example, if you were to have a div called "endOfPage" by an ID, you could link to the page in a manner such that clicking the link would take you to the start of that division. Like so:

<a href="#endOfPage"> Go to the End of the Page. </a>

This is especially useful when you're linking within your own document and working with the aforementioned single-page designs.

You refer to identifiers with a pound sign and to classes using a period, just for the record.

Another important sectional divider that you should probably know is the *footer* element. This allows you to designate in clear language the *footer* of a given page. This works just like the nav, section, and div elements do.

With that, we've covered most of the major division elements that you're going to need to get started with HTML. You can style according to these division markers and then have a very expressive markup document that will clearly show what is what and where.

# Conclusion

Thank you again for purchasing *HTML: Basic Fundamental Guide for Beginners*, and congratulations on making it to the end! Hopefully, you've gained some insight into how HTML uses tags, elements, and attributes to tell a browser how to display a web page, and had some fun designing your very own web page from scratch.

The next step is to let yourself get creative. Have an idea for a cool new web page? Try using your new HTML skills to bring it to life! As with any other skill, if you really want to continue progressing with HTML, the best way is to practice using it every chance you get—there are a ton of websites out there just waiting to be made, and that means a ton of opportunities for you.

Finally, if you found this book useful as you began on your HTML journey, please take a moment to review it on Amazon. Thank you, good luck, and enjoy your new website!

# CSS

## *Basic Fundamental Guide for Beginners*

# Introduction

Congratulations on purchasing *CSS: Basic Fundamental Guide For Beginners* and thank you for doing so! Whether you're interested in learning CSS to enhance a personal website or you'd just like to gain a better understanding of how your browser does what it does. This book is a great starting point. With its many examples and simple to understand explanations, you'll soon be on your way to creating unique web pages that function smoothly and efficiently!

Before diving into this book, a basic idea of HTML is a plus and how to use it to create a simple web page. Combine that knowledge with an editor and a browser and you're ready to get started! Over the course of this book, you'll not only learn the art of using CSS selectors in making our HTML web pages more interactive, you'll also discover techniques for creating beautiful page layouts. When it comes to interacting with users, having an approachable and easy-to-use website is crucial. By the end of this book, you can be confident that your web pages are just as simple to navigate as they are appealing to view.

There are many books available on this subject, so thanks again for choosing this one. Good luck, and have fun taking off with CSS!

# Chapter 1

# Taking Off With CSS

I f you have ever written HTML to create a web page previously, it is highly likely that you've also used CSS. CSS stands literally for Cascading Style Sheets, and it is used in web pages alongside HTML to define page styles and layouts. Need to change the default font of a paragraph? Wish that picture had a border? Would a cool animation really bring your page to life? You can do all of that using CSS!

With the examples here, just get one text editor (like Notepad or TextEdit) to write some HTML and CSS and a browser (like Google Chrome, Internet Explorer, or Mozilla Firefox) to view what you've written.

### How do CSS and HTML work together?

Generally speaking, your web browser will use the rules that you set within your CSS to determine how to display a web page. An HTML file will provide the content and define the content's type, and a CSS file will assign different styles to those different content types. CSS uses what are called properties and selectors to assign these styles. A property can be something like an element's size or color. A selector is what CSS uses to refer to an element or group of elements in order to assign them a style.

You can contain all of the rules for how to display the elements in your HTML document within a separate file called a stylesheet. A stylesheet will have a .css file extension, and you will link to it within the <head> element of your HTML file. For instance, consider the following HTML:

338

```
<!DOCTYPE html>
<html>
    <head>
            <title>A CSS Example!</title>
    </head>
    <body>
            <h1>A big important heading</h1>
            <p>An ordinary paragraph</p>
    </body>
</html>
```

If you save the above HTML in a file with a .html extension and then open it using a browser, it won't look very impressive -- just black text on a white background. However, you can change that with a little bit of CSS. Take a look at the following:

```
h1 {
    background-color: red;
    color: white;
    border: 2px dashed blue;
}
p {
    background-color: grey;
    color: aqua;
}
```

Save this CSS in a file called styles.css. Now, we'll just have to add one line into the previous HTML example, thereby connecting CSS stylesheet with the HTML file. In the <head> element, insert a <link> element as follows:

```
<!DOCTYPE html>
<html>
  <head>
          <title>A CSS Example!</title>
          <link rel="stylesheet" href="styles.css">
  </head>
  <body>
          <h1>A big important heading</h1>
          <p>An ordinary paragraph</p>
  </body>
</html>
```

Save this HTML with a .html extension in the same folder where you just saved styles.css. Now when you open your HTML using your browser, it will look a little more interesting:

## A big important heading

An ordinary paragraph

So what did we just do? In our .css file, we defined two rules. Both rules start with a selector and then contain declarations, which define the values for certain properties. The selector for the first rule is **h1**, and the rule contains three declarations: the first declaration generates red background color, white color emanates from the next, and the third declaration creates a dashed blue border around the element. The selector for the second rule is **p**, and it contains two declarations: the first declaration sets the background color to grey, and the second declaration sets the text color to aqua. These rules will apply to every element in your HTML file that use <h1> or <p> tags.

## How can I use CSS with my HTML?

In the last section, you put some CSS into a separate file from your HTML document and then linked to that file in order to use the styles it defined. When you use CSS in this manner, it's called an external stylesheet. In most cases, this is the method that you should use when styling your websites. Not only does this method allow you to efficiently organize all the styling rules for your web page in one place, it also allows you to use the same rules for multiple pages by linking to the same .css file from multiple .html files. That means that even if your website contains 100 pages, you can control the style for all of them just by altering a single .css file!

If for some reason you don't want to use an external stylesheet, you have a couple of other options for using CSS to style your HTML documents. Before we look at those options, first take a moment to remember how the HTML and CSS looked using the external stylesheet method.

Some HTML:

```
<!DOCTYPE html>
<html>
    <head>
            <title>A CSS Example!</title>
            <link rel="stylesheet" href="styles.css">
    </head>
    <body>
            <h1>A big important heading</h1>
            <p>An ordinary paragraph</p>
            <h2>A less important heading to introduce a list</h2>
            <ul>
                    A list of assorted objects:
                    <li>a hairbrush</li>
                    <li>a skeleton key</li>
                    <li>a cat</li>
                    <li>a gaming console</li>
                    <li>a pancake</li>
            <ul>
    </body>
</html>
```
Some CSS:

```
h1 {
    background-color: red;
    color: white;
    border: 2px dashed blue;
}
h2 {
    background-color: purple;
    color: yellow;
}
p {
    background-color: grey;
    color: aqua;
}
ul {
    text-decoration: underline;
    border: 1px solid green;
}
li {
    text-decoration: bold;
}
```

The first alternative to using an external stylesheet that we'll take a look at is called an internal stylesheet. Instead of placing a <link> element within the <head> element of your HTML document, you'll instead use a <style> element to contain the CSS declarations. To create the same page as the example above using an internal stylesheet, your HTML document would look something like this:

```
<!DOCTYPE html>
<html>
    <head>
        <title>A CSS Example!</title>
        <style>
                h1 {
    background-color: red;
```

```
      color: white;
      border: 2px dashed blue;
}
h2 {
      background-color: purple;
      color: yellow;
}
p {
      background-color: grey;
      color: aqua;
}
ul {
      text-decoration: underline;
      border: 1px solid green;
}
li {
      text-decoration: bold;
}
            </style>
      </head>
      <body>
            <h1>A big important heading</h1>
            <p>An ordinary paragraph</p>
            <h2>A less important heading to introduce a list</h2>
            <ul>
                  A list of assorted objects:
                  <li>a hairbrush</li>
                  <li>a skeleton key</li>
                  <li>a cat</li>
                  <li>a gaming console</li>
                  <li>a pancake</li>
            <ul>
      </body>
</html>
```

This method has the benefit of containing all of the styling information you need in the same document as your HTML. Changing the styles within the <style> element will apply them to the <h1> and <p> elements throughout your .html document. However, if you want to create multiple pages with the same style rules, you'll have to put the CSS into each file individually. Then, if you decide you want to change something, you'll have to change it in multiple files.

A third option for applying CSS to you HTML document is via inline styles. Inline styles only affect a single HTML element, and they are defined within the **style** attribute in the start tag of an element. To create the same page as above using inline styles, you would have to do the following:

```
<!DOCTYPE html>
<html>
   <head>
          <title>A CSS Example!</title>
   </head>
   <body>
          <h1 style="background-color: red; color: white; border: 2px dashed blue;">A big important heading</h1>
          <p style="background-color: grey; color: aqua;">An ordinary paragraph</p>
   </body>
          <h2 style="background-color: purple; color: yellow">A less important heading to introduce a list</h2>
          <ul style="text-decoration: underline; border: 1px solid green;" >
                  A list of assorted objects:
                  <li       style="text-decoration:       bold;">a hairbrush</li>
                  <li  style="text-decoration:  bold;">a  skeleton key</li>
                  <li style="text-decoration: bold;">a cat</li>
```

```
                <li    style="text-decoration:    bold;">a    gaming
console</li>
                <li         style="text-decoration:         bold;">a
pancake</li>
        <ul>
</html>
```

Although this might be a reasonable option in certain restrictive circumstances, it is generally not a good idea to use inline styles. If you decide to change any of the styles on your website, you won't just have to update each affected page -- you'll have to update each affected *element*. Additionally, having the styles defined within the start tag of each element tends to clutter up your HTML file and make it harder to read and understand.

## How should I format my CSS?

You've already seen a couple of simple examples of how to properly format your CSS in the previous sections. Take a look at the following components to gain a better understanding of CSS syntax:

**Property:** A property is an identifier that is used to indicate what feature of an element you want to style. Properties are descriptive and meant to be easy for a human to read and understand. Some examples of properties include size, font, color, and border. There are over 300 properties available to use in CSS! CSS properties are case sensitive and they all use US spelling -- color doesn't work, but color does.

**Value:** A value is assigned to a property to define what its specific style should be. A color property could have a value of blue or red, for instance. The available values depend on which property they're defining. Like properties, values are case sensitive.

**Declaration:** A CSS declaration is the pairing of a property with a value. A declaration is formatted as follows, with the property first, a colon, and then the value:

345

color: blue;

background-color: purple;

width: 100%;

font-family: courier;

It's worth noting here that not every value is valid for every property. Each property has its own list of acceptable values. If you try to use an invalid property or value in your declaration, the browser will simply ignore the whole declaration.

**Declaration block:** A declaration block contains zero or more CSS declarations. The declaration blocks are contained in {} brackets and separated by semicolons. The final declaration in a declaration block doesn't need to end with a semicolon, but that is better to ensure consistency:

```
{color: blue;
    background-color: aqua;
    border-left: 1px dashed green;
    width: 100%;
    text-decoration: underline;
}
```

**Ruleset:**      A ruleset or rule is the pairing of a declaration block with a CSS selector or group of selectors. This pairing is accomplished simply by placing the selector or group of selectors before the opening {bracket of the declaration block. Each selector in a group of selectors should be separated by a comma:

```
h1 {
    background-color: black;
    color: white;
    font-family: courier;
}
```

```
h2, p {
    background-color: grey;
    color: aqua;
    font-family: verdana;
}
```

If any of the selectors in a group of selectors is invalid, the browser will skip over it. However, the browser will still apply the styles set in the declaration block to the remaining selectors in the group.

In addition to understanding and properly formatting your CSS rules, it is also generally a good idea to use whitespace to your advantage within your .css files. Although it isn't necessary to create a functioning web page, using line breaks, tabs, and spaces in your file can make it readable and simple to alter if the need arises. For instance, this CSS:

```
h1 {
background-color:red;
color:white;
font-family: courier;
border:2px dashed blue;
}
p {
background-color:grey;
font-family: verdana;
color:aqua;
}
```
and this CSS:
```
h1 {background-color:red;color:white;font-family:courier;border:2px      dashed      blue;}p{background-color:grey;font-family:verdana;color:aqua;}
```

will both define the same styles for your web pages. However, it is much easier to see and understand what is being done in the first example, and it would be much easier to make any changes if needed.

# Chapter 2

# Using CSS Selectors

In the last chapter, you had a chance to work with some basic CSS examples, and you learned that one or more selectors should come before a declaration block. Now, let's take a look at some of the different selector types and how they can be used to apply styles to your web pages:

## Simple Selectors

A simple selector is used to refer to a single or multiple elements based on their ID, their class, or their type. A simple selector could look like any one of the following:

p

h4

ol

.someclass

.important

p.error

#q1

#input4

*

The first kind of simple selector is very common and is called a type selector or an element selector. Type selectors are not case sensitive, and they are a simple way to refer to all of the elements of the same type within an HTML document, like all the type 1 headings or all the ordered lists. For the following HTML:

```
<!DOCTYPE html>
<html>
   <head>
          <title>CSS Type Selectors</title>
          <link rel="stylesheet" href="styles.css">
   </head>
   <body>
          <p>A paragraph with a defined color and background
color</p>
          <ol>
                 A list with a border:
                 <li>square</li>
                 <li>circle</li>
                 <li>triangle</li>
          </ol>
   </body>
</html>
```

the following CSS uses the type selectors **p** and **ol** to style the <p> and <ol> elements:

```
p {
    background-color: blue;
    color: yellow;
    font-family: courier;
    text-decoration: bold;
}
ol {
    border: 1px solid green;
}
```

Another simple selector is the class selector. Instead of using the element type, the class selector uses a class name to refer to an element. In the .css file, the class selector is a period followed by the class name. In the .html file, the class name is written in the **class** attribute within an element's start tag. For example, for the following HTML:

```
<!DOCTYPE html>
<html>
    <head>
            <title>CSS Class Selectors</title>
            <link rel="stylesheet" href="styles.css">
    </head>
    <body>
            <ul>
                    A list with items of different classes:
                    <li class="shape first important">square</li>
                    <li class="shape second important">circle</li>
                    <li class="shape third">triangle</li>
            </ul>
    </body>
</html>
```

the following CSS uses the .shape, .first, .second, .third, and .important class selectors to style the items in the list. An element can have multiple classes, and it will use the styles assigned to all of its classes:

```
.shape {
    background-color: red;
    color: aqua;
}
.first {
    text-decoration: underline;
}
.second {
}
.third {
```

```
    font-family: courier;
}
.important {
    font-weight: bold;
}
```

The resulting list will look like so:

A list with items of different classes:
square
circle
triangle

You can also use class selectors such as **p.error** or **p.valid** to refer to classes within a certain type of element. In this way, you could set a style for the error class that displays differently when it is a <p> element as opposed to a <div> or another type of element.

The third kind of simple selector is the ID selector. Similar to a class selector, an id selector refers to an id that is defined within the start tag of an element. However, while multiple elements can have the same class, only one element can have anID. If you attempt to assign the same id to multiple elements, you might encounter errors, or the browser might only accept the first instance. Take a look at the following HTML:

```
<!DOCTYPE html>
<html>
    <head>
            <title>CSS Class Selectors</title>
            <link rel="stylesheet" href="styles.css">
    </head>
    <body>
            <p id="george">George likes the color blue.</p>
            <p id="amy">Amy likes green.</p>
    </body>
</html>
```

and the following CSS:

```
#george {
color: blue;
}
#amy {
color: green;
}
```

In the above example, you can see thatID selectors are written using the # symbol followed by the id value. Any element can be assigned a unique id within its start tag.

The final kind of simple selector that we will cover in this book is called the universal selector, which is simply written as the * symbol. The universal selector applies the styles defined in its declaration block to every element on the page. It is very uncommon to have a situation in which you should use the universal selector, and it can cause large web pages to have significantly poorer performance. A simple example could use the following HTML:

```
<!DOCTYPE html>
<html>
    <head>
            <title>CSS Class Selectors</title>
            <link rel="stylesheet" href="styles.css">
    </head>
    <body>
            <h1>A large and important heading</h1>
            <p>A regular paragraph with some <b>bold</b>,
<i>italicized</i>, and <u>underlined</u> elements.</p>
    </body>
</html>
```

and the following CSS:

```
* {
    border: 1px double black;
    color: purple;
}
```

to create a page that looks like this:

## Attribute Selectors

A somewhat more complex kind of selector is called an attribute selector, and it works by matching the value of an element's attribute. The attributes are contained within the start tag of an element in the .html file and are written in [] brackets in the .css stylesheet. For instance, take a look at the following HTML:

```
<!DOCTYPE html>
<html>
    <head>
        <title>CSS Class Selectors</title>
        <link rel="stylesheet" href="styles.css">
    </head>
    <body>
        A list of assorted things:
        <ul>
            <li          thing-category="shape"          thing-
color="blue">square</li>
            <li          thing-category="number"          thing-
color="none">four</li>
            <li          thing-category="number"          thing-
color="none">17</li>
```

```
              <li         thing-category="shape"          thing-
color="green">circle</li>
              <li         thing-category="animal"         thing-
color="white">bunny</li>
          </ul>
      </body>
</html>
```

and the following CSS:

```
[thing-category] {
    background-color: aqua;
}
[thing-category=shape] {
    text-decoration: bold;
}
[thing-color] {
    color: red;
}
[thing-color=blue] {
    color: blue;
}
[thing-color=green] {
    color: green;
}
```

When viewed with a browser, your page should look similar to this:

A list of assorted things:

- square
- four
- 17
- circle
- bunny

In the above example, you can see how you can use attribute selectors in a couple of different ways. If you only list the attribute as the selector, the corresponding declaration block applies the contained styles. It does this to all, irrespective of the attribute value. On the other hand, if you list both an attribute and a value as the selector, the styles in the declaration block are only applied to elements that have that attribute set to that value.

## Multiple Selectors

If you would like to use the same styles for more than one set of elements, you can pair multiple selectors with the same declaration block by separating them with commas. For example, if you use the following HTML:

```
<!DOCTYPE html>
<html>
    <head>
            <title>CSS Class Selectors</title>
            <link rel="stylesheet" href="styles.css">
    </head>
    <body>
            <h1>A big and important heading</h1>
            <h2>A less important heading</h2>
            <h3>An even less important heading</h3>
            <h4>A somewhat unimportant heading</h4>
            <h5>An even more unimportant heading</h5>
            <h6>A small and very unimportant heading</h6>
    </body>
</html>
```

with the following CSS:

```
h1, h3, h5 {
    background-color: grey;
}
h2, h4, h6 {
    color: blue;
}
```

your output will look something like this:

## A big and important heading

### A less important heading

#### An even less important heading

##### A somewhat unimportant heading

###### An even more unimportant heading

A small and very unimportant heading

Great! You now have an idea of how to use some common and useful selectors to apply custom styles to elements and groups of elements. Play around with the techniques you just learned. Can you figure out how to assign the same style to a class and an id without rewriting the declaration block? How does an element display if you assign different values to the same property within different declaration blocks? What happens if an element is nested within another element? Set up these scenarios in your text editor and find out!

# Chapter 3

# CSS Layout Basics

In the last chapters, you've had the opportunity to use CSS rules to define the styles for elements in your HTML documents. CSS doesn't just define appearance attributes like colors and borders, however. It is also a valuable tool in deciding how elements are laid out on a web page. CSS uses a box model to determine where to place each element -- every element is considered as a rectangular box shape, and those boxes are placed in relation to one another. Each element "box" contains the element content, some space called padding between the content and a border, the border itself, and then surrounding space called a margin. Take a look at some of the following defining properties:

**Width and Height:** The height and width properties set the height and width of the area where the content of an element box is displayed. This content can be something like the text or image content of an element, or it could include other boxes nested inside. Widths are measured using either pixels (written as 100px, for instance) or by the percentage of the page they cover (a box with a width of 50% would span half the total page width). Heights are measured using pixels and don't use percentages.

You can also set maximum or minimum values for your content boxes instead of defining a size using pixels or percentages. These maximum and minimum values can be set using properties like max-width, max-height, min-width, and min-height. Play around with these attributes to determine which are best for managing the content of your specific web page. Check out the following examples for defining the size of a <div> element:

```
div {
    height: 225px;
    width: 50%;
}
div {
    max-height: 500px;
    min-height: 20px;
    max-width: 300px;
    min-width: 15px;
}
```

Do not set the width or height of your content box to a value that is greater than the size of the browser window in which you are viewing your page. If you do so, the content box will overflow outside of the window and you will need to use the up/down and left/right scroll bars to view the entire box.

**Padding:** The padding of a content box is the space between the content itself and the edge of the box where a border would be. You can define the padding on each side of your content box individually by using the padding-left, padding-right, padding-top, and padding-bottom properties. Alternatively, you can set the padding for all four sides at once by using the padding property followed by the top, right, bottom, and left padding values. Take a look at each of these methods below for styling a <div> element:

```
div {
    padding-left: 125px;
    padding-right: 20px;
    padding-top: 55px;
    padding-bottom: 110px;
}
div {
    padding: 55px 20px 110px 125px;
}
```

Both of the above rulesets accomplish the same thing. You can also have a padding property that contains 3, 2, or even 1 value instead of 4. If a padding property contains 3 values, the first value corresponds to the padding-top value, the second value corresponds to the padding-right and padding-left values, and the third value corresponds to the padding-bottom value. If a padding property contains 2 values, the first value corresponds to the padding-top and padding-bottom values and the second value corresponds to the padding-left and padding-right values. If a padding property only contains a single value, that value is used for all four sides.

**Border:** The border for a content box is located between the padding and the margin of the box. The default border size for an element is 0, which would display as nothing, or invisible. However, you can use border-width, border-color, and border-style properties to define a border with a specific thickness, style, and color. You can also use the border, border-left, border-right, border-top, or border-bottom properties to define the style, color, and thickness of a border on one or all sides of your content box. If you'd like to instead set a specific border property on only one side of your content box, you can do that as well by using properties such as border-top-width, border-top-color, or border-top-style. Take a look at some of the ways you might define the styles for the border of a <div> element:

```
div {
    border-left: 2px solid black;
    border-right: 5px solid black;
    border-top: 1px solid red;
    border-bottom: 3px solid red;
}
div {
    border: 2px dashed green;
}


div {
    border-top-style: dotted;
    border-top-color: green;
```

```
      border-top-width: 4px;
      border-bottom-style: double;
      border-bottom-color: purple;
      border-bottom-width: 1px;
      border-left-style: dashed;
      border-left-color: yellow;
      border-left-width: 3px;
      border-right-style: ridge;
      border-right-color: aqua;
      border-right-width: 2px;
   }
   div {
      border-weight: 2px;
      border-color: blue;
   }
```

It is worth noting here that, by default, the background color of an element will extend to the outer edge of the border.

**Margin:** An element box's margin envelopes the outside margin and demarcates the box from other entities, sort of like an outer padding. You can set the top, right, left, and bottom margins for an element all at once using the margin property, or you can set them individually using the margin-top, margin-bottom, margin-left, and margin-right properties.

The margins from separate elements within a web page can push up against one another and use margin collapsing when they touch. With margin collapsing, the distance between two touching element boxes becomes the larger of the two touching margins instead of the sum of the two touching margins.

Some examples for defining the margins of a <div> element are as follows:

```
   div {
      margin: 20px 30px 15px 10px;
```

```
}
div {
    margin-top: 20px;
    margin-right: 30px;
    margin-bottom: 15px;
    margin-left: 10px;
}
```

Similarly to the padding property, the margin property can have anywhere from one to four values. If the margin property has four values, they correspond to the margin's top, right, bottom, and left values, in that order. If the margin property has three values, the first value corresponds to the top margin, the second value corresponds to the left and right margins, and the third value corresponds to the bottom margin. If the margin property has two values, the first value corresponds to the top and bottom margins, and the second value corresponds to the left and right margins. If the margin property only has one value, that value corresponds to all the four margins of the element box.

Using the box model, it is easy to determine to a total actual size that an element will take up on a page. To determine the element's height, add the content box height, the top padding, the bottom padding, the top border, the bottom border, the top margin, and the bottom margin. Similarly, to determine the element's width, add the content box width, the left padding, the right padding, the left border, the right border, the left margin, and the right margin. Note that this method will give you the total space that an element will take up on the web page. If you would instead like to know how big the element will look, perform the same calculations as above without adding in the top margin, the bottom margin, the left margin, or the right margin.

**Position:** With the position attribute, you can define the location of an element on your page. There are several different values for the position attribute, including static, fixed, relative, absolute, and sticky. These positions are then defined using the top, bottom, right, and left attributes to set the top margin edge, bottom margin edge, right margin edge, or left margin edge location within your page.

The static value is the default for the position attribute, and doesn't really do anything special to the positioning of the element; it will just flow normally with the page:

```
div {
    position: static;
}
```

The fixed value puts an element in a fixed position relative to the viewing port for your web page, and uses the top, bottom, left, and right attributes to define the said position. The following example would place the <div> element into the bottom right corner of your browser window:

```
div {
    position: fixed;
    width: 75px;
    height: 50px;
    right: 0;
    bottom: 0;
}
```

The relative value sets an element's position relative to where it would normally be located on the page and leaves a space in the page where the element would normally be. The following example would move the <div> element over 75 pixels from its default position:

```
div {
    position: relative;
    left: 75px;
}
```

The absolute value allows an element to be positioned in a specific location based on an ancestor's location or the body of the document if no ancestor is present. The following example could be used to position the "little" div in the bottom right corner of the "big" div:

```
div.big {
    position: relative;
    width: 450px;
    height: 250px;
}
div.little {
    position: absolute;
    bottom: 0;
    right: 0;
    width: 150px;
    height: 75px;
}
```

```
<!DOCTYPE html>
<html>
    <body>
            <div class="big">
This div is big and has a relative position
<div class="little">
This div is smaller and its position is relative to the big div it is
contained in</div>
</div>
</div>
    </body>
</html>
```

The sticky value allows an element to have a position based on a user's scroll position. A sticky element will have a relative position until a user scrolls past it, and then it will "stick" to one position in the viewing window. The following example will cause the <div> element to stay 50 pixels down from the top of the screen once a user scrolls to it:

```
div {
    position: sticky;
    top: 50px;
}
```

**Float:** The float property in CSS can be a useful tool when defining your page layouts. One of the most common uses of the float property is to wrap text around images or display images side by side. Or, if you'd like, you can even use the float property to set the layout of your entire web page! The following CSS would cause the <img> elements to float to the right of the text within a paragraph, and allow the text to wrap around the image naturally once it gets long enough:

```
img {
    float: right;
}
```

```
<!DOCTYPE html>
<html>
    <body>
            <p><img src="shapes.png">A bunch of text!</p>
    </body>
</html>
```

**Clear:** The clear property is used along with the float property to further control the layout of a web page. By using the clear property, you can disallow floating elements to the left and right of an element. For instance, the following CSS would make it so that no elements are allowed to float on either side of the <div> element:

```
div {
    clear: both;
}
```

By default, the clear property has a value of none; that is, floating elements are allowed both to the left and to the right of the element.

Let's take a look at some examples of web pages using the properties discussed in this chapter. For the first page, copy and paste or manually type the following HTML into your text editor and save it with a .html extension:

```html
<!DOCTYPE html>
<html>
   <head>
          <title>CSS Layout Example</title>
          <link rel="stylesheet" href="styles.css">
   </head>
   <body>
          <div class="news">
                 This could tell users about a cool new update for
your site!
          </div>
          <div class="pageheader">
                 <h1>The header for your webpage!</h1>
          </div>
          <div class="column menu">
                 <ul>
                        <li>An item in your page menu</li>
                        <li>A    second    item    in    your    page
menu</li>
                        <li>A third item in your page menu</li>
                        <li>A fourth item in your page menu</li>
                        <li>A fifth item in your page menu</li>
                 </ul>
          </div>
          <div class="column content">
                 <h1>This could be a heading for some content on
your page</h1>
                 <p>This paragraph could welcome users to your
website.</p>
                 <p>This could be an interesting paragraph about
a hobby or an interest that your page is about.</p>
                 <p>This could be a followup paragraph for the
first.</p>
                 <p>This   paragraph   could   give   users   some
instructions on how to navigate your website.</p>
```

```
        </div>
        <div class="pagefooter">
                <p>Here is some text in the footer of your
webpage!</p>
                </div>
    </body>
</html>
```

Then, copy and paste or manually type the following CSS into a separate file in your text editor and save it at styles.css:

```css
.pageheader, .pagefooter {
    clear: both;
    background-color: black;
    color: white;
    padding: 20px;
}
.column {
    float: left;
}
.menu {
    width: 20%;
    padding: 10px;
}
.content {
    width: 75%;
}

.menu ul {
    list-style-type: none;
    margin: 0;
    padding: 0;
}
.menu li {
    padding: 10px;
    margin-bottom: 10px;
```

```
        background-color: blue;
        color: aqua;
        text-decoration: bold;
        text-align: center;
}
.news {
        position: sticky;
        background-color: yellow;
        text-align: center;
        top: 20px;
        margin: 0px 5%;
        height: 20px;
        width: 90%;
        border: 2px dashed green;
}
```

Make sure that you saved the HTML file and the CSS file in the same folder, or put the CSS into the <head> element of your HTML document, as in this case:

```
<!DOCTYPE html>
<html>
    <head>
            <title>CSS Layout Example</title>
            <style>
.pageheader, .pagefooter {
    clear: both;
    background-color: black;
    color: white;
    padding: 20px;
}
.column {
    float: left;
}
.menu {
    width: 20%;
```

```css
        padding: 10px;
}
.content {
    width: 75%;
}
.menu ul {
    list-style-type: none;
    margin: 0;
    padding: 0;
}
.menu li {
    padding: 10px;
    margin-bottom: 10px;
    background-color: blue;
    color: aqua;
    text-decoration: bold;
    text-align: center;
}
.news {
    position: sticky;
    background-color: yellow;
    text-align: center;
    top: 20px;
    margin: 0px 5%;
    height: 20px;
    width: 90%;
    border: 2px dashed green;
}
        </style>
    </head>
    <body>

        <div class="news">
                This could tell users about a cool new update for
your site!
```

```
        </div>

        <div class="pageheader">
                <h1>The header for your webpage!</h1>
        </div>

        <div class="column menu">
                <ul>
                        <li>An item in your page menu</li>
                        <li>A    second    item    in    your    page
menu</li>
                        <li>A third item in your page menu</li>
                        <li>A fourth item in your page menu</li>
                        <li>A fifth item in your page menu</li>
                </ul>
        </div>

        <div class="column content">
                <h1>This could be a heading for some content on
your page</h1>
                <p>This paragraph could welcome users to your
website.</p>
                <p>This could be an interesting paragraph about
a hobby or an interest that your page is about.</p>
                <p>This could be a followup paragraph for the
first.</p>
                <p>This    paragraph    could    give    users    some
instructions on how to navigate your website.</p>
        </div>

        <div class="pagefooter">
                <p>Here  is  some  text  in  the  footer  of  your
webpage!</p>
        </div>
    </body>
```

</html>

Then, open the HTML file with your browser. The resulting page should look similar to this:

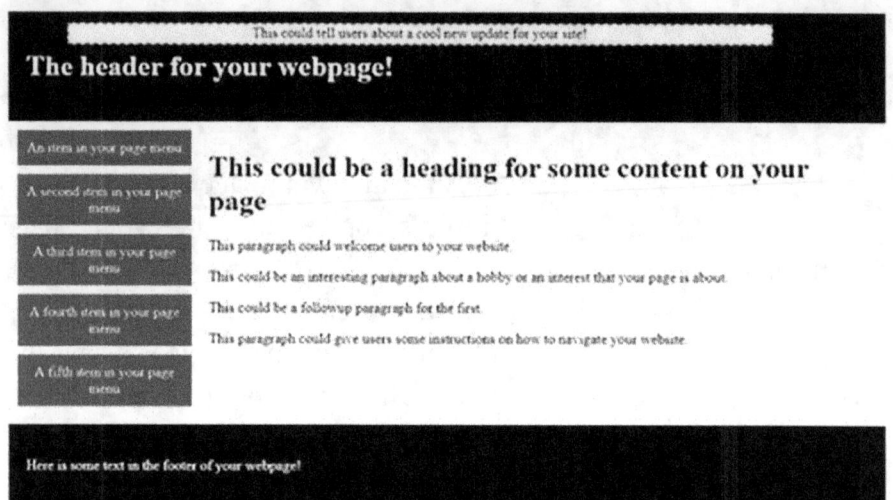

For this next example, copy and paste or manually type the following HTML into your text editor and save it with an .html extension:

```
<!DOCTYPE html>
<html>
    <head>
            <title>CSS Layout Example</title>
            <link rel="stylesheet" href="styles.css">
    </head>
    <body>

            <div class="pagealert">
                    This box will always show at the bottom of the
page. Use it for news or alerts!
            </div>

            <div class="pageheader">
```

```html
        <h1>Put some text here to display in your page
header!</h1>
        </div>

        <ul>
        <li><a  class="active"  href="#home">A  menu
item</a></li>
        <li><a    href="#page1">A    second    menu
item</a></li>
        <li><a    href="#page2">A    third    menu
item</a></li>
        <li><a    href="#page3">A    fourth    menu
item</a></li>
        </ul>

        <div class="content">
        <h1>This could be a heading for some content on
your page</h1>
        <p>This paragraph could welcome users to your
website.</p>
        <p>This could be an interesting paragraph about
a hobby or an interest that your page is about.</p>
        <p>This could be a followup paragraph for the
first.</p>
        <p>This    paragraph    could    give    users    some
instructions on how to navigate your website.</p>
        </div>

        <img class="galleryitem" src="shapes.png">
        <img class="galleryitem" src="rectangle.png">
        <img class="galleryitem" src="triangle.png">
        <img class="galleryitem" src="oval.png">
        <img class="galleryitem" src="shapes.png">
        <img class="galleryitem" src="rectangle.png">
        <img class="galleryitem" src="triangle.png">
```

```
<img class="galleryitem" src="oval.png">
<img class="galleryitem" src="shapes.png">
<img class="galleryitem" src="rectangle.png">
<img class="galleryitem" src="triangle.png">
<img class="galleryitem" src="oval.png">
<img class="galleryitem" src="shapes.png">
<img class="galleryitem" src="rectangle.png">
<img class="galleryitem" src="triangle.png">
<img class="galleryitem" src="oval.png">

<div class="content">
        <p>This paragraph could contain descriptions
about the photos in your gallery.</p>
        </div>

<div class="pagefooter">
        <p>Here is some text in the footer of your
webpage!</p>
        </div>
    </body>
</html>
```

Then, copy and paste or manually type the following CSS into a separate file in your text editor and save it at styles.css:

```
.pageheader, .pagefooter {
    clear: both;
    background-color: grey;
    color: aqua;
    font-family: arial;
    padding: 15px;
}
.pageheader {
    font-size: 28px;
```

```css
}
.pagefooter {
    margin-bottom: 50px;
    text-align: center;
}
.galleryitem {
    float: left;
    width: 31%;
    margin: 1%;
    border: 1px solid green;
}
.content {
    float: left;
    width: 100%;
}
ul {
    list-style-type: none;
    margin: 0;
    padding: 0;
    overflow: hidden;
    background-color: #333;
}
li {
    float: left;
}
li a {
    display: inline-block;
    color: white;
    text-align: center;
    padding: 14px 16px;
    text-decoration: none;
}
li a:hover {
    background-color: orange;
}
```

```css
.active {
    background-color: black;
}
.pagealert {
    position: fixed;
    background-color: red;
    text-align: center;
    text-decoration: bold;
    color: white;
    bottom: 20px;
    margin: 0px 25%;
    width: 50%;
    border: 3px double black;
}
```

Make sure that you saved the HTML file and the CSS file in the same folder, or just include the CSS in the HTML <head> element, like so:

```html
<!DOCTYPE html>
<html>
    <head>
            <title>CSS Layout Example</title>
            <style>
.pageheader, .pagefooter {
    clear: both;
    background-color: grey;
    color: aqua;
    font-family: arial;
    padding: 15px;
}
.pageheader {
    font-size: 28px;
}
.pagefooter {
    margin-bottom: 50px;
    text-align: center;
```

```css
}
.galleryitem {
    float: left;
    width: 31%;
    margin: 1%;
    border: 1px solid green;
}
.content {
    float: left;
    width: 100%;
}
ul {
    list-style-type: none;
    margin: 0;
    padding: 0;
    overflow: hidden;
    background-color: #333;
}
li {
    float: left;
}
li a {
    display: inline-block;
    color: white;
    text-align: center;
    padding: 14px 16px;
    text-decoration: none;
}
li a:hover {
    background-color: orange;
}
.active {
    background-color: black;
}
.pagealert {
```

```
position: fixed;
background-color: red;
text-align: center;
text-decoration: bold;
color: white;
bottom: 20px;
margin: 0px 25%;
width: 50%;
border: 3px double black;
}
        </style>
</head>
<body>

        <div class="pagealert">
                This box will always show at the bottom of the
page. Use it for news or alerts!
        </div>

        <div class="pageheader">
                <h1>Put some text here to display in your page
header!</h1>
        </div>

        <ul>
                <li><a class="active" href="#home">A menu
item</a></li>
                <li><a href="#page1">A second menu
item</a></li>
                <li><a href="#page2">A third menu
item</a></li>
                <li><a href="#page3">A fourth menu
item</a></li>
        </ul>
```

```html
<div class="content">
        <h1>This could be a heading for some content on your page</h1>
        <p>This paragraph could welcome users to your website.</p>
        <p>This could be an interesting paragraph about a hobby or an interest that your page is about.</p>
        <p>This could be a followup paragraph for the first.</p>
        <p>This paragraph could give users some instructions on how to navigate your website.</p>
</div>

        <img class="galleryitem" src="shapes.png">
        <img class="galleryitem" src="rectangle.png">
        <img class="galleryitem" src="triangle.png">
        <img class="galleryitem" src="oval.png">
        <img class="galleryitem" src="shapes.png">
        <img class="galleryitem" src="rectangle.png">
        <img class="galleryitem" src="triangle.png">
        <img class="galleryitem" src="oval.png">
        <img class="galleryitem" src="shapes.png">
        <img class="galleryitem" src="rectangle.png">
        <img class="galleryitem" src="triangle.png">
        <img class="galleryitem" src="oval.png">
        <img class="galleryitem" src="shapes.png">
        <img class="galleryitem" src="rectangle.png">
        <img class="galleryitem" src="triangle.png">
        <img class="galleryitem" src="oval.png">

<div class="content">
        <p>This paragraph could contain descriptions about the photos in your gallery.</p>
</div>
```

```
        <div class="pagefooter">
                <p>Here is some text in the footer of your
webpage!</p>
                </div>
        </body>
</html>
```

Now, open the HTML file with your browser. The resulting page should look similar to this:

Once you have this page opened in your browser, see what happens if you scroll down the page or resize the browser window. For some practice, see if you can create a .css file that contains elements that retain their size when the window is made smaller or larger.

# Chapter 4

# Polishing Your Web Pages With CSS

In order to ensure that your web pages are displaying properly, it's important to frequently check your HTML and CSS files and debug them when necessary. Both HTML and CSS are permissive, so you don't have to worry about "breaking" you web page if you make a mistake. Even, if you use an invalid CSS declaration or an unsupported feature your browser will simply ignore the error and proceed to the next declaration. This can often be beneficial since a single error won't bring down your entire page -- the browser just won't display your content as expected. However, it can sometimes be difficult to figure out how to fix an improperly displayed element if you aren't sure what is causing the discrepancy. Fortunately, there are a couple of different ways to handle this issue.

The first way to try and debug a problematic web page is by using your browser's page inspector tool and CSS editor. To open up the page inspector tool, simply right click within a web page. In this example, we'll be using a Chrome browser to inspect one of the web pages you created in the previous chapter. If you aren't using Chrome, that's okay! Other browsers will offer you the same features, although they might be accessed in a slightly different way. With Chrome, once you right click within a web page, you simply need to choose "Inspect" from the pop up menu to open the page inspector tool. It will look something like this:

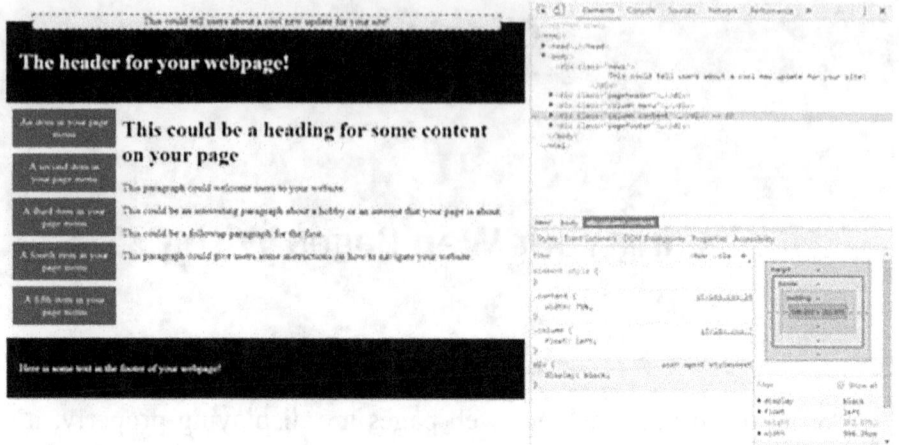

You can also use Ctrl + Shift + I to open the inspect panel in Google Chrome.

Now, take a look at the panel that has opened up. In the top portion, you can view the HTML that is used to display the page. In the lower right portion, you can view a graphical representation of each element's size, padding, border, and margin. In the lower left portion, you can see a block with tabs labeled Styles, Event Listeners, DOM Breakpoints, and Properties. We'll be working in the tab labeled Styles for this example.

To use the CSS Editor tool, first, click on an element in the top portion of the Inspect panel (where the HTML is displayed). For instance, let's click on the line that says <div class="news">. When you do so, you should see the contents of the Style tab below change to reflect the CSS that is used when displaying that element. If a CSS declaration is invalid for any reason, it will appear with a line through it in this window, along with a warning symbol. Also, if you hover over the attributes in this window, you will notice that they each have a checkbox to their left. You can click this checkbox to toggle the CSS attribute in the page.

Try this out now. Click the checkbox next to the text-align attribute and notice how this affects the way the news alert box displays on your web page on the left of the screen. The property will have a line through it when you click the checkbox to toggle it off. If you click on the value to the right of the properties in the Style tab, you are given the option to

380

enter a new value. You can also click on the colored boxes next to properties with a color value to change the color and instantly view how your page will be affected.

You can probably already understand how this can be a useful tool when trying to find and fix errors in your CSS. Not only can you instantly view any invalid CSS, you can easily manipulate the values for each of the properties of any element. By this, you can see how they affect how that element is displayed. You can easily view all of the CSS that is associated with an element. This is especially beneficial when working with elements that use multiple classes. You can even choose to temporarily ignore a certain property to check whether or not that is causing your page to display incorrectly. With these tools, you have a huge advantage in finding errors within your CSS over simply reading through your .css file manually!

If you'd rather not use the Page Inspector and CSS Editor in your browser, another option for finding errors in your CSS is to use a CSS Validator. You can find a CSS Validator online with a simple Google search. The validator should allow you to upload your CSS file, link to a web page online, or manually type some CSS into a text area. Then, the validator will comb through your CSS and display any errors it encounters along with the line numbers where they are located and the selectors that are associated with them. For instance, your CSS validator tool might tell you that there is an error in your .news class on line 35 that has occurred due to a missing semicolon or a misspelled property name.

Although using a CSS validator tool can be beneficial in some circumstances, there are many times it won't be able to provide you with the information you need to fix your display issues. For instance, if your page is displaying incorrectly because you typed the wrong value into your CSS file, the validator won't display an error since the syntax of the declaration is technically correct. Similarly, if you use the wrong selector when defining the styles for your page, the validator won't catch the error since nothing is syntactically incorrect. The best use of a CSS validator is probably as a precursor to using the Page Inspector method above -- the CSS validator will catch any basic errors in the syntax of your CSS, and you'll be able to fix them before addressing selector, property, and value issues with the built in browser CSS editor.

Try running a few of the examples from this book through a CSS validator and then view them with your browser's Inspect feature to familiarize yourself with both methods. That's it! Now you're ready to create, view, and debug your own HTML and CSS projects.

# Chapter 5

# CSS Animations

One of the cool and more recent things to come into CSS is the concept of CSS animations. CSS animations are great because they allow your site to be fluid and allow you to, as it sounds, animate your HTML code.

In the past, animating your code was pretty tedious. It was something you had to do through a combination of JavaScript code and clever CSS/HTML scripting. That or, in even older days, you'd have to animate your site through the use of Flash. This led to sites being extremely clunky, hard to interact with, tacky, and altogether much lower quality than they are today.

That all changed with the advent of CSS3. CSS3 now allows you to subtly animate your site in various ways that weren't available to programmers before. This is great because it means that there's an even greater chance that your site can be run without cumbersome scripts or anything of that nature.

The first part of CSS animations rests in keyframes. Keyframes allow you to set important events that happen throughout the course of an animation. You can name your keyframes and then refer to those at a later point. Let's say, for example, that we wanted to shift the text color from black to aqua. We could do this like so:

```
@keyframes myText {
    from {color: black;}
    to {color:yellow;}
}
```

You could then refer to this at a later point using *myText* as the animation name. You can give a certain animation description to an element by defining the animation name and then defining the length of the duration.

Note also that you can actually instead of using *from* and *to*, define the *percentages* at which these keyframes will take place. 0% describes the starting state, 100% describes the ending state, and anything between will ensure that the element takes on that property at that point within the overall duration of the animation.

Let's say we had an element called *myDiv* that we wanted to use our previous animation with:

```
#myDiv {
    animation-name: myText;
    animation-duration: 2s;
}
```

You can take this a step further by using CSS selectors. CSS selectors allow you to change the state of a given element when a certain event happens. Let's say, for example, that you wanted to specify an animation to happen exclusively when you hovered over a certain div. You could do so using the *hover* selector. Then, within the element description for the hover selector, you would put the animation data.

```
#myDiv {
    // raw data goes here
}
#myDiv:hover {
    animation-name: myText;
    animation-duration:2s;
}
```

This would cause the on-load data from the initial definition to happen when the page is loaded. The style of the element would change whenever the element was hovered over, thanks to the hover selector.

Therefore, whenever the element with the ID "myDiv" was hovered over, the specified animation would take place. Make sense? It's pretty simple!

There are a number of different CSS selectors that you can use.

*hover* will become active whenever the element is hovered over.

*active* is used in reference to anchor links and refers to the page that you're actively on. *a:active* will select any links on the page that link back to the page you are currently on and then style them in the way that you specify.

*::after* will insert data after the content of any given specified element.

*::before* will insert data before the content of any given specified element.

There are many more, but these are the most common ones and are therefore the ones that you are most likely going to be seeing often. Hover especially is the one that you'll most likely make the most use of.

With that, we've covered the basics of CSS animations. In the following chapter, we're going to be talking about how you can actually implement everything we've covered so far in this book in a few more modern web design paradigms. Stay tuned!

# Chapter 6

# Trends in CSS - Fixed Width Sites

One of the older trends in website design is actually essential to cover because it will give you a prime basis and starting point for the rest of your website design. One thing that we haven't really talked about at this point is actually culminating everything that you've worked with into a cohesive design, so we're going to be doing that in this chapter as we try to shamble together a lot of the concepts that we've covered into one bigger vision.

Web design is all about presentation. It's important that in your design path, you choose a way which presents your end vision in a way that makes it appealing to anybody who might come across your site. The most immediate way to get practice with this - and, indeed, the easiest - is to start with the most simple form of higher-level website design in CSS that is still applicable in today's web design market.

While you aren't going to come across many sites from established designers that utilize fixed-width constructions these days, it's still important that you understand the methodology and the thought process because it will actually teach you quite a bit about design in the process.

Fixed width designs have their basis in the fact that when you design a website, you want its presentation to be uniform. You want what the users see to be what you see. This can be difficult when you're dealing with all of the different computers and display resolutions out there. The way that early web designers would deal with this problem was by designing sites in such a way that anybody with any computer would see the same exact thing, provided that their viewport was beyond a certain width.

As at the time of writing this book, there really aren't many computers out there running on hardware updated enough to use a modern web browser that will have a smaller resolution than 1280x1024 - even mobile devices normally have a greater width than 960. If you go really old, such as iPhone second generation and prior, you'll run into widths that are in the 400s, but there's running on 10-year-old technology and very, very old mobile phones. So, you can trust that most people who would be accessing your site in the current climate would have a width greater than 960.

Most resolutions for computers generally have a width of at least 1366, with most desktop computers having a resolution width of at least 1920.

So what does this mean? This means that by finding a resolution that all of these devices can display and then show everything within that width, you assure that any device that has a resolution of that size or greater can display the content of your website in a seamless and uniform manner.

You've almost certainly in your time on the internet come across sites that do this in a pretty subtle way. One of the more popular web design magazines/periodicals, for example, uses this format in such a way that a given user would find it difficult to tell that this was the design principle. Because of the subtlety, regularity, and simplicity, this is a great place for future would-be web designers to start off.

So how does this work? The main philosophy of fixed-width design is having everything on your site fit within a certain container. This container sits on top of your background but contains all of your content. It will normally have a certain width affixed to it. A width of 900 or 1000 pixels is considered both standard and safe. Your code may end up looking like this:

```
<!DOCTYPE html>
```

```html
<html>
    <head>
        <title>My site</title>
        <style>
            html, body, background {
                margin:0px;
                padding:0px;
                background:#d0d0d0;
            }
            #container {
                width:900px;
                margin-left:auto;
                margin-right:auto;
                border-left:1px solid #efefef;
                border-right:1px solid #efefef;
            }
        </style>
    </head>
    <body>
        <div id="container">
            Container example.
        </div>
    </body>
</html>
```

The automatic left and right margins would center the div element. Your content would then fit pretty safely within this container. Your content could go in here and you could scale your content according to these widths. This means you could use exact pixel numbers and ensure that the design would actually look the same regardless of the platform that it was being viewed on. This is of the utmost importance in terms of overall usability and presentation and was, in fact, one of the main draws in using a fixed width design.

There are numerous drawbacks to using a fixed width design, though. The first of them is that it simply doesn't look as good as certain other kinds of designs do. For example, using exact widths means necessarily that your design won't be able to scale up to the beautiful and breathtaking artistic designs of the responsive designs that we'll be discussing in the next chapter.

This can be a massive drawback because as a web designer, you want your end result to look pretty. You want it to be flashy, effective, and showcase your abilities as well as the key point that the site is trying to convey. You want to show what you're able to do because web design is an artistic medium like any other form of design.

However, there are many cases where the simpler design and faster turnaround time and more exact and simplistic nature can be preferable. For example, many industrial designs will prefer, to one extent or another, the fixed-width design because it's less distracting and flashy. It lets people just do what they need to do with minimal intervention on the design side. It is an effective and simple design which gets out of the way and works even on older browsers and legacy systems.

# Chapter 7

# Trends In CSS - Responsive Design

The point of this book is to get you up to speed with CSS and feeling like you understand what you're doing. The hope is that by the end, you'll feel confident enough with the essential information pertaining to CSS and related disciplines that you'll be able to start designing your own sites.

One of the key parts of this is that we cover what could be considered the primary trends in CSS and web design at the moment. These are the most common as at the time of writing this book, but it does exclude certain frameworks which one could consider to be beyond the scope of this book, like React.JS or things similar in nature.

The first thing that we're going to talk about is *responsive web design*. Responsive web design arose in reaction to the trend of smartphone market dominance in web design. More and more people are having access to smartphones. They also have access to instantaneous web access regardless of where they were. Consequently, it began to become necessary to create intricate mobile designs which went beyond the low-data mobile versions of yesteryear from the eras of Blackberries and Palm Pres. In the face of high resolution mobile browsers and smartphones such as the iPhone and Samsung Galaxy, it was necessary to have a way for web design. This way, it could mimic the strengths of these mobile browsers and remove the need for a separate mobile version of the site. In the alternative, we are opting for a version of the site relative to the screen resolution of the device being used.

While this hasn't completely invalidated the mobile versions of sites, it does create a sort of situation where one can address them in a different way. Before, mobile sites were addressed by a JavaScript or HTML preprocessor directive that would cause the page to redirect if a certain browser was detected. With the advent of CSS3, it became possible to detect screen resolutions and automatically adjust the site in response rather than having a site being entirely readjusted.

Part of responsive design involves having designs that are artistically and aesthetically pleasing rather than just being fully functional. In this capacity, responsive designs serve as a means to make designs more expressive on the designer's end and more interactive and intuitive on the user's end.

So, what is responsive design? You've more than likely see the the responsive design before. If you've run into a web page that takes up the entire width and height of your browser window and that scales appropriately regardless of how large your browser window is at any given moment.

The way that responsive design works can take many different forms but the essence of responsive design comes down to essentially just everything being efficiently and easily scalable. It also should respond to the size of the viewport, or the overall viewing resolution of the browser. You can test out different viewport sizes in a responsive design by actually sizing your browser up and down both vertically and horizontally using your operating system's built-in sizing mechanisms.

Responsive designs work on the basis of things scaling with width and height values. You can accomplish this by using percentage-based sizing in your document. This is the basic idea, anyhow; the rest of it - which is a little bit beyond the scope of a beginner book - is actually using CSS commands in order to change the style of the document if, for example, the viewport were less than a certain width or height. For right now, we're just going to focus on how to implement scaling heights and widths.

The first thing you need to bear in mind is that when you test this out by scaling your window size up and down, you will notice that the size of the divisions will actually grow larger and smaller. This is perfect! It is exactly what is meant to happen.

The first thing that you need to realize about CSS width and height properties is that they inherit from the element larger than them. So, for example, you can't just say that divs of a certain class will have a height of, say, 20%. There is no definition of what 20% is even *of*. 20% of… what, exactly? In order for this statement to have any sort of meaning behind it, you need to realize that 20% is supposed to be a percentage of something else. If you say 20%, then this statement is somewhat inherently meaningless unless you indicate the 20% is a percentage of.

The way that you do this is by defining some parent object with a percentage. The greatest parent object is the *body* element, so any elements located within the *body* element can only be based on the *percentage* that is defined for the *body* element. Make sense? So if you want something to be 20%, then the body element has to have a parent height that this can be based on.

The body element will automatically use percentage based heights as a function of the viewport's size. However, if you were to define the body height as something like 1000 pixels, and had a div that was 20% height, then the div would base its 20% of the nearest parent element - here, body - and therefore have a height of 200 pixels.

Let's look at this a little bit more in-depth. The first thing you would have to do for scaling heights and widths is defined your body height as the height of the viewport. This will let everything else be a function of that when you define their heights and widths with percentages. In order to define your body as the height and width of the viewport, you're going to want to put the following in your code:

```
html, body, background {
    height:100%;
```

```
    width:100%;
}
```

Every div that you define afterward that has the body element as its most immediate parent element (as in, it isn't nested within another div element) will scale based on this. So, if you were to make a div now that was set to have a height of, say, 50%, it would take up 50% of the screen height.

In modern web design, this really comes to present itself in two different ways. The first is through the development of one-page designs, and the other way is through the development of grid-based design layouts. We'll spend a brief moment going over both of these so you have an idea of how they work.

One-page designs essentially are divided into sections. They'll usually have a splash opener to the site that talks about the site and its primary purpose, as well as a navigational bar or button you can click in order to open a navigational panel. Both of these will move with the page as you scroll down.

Now, you can start to move down the web page. Generally, all of the sections are the size of one viewport. There are often some neat transitions added in or other things that will cause the scrolling between sections to feel easy or even seamless. Others, still, will use parallax scrolling techniques in order to make the background stay exactly where it is as the user scrolls down the page.

Let's talk for a second about parallax scrolling before we move on to the next section of this chapter. Parallax scrolling is relatively intuitive and also pretty beautiful in its own right when done correctly. It's a snazzy feature that can be seriously cool when implemented well.

Parallax scrolling is essentially when the background moves in some way in response to the user scrolling. This runs counter to the standard wherein the background image or background of a given section doesn't necessarily stay with the user as they scroll. This might sound difficult, but it's actually rather simple.

You can implement parallax scrolling by setting a background image for the given section and then fix its position:

background-position: fixed;

This will lead the background position to scroll with the user as they move up and down the page. Interspersed with clever design, this can be an absolutely killer way to showcase your design abilities while not roughing up your code or making it excessively difficult. Bare this in mind, because this is a massive trend in web design these days and you're going to be seeing it a lot.

Through other CSS features and JavaScript events, you can add even more things to implement within your code base which will make your design more appealing or more intuitive. The combination of HTML5, CSS3, and JavaScript is extremely powerful. Some people have even created full-on games in just these 3 languages. So, it's important that you have a grasp on them and how they work because by doing so, you're setting yourself up for success in terms of long-term design potential.

The other way that these responsive designs tend to be implemented is through the use of grid-based layouts. Grid-based layouts are becoming more and more common as time presses on. Their particular handiness comes from the fact that, first and foremost, they offer a very convenient modular method of development. Moreover, they allow you to design a simple and beautiful site using pre-developed and prefixed dimensions. This makes your entire development process far easier.

An example of a grid-based layout would be something which, for example, uses a 3 wide grid where 3 elements are fit into one row. In addition, these rows are roughly 30% width each, perhaps with a 3% margin on either side and a 2% margin in between. This would allow the information to be presented in a clean and pragmatic manner.

The grid-based layout is one of the other very popular methods of design because it allows for the combination of multiple different manners of layouts within the context of a grid-based system.

Grid-based designs fill, to some degree, the industrial void that fixed-width sites used to fill. While fixed-width sites do still exist, when simple and effective designs that look modern are needed, they are usually accomplished using some form of grid-based design. This also is an ideal choice for online store fronts because it's unpretentious and rather easy to use.

With that, we've covered the other monolith of modern web design: the responsive website. As I said, there's quite a bit more to it than all of this, but it's something that you're mainly going to get experience and exposure to through practice.

# Conclusion

Thank you again for purchasing *CSS: Basic Fundamental Guide For Beginners*, and congratulations on making it to the end! Hopefully, you've gained some insight into how to use CSS selectors, discovered how to effectively create layouts for your web pages, and had some fun exploring the different ways CSS can enhance your websites.

The next step is to let yourself be creative. Have an idea for a unique new web page? Try to apply the techniques you learned throughout this book to make it a reality! Practice makes perfect, just like with any other skill, so be sure to put in the time to polish your techniques. There are countless new websites out there just waiting for someone to create them, and that means countless opportunities for you to hone your skills.

Finally, if you found this book useful as you began on your CSS journey, please take a moment to review it on Amazon. Thank you, good luck, and enjoy your new and improved websites!

www.ingramcontent.com/pod-product-compliance
Lightning Source LLC
Chambersburg PA
CBHW071247220526
45468CB00001B/31